LAND OF NO BUDDHA

RICHARD P. HAYES

LAND OF NO BUDDHA

Reflections of a Sceptical Buddhist

WINDHORSE PUBLICATIONS

Also by Richard P. Hayes
Dignaga on the Interpretation of Signs

Published by Windhorse Publications
11 Park Road
Birmingham
B13 8AB

© Richard P. Hayes 1998

The right of Richard P. Hayes to be identified as the author of this work has been asserted by him in accordance with the Copyright, Designs and Patents Act 1988

Cover design Dhammarati
Cover image © John Wilkes, Photonica
Printed by Interprint Ltd, Marsa, Malta

British Library Cataloguing in Publication Data:
A catalogue record for this book is available from the British Library

ISBN 1 899579 12 5

The publishers acknowledge with gratitude permission to quote extracts from the following:

pp. 22–3: Thomas Cleary (trans.), *The Dhammapada: Sayings of the Buddha*, Bantam Books, New York 1995

pp. 94–5: Garma C.C. Chang (ed.), *A Treasury of Mahāyāna Sūtras: Selections from the Mahāratnakūṭa Sūtra*, Pennsylvania State Press, University Park and London 1983

pp. 113, 210, 264–5: *The Long Discourses of the Buddha: A Translation of the Dīgha Nikāya*, © Maurice Walshe 1987, 1995. From the Teachings of the Buddha series, courtesy of Wisdom Publications, 199 Elm Street, Somerville, MA 02144

pp. 234–5: H. Saddhatissa (trans.), *Sutta Nipāta*, Curzon Press, London 1985

CONTENTS

About the Author ix

Author's Note 1

Preface 5

1 On Being Dharma-centric 13

2 Bodhisattvas in Blue Jeans 39

3 A Dialogue on Rebirth 73

4 Teachers 83

5 Dr Ambedkar's Social Reform Through Buddhism 97

6 Christianity and Buddhism 125

7 Some Reflections on Words 139

8 Buddhism in the New Dark Ages 153

9 Does a Logician have Buddha Nature? 165

10 What is a Friend? 179

11 Farewell to the Raft 209

12 Perils of a Raft-dodger 249

Notes 263

Bibliography 267

Index 271

About the Author

In January 1967, at the age of 21, Richard Hayes attended four talks on Buddhism and a month-long seminar on the trial and death of Socrates, both at the family Unitarian Church. Afterwards, he felt quite comfortable telling his friends that he was a Buddhist, albeit a rather Socratic one. After migrating to Canada a month later, his personal alternative to answering the call to appear for induction into the US military, Hayes found himself in the company of Quakers, whom he joined regularly for silent worship. As his Quaker friends bore silent witness to their Christian faith, he practised Buddhist meditation exercises he had read about in a book.

Until he met other Buddhists, Hayes studied on his own and eventually took academic courses in Buddhism, which led him to study Sanskrit, Pali, and Tibetan. In 1982, after studying Indian philosophy for ten years, including two years in Japan, he earned a PhD from the department of Sanskrit and Indian Studies at the University of Toronto. Since 1988 he has been teaching Sanskrit language and Indian Buddhist philosophy at McGill University.

During his years in Toronto, Hayes practised in a Korean Zen context. He discovered the FWBO in 1987 and, despite the distance between Montreal and the nearest FWBO centre (about eight hours by bus) he has become increasingly involved with the movement. He lives a quiet life with his wife, Geri, and a number of cats and rabbits. Among his family and friends his playful and slightly mischievous sense of humour has earned him the nickname Coyote. He still thinks of himself as a Socratic Buddhist.

About the Author

I tell you that to let no day pass without discussing goodness and examining both myself and others is really the very best thing that a man can do, and that life without this sort of examination is not worth living.

Socrates, Apology 38a

Let one's thoughts of boundless love pervade the whole world: above, below, and across without any obstruction, without any hatred, without any enmity. Whether one stands, walks, sits, or lies down, as long as one is awake, one should develop this mindfulness. This they say is the noblest living here.

Sutta Nipāta 150–1

AUTHOR'S NOTE

ALL BUT ONE of the essays in this collection were written in the mid-1980s. In 1989 I collected them together, wrote a preface, and circulated the manuscript to a dozen carefully chosen publishing companies. Although two of the companies showed more than passing interest, both finally decided against publishing the essays. Wanting to turn my attention to other matters, I stuck the manuscript in a filing cabinet and forgot about it for several years.

It was not until October 1994 that I gave the collection of essays another thought. In the summer of that year, I had gone on a meditation retreat at Aryaloka Buddhist Retreat Center in Newmarket, New Hampshire, where I had renewed old friendships with Manjuvajra and Saramati (Prof. Alan Sponberg), both members of the Western Buddhist Order. Attending the retreat and meeting again with these two old friends had rekindled my earlier interest in the Friends of the Western Buddhist Order. Then in October of that year, Sangharakshita made a visit to Aryaloka, and, since I had never met him in person, I drove from Montreal to make his acquaintance. On an impulse as I was about to set out for New Hampshire, I dug the manuscript of these essays out of the filing cabinet and pushed it into a battered envelope with the idea that I might leave them with Manjuvajra to read at his leisure. Manjuvajra read them and passed them on to a few other people to read, and eventually it was suggested that I might consider publishing them through Windhorse Publications.

No sooner was the decision made to publish than a number of problems became apparent. The most serious of these was that my way of viewing many things has changed since the essays were written, and even when my views have remained more or less as they were, I would now strive to find different ways of expressing them. In the 1980s I was a much more frustrated and angry man than I am now, and much of that previous mentality shows through in a more strident and mordant manner of expression than I would now use. Indeed, for some time I was of a mind to withhold the essays from republication altogether; it seemed enough to me that most of them had been in print before during times best forgotten. Various people persuaded me, however, that the collection of essays chronicle a stage in my own development as a Buddhist, and that many other Western Buddhists have gone through, or are now going through, a similar stage of development. If nothing else, the collection might be a record of how at least some North American Buddhists were thinking towards the end of the twentieth century. The decision was made, then, to let these essays stand almost exactly as they were written ten years ago. Only a few very minor stylistic changes have been made in the hope of making the essays easier and more pleasant to read. No substantial changes in content have been made in the bodies of the essays themselves.

While the decision to leave the bodies of the essays intact seemed most satisfactory in general, it did leave the problem of how to indicate in what ways my thinking has changed during the past ten years. The solution that was finally settled upon was to append a final essay that brings my thinking up to date, in at least very broad outline. In addition, I have added explanatory paragraphs at the beginning of each essay, and in some cases have added a postscript as well. Elsewhere, I have also added endnotes to draw attention to very specific points that can be dealt with briefly. Even these measures will do no more than outline ways in which my thinking about Buddhism has changed. To provide a more detailed account will require writing an entirely new set of essays, which I may do within the next few years if it seems advisable and if circumstances permit.

Everything more that needs to be said by way of introduction to the essays is found in the Preface that follows. In addition to the people who are thanked there for their help and inspiration, I now have the pleasure of acknowledging the gracious editorial help and gentle but persistent encouragement of Nagabodhi, without whom I probably would not have carried this task through. I also derived benefit from comments made by Saramati and Manjuvajra, whose friendship over the years has been invaluable to me. Stephen Batchelor made a number of very useful comments when this manuscript was first circulating in 1989, and following several of his suggestions has resulted, I think, in an improved collection of essays. Finally, it is a joy to acknowledge the sustenance I have received from my most honest critic and constant Dharma companion, Geraldine Day Hayes, to whom I also have the good fortune to be married.

Montreal, Quebec
June 1997

PREFACE

THE TITLE OF this collection of essays, most of which are about Buddhism in the context of North American culture, may require a certain amount of explanation. In one sense, of course, it is obvious that essays about North America should be called 'Land of No Buddha', for Buddhism is relatively foreign to this soil and probably always will be. But there is a further reason for the title, which can only be told by telling a little about myself.

In the days of my obdurate youth, running with the pack was just not my style. Although attracted to the teachings of Buddhism at the age of about twenty, I had little interest in deliberately congregating with Buddhists or seeking out their counsel, even after deciding that one way or another I would devote my life to studying Buddhist texts in their original languages and would do my best to live according to Buddhist moral standards. If anyone asked what my religion was, I would usually make a joke to the effect that I was a follower of the *Pratyeka-yāna* school of Buddhism. Pratyeka-yāna of course is not really a school of Buddhism at all but a term of contempt used by early Mahāyāna Buddhists for those solitary wanderers who sought enlightenment without the benefit of teachers and refused to teach others when and if they achieved that lofty goal.

Even while staying away from formal Buddhist groups and teachers, I always had a secret longing to be given a Buddhist name. Being a student of Sanskrit, Pāli, and Tibetan I could easily have invented a name for myself, but giving a name to oneself is not the same somehow as being given a name by someone else. In fact, picking a name for oneself seems downright immodest. A name, after all, and especially a religious name, should be given on the basis of some virtue in the person who receives it, and in polite society one should not be sufficiently conscious of one's own virtues to be able to find the right words for them. So for many years I wandered around the wildernesses of *saṁsāra* as an anonymous Pratyeka-yāna Buddhist, wondering what my name would be if I had one.

Eventually, for a variety of reasons, my attitudes about running with the pack changed somewhat, and I began looking around for the right setting in which to practise meditation with others under the guidance of a qualified teacher. Finding the right setting was not at all easy, because too many years of being a cranky academic had filled me with impatience with everyone's imperfections except my own. I had managed to become a little tolerant of my own shortcomings, in fact, only out of resignation born of the exhaustion of trying to escape them. Coexisting graciously with foolishness has never been my strong suit, and in my experience with Buddhist groups there was rarely less foolishness among those seeking enlightenment than there was among the totally unenlightened; indeed, I preferred the foolishness of the ordinary person who is at least not pretending to be spiritual. So, while actively looking for a number of years for a proper setting in which to pursue meditation practice with others but finding no teacher with whom to study or from whom to receive a proper name, I still had no idea what my name was.

All situations change sooner or later. One day a good friend of mine dragged me off to a celebration of the Buddha's birth at a Zen temple in Toronto, an event that my friend seemed very much to want to attend but about which I felt lukewarm and cynical. Much to my surprise, I actually found the atmosphere of the Zen Buddhist Temple inviting. Accustomed as I had become to a sort of cloying piety and soft-headed credulity among North American Buddhists, I was immediately struck by a very different atmosphere in the Zen Buddhist Temple. The people were obviously very hard working in general and serious about and dedicated to their practice in particular, but their devotion was spiced with just the right amount of wry wit and self-effacing humour to prevent anyone from taking his own spiritual odysseys too seriously. It was a place well grounded in common sense, a rare commodity in North American Buddhist circles. Right away I knew I had found a place to come to park my bones for a while.

It came as quite a surprise to me to learn that the Zen Buddhist Temple is run under the supervision of Ven. Samu Sunim, a monk originally from Korea whom I had seen years earlier hanging around the East Asian Studies library of the University of Toronto. During my time as a graduate student, this Korean Zen monk had always been an intimidating figure to me, because he looked like a person who would brook no nonsense, and nonsense was the only thing I had to offer. So because of shyness I never made much effort to get to know him, but I had thought more than once that if I ever did get around to serious meditation practice, I would like to do it with a person of Samu Sunim's qualities. And so it really struck me as quite a coincidence that this Temple that I had been dragged to visit, and which turned out to feel so much like home, was Samu Sunim's. Many weeks after that initial visit I dropped by the Temple for a cup of tea, and a member of the staff introduced me to Sunim as a scholar in the area of Buddhist studies. He said, 'We don't have much need for scholars around here.' It was then that I really knew I had found the right person to give me my name.

It so happened that about six months after I started hanging around the Zen Buddhist Temple there was a precept-taking ceremony, which is held there every two years and which in that tradition is the means by which one formally becomes a Buddhist. It was at that ceremony that I finally was given a Buddhist name. Solemn though the ceremony was, I could not help laughing when the name was conferred. Sunim had given me the name Mubul, which is the Korean pronunciation of two Chinese characters that mean 'no Buddha' or 'without a Buddha'. My first interpretation of the name was that it meant having no Buddha-nature, that is, altogether lacking the potential to become enlightened, and I thought the name suited me perfectly, for I have always known it would be easier for a granite gargoyle to wipe the silly grin off its face than it would be for me to acquire even a shred of wisdom.

It is this quality of being impervious to wisdom that makes me fit in with my fellow citizens of North America, for we have become an entire society that dreads wisdom and civilizing influences of any sort. Having lived the first twenty-two years of my life in various parts of the United States (New Mexico, Virginia, Maryland, Colorado, Wisconsin, and California) and the next twenty-two years in various parts of Canada (Manitoba, British Columbia, Alberta, Ontario, and

Quebec), I am a child of North America. It is my land, the land of Mubul, the land of No Buddha, a land in which I have always felt a little like a stranger no matter which part of it I have lived in or travelled to, but a land for which I have a great deal of affection and warmth of feeling, and on rare occasions even a little hope. To this land I present this collection of essays as a series of humble offerings.

Although I earn my keep as a university professor teaching Buddhist studies, this book is not intended to be a 'professional' monograph to be read by other scholars. When professional scholars of religion deal with their subject matter in a university setting, they are required to handle it clinically, antiseptically, and at great personal distance, in approximately the way that one might handle the carcass of a cockroach. Meditation, prayer, and devotional exercises must be talked about as things that other people do, and faith and belief as things that other people have. There are, I suppose, good reasons for this distance from the subject matter, and in a university setting I do my best to play by the rules. But these essays were written while I was 'off duty' in the privacy of my own home. Although I have made every attempt to apply the same standards of accuracy in presenting information as I would in plying my trade as an academic, I have not felt at all constrained to treat Buddhism or any other religion at a remove from my own personal feelings and judgements. On the contrary, I have dared to treat Buddhism as the religion that I have deliberately chosen as my own. Moreover, I have not restricted myself to discussing Buddhism in North America descriptively, for my interest has been less to show Buddhism as it actually is in North America than to show it as I think it ought to be. And in talking about Buddhism as I think it ought to be in North America, I have also perforce talked about North American society as I think it ought to be.

Many of these essays have appeared before in the pages of *Spring Wind: Buddhist Cultural Forum*, a magazine that used to be published at the Zen Buddhist Temple in Toronto. Encouraged by a number of kind readers who have expressed their appreciation for some of the things I have written, and encouraged above all by Samu Sunim, I have decided to make some of my *Spring Wind* writings available again to a different readership. Few of the original *Spring Wind* items appear here exactly as they first appeared there. All have been revised to some extent, some having been significantly shortened and some significantly expanded. Not all the essays collected here were written for *Spring Wind*. Some were written by invitation for particular occasions, and two were written especially for this book.

Because the occasions for the actual writing of these essays have been so various, the styles of the essays are by no means uniform. Some have a rather light mood, others may strike some readers as having a more petulant tone, and still others are merely straightforward presentations of information. Much of the information in these essays, incidentally, was gathered for me by Samu Sunim, who reads widely and often presented me with large piles of books, magazines, and newspaper clippings dealing with various themes of interest. Without his energetic skills at gathering information and generating ideas, these essays would be much poorer, and some would not have existed at all without his instigation.

Regardless of the tone that any given essay may have, each is presented with the same purpose, which is not so much to persuade people to adopt my point of view as to encourage people to give further thought to a variety of features of North American society that deserve prolonged and careful reflection. The themes of Buddhism are woven into all the essays, but they are by no means the only themes. North American society is founded primarily on the principles of post-medieval Christian thought, and one cannot say much about North America without speaking of her intellectual and spiritual roots. There is, therefore, quite a bit said about Christianity in these pages. So it is hoped that North Americans of all creeds and modes of practice will find something to think about in these pages, and it is expected that much of their thinking will take the form of informed disagreement and reasoned opposition.

Speaking further of the tone of the essays, the faint-hearted reader should be warned in advance that I do occasionally inadvertently ride roughshod over people's most dearly held sentiments and prejudices. My sense of indignation at some forms of human folly and injustice does not always find gentle and diplomatic expression, partly because I think the crises we face in this world are so urgent that we no longer have time always to be superficially polite. But even when my expression seems harsh, it is never my intention to hurt any reader's feelings or to stir up anyone's anger against anyone else. Above all, I never intend to direct my invective towards any particular person or group of people; rather, the intended target is always folly as such, a property in which we all have a share from time to time. Despite these intentions, I do occasionally learn that a reader has been offended by something I have written. Let me apologise in advance for any offence that may be taken by any reader of my words.

An apology is also in order for the inordinate amount of autobiographical material in these essays. It is there not because there is anything about my own experiences and reflections that makes them especially worthy of recording for posterity, but for the simple reason that I cannot easily escape the intimately familiar prison of my own memories. It is hoped that the autobiographical material will not be obtrusive but will be heard as just one more indistinguishable voice in the choir made up of those who have watched in dismay as the human race has accelerated the destruction of an entire planet through individual and collective forms of greed, through ideological blindness, through national and ethnic arrogance and individualistic complacency, and through a genetic and inescapable short-sightedness that predisposes all of us to experience the vast problems of life as a series of stereotypical images to which we can only react by gluing stickers on the bumpers of our cars, croaking shallow slogans, and raising our fists against the many demons that we ourselves invent to blame for all that goes wrong. During the decades that I have been alive I have heard these demons called by such names as the Communist threat, capitalist imperialism, fundamentalist intolerance, secular humanist amorality, or patriarchal misogyny; if I live another decade or two, I expect I shall hear the demons renamed several times over.

There are those who have come to realize that no one has any solutions to the human condition and who with all their remaining strength resist being led astray by the hysterical spiritual leaders, demagogues, despots, and totalitarians who would have us believe that there are simple solutions or any solutions at all. And among those who resist the purveyors of simple-minded panaceas, there are some who nevertheless refuse to yield to despair but who seek instead to face whatever form the horror of humanity may take with some degree of humour and cheerful dignity and an unimpaired sense of beauty and justice. Let mine be a voice in their choir. And let them forgive me for occasionally being off-key.

No preface is complete without acknowledgement of those who have helped the author in various ways, and it is with special pleasure that I complete this one by offering my heartfelt thanks to the many good friends I have been fortunate enough to have along the way. I have benefited immeasurably from many hours of conversation from my colleagues Leonard Priestley, Graeme Hunter, Brendan Gillon, and John V. Canfield, with all of whom I have had the pleasure of discussing issues in religion and philosophy. Mention has already been made of the Venerable Samu Sunim, whose methods of training students did much to clarify my perspective during the time I spent with him. As every Buddhist knows, every complex thing is impermanent and must eventually come to an end. Among the complex things of the world are one's relationships with other beings, such as teachers. All relationships must end in due season with no regrets. I am among those who believe that the perfect relationship with a meditation teacher is like the perfect relationship with a dentist: as efficacious and as brief as conditions will permit. The Buddhist teacher's responsibility is to help the student become able, as quickly as possible, to live by the frequently repeated dictum of the Buddha to his disciples: 'Be an island (or lamp) unto yourself, taking nothing but wisdom itself as your guide.' I shall always be grateful for the years Sunim and I had of working closely together. It is not only to Sunim, but to all the members and associates of the Zen Buddhist temples of Toronto and Ann Arbor that I offer my deep appreciation for years of joyful friendship. During the five years that I was a member of the Zen Buddhist Temple, no one was a greater source of constant good cheer and kind encouragement through occasionally difficult times than Sujata Linda Klevnick, who was then priest and director of the Toronto temple. She is the kind of friend that most people spend their entire lives hoping to find. To all these people I offer my gratitude, and with them I extend my sincere wish that all beings may find true and lasting peace.

Montreal, Quebec
May 1989

1

ON BEING DHARMA-CENTRIC

This essay was written in 1986 as a response to a request from Ven. Phra Sunthorn Plamintr, a Theravādin monk originally from Thailand and then working in Illinois, to write an autobiographical account of my life as a Buddhist. Phra Sunthorn was hoping to collect several such autobiographical sketches by Western Buddhists, because he thought they might be inspiring to other Buddhists, in Thailand as well as in the West. Although I felt awkward trying to write a 'spiritual autobiography' at the tender age of forty-one, I found it impossible to refuse the request of this gentle and soft-spoken monk. So this was how my life looked to me when I was in my early forties. Eleven years later, I find that the past has changed somewhat since I was last there. Everything is impermanent, perhaps most of all memories. That notwithstanding, the only changes made to the text are the replacement of an older translation of the Dhammapada with a more recent one.

I USED TO have a type of nightmare that haunted me again and again. At some point during a dream, usually a perfectly ordinary one in which everything was slightly distorted but not necessarily in a frightening way, I would suddenly realize that I was in fact just dreaming, and a slow panic would begin to invade the dream. This would grow stronger, and I would be overcome by a feeling that I must wake up immediately. But the harder I tried to wake up, the more hopelessly I would become entangled in the dream. Trying to yell for help or bang my hand against the wall, I could not make a sound or a movement. During times of stress the dreams were more frequent and more intense, and I would often dream that I had finally managed to wake, only to discover that I was in a different dream. Sometimes I had to go through as many as four or five dreams before I finally woke up in a sweat, and it would take several minutes before I could assure myself that I was really awake at last. On several occasions I woke up in a different room from where I had gone to sleep, evidently having walked in my sleep.

On one very cold winter night I had this experience of going through dream after dream, trying desperately to wake up, and I found myself standing naked on the ledge of the window of my room several floors above the ground. At first it seemed simply like another nightmare on the way to becoming awake, but the cold air soon brought me fully to my senses. I gingerly crawled back into my room and listened for a long time to the pounding of my heart, all too aware that I could easily have fallen to my death. Sleeping began to seem like an enormously risky and terrifying undertaking, and I hated the very thought of it. But the more I forced myself to stay awake at night, the more nightmares I would have when sleep finally conquered me. It seemed as though I was spending all my time climbing through veils of dreams.

The year in which these panic-filled multiple dreams were at their worst happened to be the first semester of my final year in Beloit College, a small liberal arts college in southern Wisconsin. It was the autumn of 1966. Practically every American male I knew was preoccupied with the steadily increasing involvement of the United States in the war in Vietnam, but few young people had a clear idea of what was taking place over there. In fact not many young people even among those who were supposedly well educated had a clear idea where exactly Vietnam was. It was just 'over there' somewhere. Some people talked with such alarm about the danger to American freedom posed by Communism in Vietnam that one could easily get the idea that it must be an island five miles off the coast of California. People argued constantly about the war, and several friendships came to an end as people took different sides on the issue of whether the United States had any business being involved in a war 'over there', but hardly anyone was informed about the history of the conflict or the culture of the Vietnamese people. People just argued, blindly and stupidly shouting slogans at each other and accusing each other of being either fascist warmongers or un-American Communist sympathizers.

I was definitely in the latter category, not only in the eyes of people who favoured the US involvement in the war, but also in my own mind. Filled with a blind hatred of the nation of my birth, enraged by the mindless and incessant greed for power and material wealth and prestige that so many of my peer group displayed, outraged by the racism and intolerance and xenophobia of the society around me, I took consolation only in fantasies about destroying the evil American giant. Utopian visions, undoubtedly the legacy of my deep Yankee Puritanical roots, dominated my thinking and drove me to read the poetry and essays of the alienated Beat Generation, the American Transcendentalists, the Marxists and the Maoists. Reading such literature honed my contempt for the generation of which I was a part, a pampered and overfed generation whose social values and human sensibilities had been formed by the insipid vicariousness and complacent self-indulgence of a Hollywood motion picture and television culture that paradoxically celebrated both the superheroes of American mythology and the tasteless mediocrity of the suburban family next door.

Among the many things that I read in my struggle to remain at war with my own generation was an anthology of writings by the ancient Stoics. I was deeply impressed when I read that Stoic teachers made their disciples, most of whom came from wealthy families, perform humble types of work, the sort of tasks ordinarily left to slaves. Only when disciples learned to bear the physical hardships and social embarrassment of doing a slave's labours could they begin the arduous task of acquiring wisdom. Philosophy, which I had always regarded with a certain amount of suspicion, began to seem an enterprise of the greatest importance, for it involved using not only one's intellect but the totality of one's character towards the goal of learning how to live sensibly in an often senseless world. Upon reflection it became increasingly obvious that none of the causes I had so passionately taken up – civil rights, international peace in general and nuclear disarmament in particular, and the movement for conservation of natural resources and wildlife areas – could be achieved on the national or international level unless the population began to work first on their own individual characters. It was self-evident that before I could possibly be effective in any of these areas, I had to begin the task of reform with myself. As Gotama Buddha said, 'One who is sunk into mud cannot by himself pull out another who is sunk into mud.'[1] There was so much to be done in just this preliminary task of getting myself out of the mud that it seemed unlikely that I would ever get around to dealing effectively with the larger social issues.

Before his retirement, my father was a field geologist with the United States Geological Survey, and from him I acquired a scientific frame of mind from as early as I can recall. The type of scientific spirit that he instilled in me was an attitude of scepticism towards everything. He constantly urged me to avoid making hasty conclusions about things and to be willing at all times to modify my opinions in the face of new evidence and new experiences. Some of my earliest memories are of my father talking about vast expanses of space and time and impressing upon me how very tiny and insignificant human beings are and how very simple our minds are in comparison to the inconceivable complexity of the natural world. To think that we can really come to any sort of adequate understanding of the world and our place in it is laughable, and yet we have an undeniably strong curiosity. My father taught me to cherish this natural curiosity that is innate in living beings but to be constantly cautious of a false sense of certainty. Because of this strongly sceptical outlook, I developed from a very early age a contempt towards Christianity, partly because the only form of Christianity with which I ever came into contact was that of door-to-door evangelists who regularly came through the neighbourhood with their dire threats of hellfire for those who did not accept Jesus into their hearts. While still a young pupil in grammar school I took childish delight in shocking my religiously conservative playmates by insisting that I was an atheist.

This hostility towards religion grew stronger every year, and by the time I was an undergraduate at Beloit College I was so obsessed with my war against religion that many of my friends grew quite tired of my obnoxious raving. Whenever I encountered people with religious beliefs, my feelings towards them alternated between great anger at the stupidity of the views that had been inflicted upon them and that they would inflict upon others, and pity for their minds that were so mired in dogmas; at other times I was amazed at the moral strength of these same people who angered me and evoked in me feelings of sympathetic sorrow, and I had to admire them, however grudgingly. What impressed me in particular about many of these Christians was that they could accept my atheism much more easily than I could accept their Christianity. Their tolerance sometimes made me feel ashamed of my own intolerance.

The literature of the ancient Stoics, which led me to look also into the Cynics and the Sceptics and the other neo-Socratic traditions, provided me with the most important dimensions of religion and philosophy, namely, a deep sense of concern for the causes of justice and morality (which I had often admired in my Jewish and Christian friends) and a sense of intellectual integrity, a freedom from the chains of ideology and dogma, that good scientists usually managed to cultivate. The only thing I found disappointing in the ancient philosophers was that they had somehow managed to become extinct, and there was nowhere to turn to find an authentic teacher in the classical traditions of Cynicism and Scepticism. Reading about them in books was inspirational but hopelessly vicarious. What one really needs is good human teachers.

It was not long after I began to find great comfort in the ancient Hellenistic thinkers that I came into contact with Buddhism. The time was only a few weeks after the incident described above in which I had fought my way out of a dream only to find myself standing naked on a window ledge. Not long after that incident I left school, having decided not to complete the requirements for a degree, and went to live with my parents to await a call from the United States Army to appear for induction. While staying with my parents for that period of about two months, I enrolled in two seminars at the local Unitarian Church. One was on the trial and death of Socrates, which I found very moving, and the other was on the teachings of Buddhism. The seminar on Buddhism was led by a series of Buddhists who had come to live in the Denver area from various parts of Asia. All of them happened to be scientists, and each of them in his own way placed emphasis on how little conflict there was between the scientific mentality and the Buddhist mentality. Buddhism, they said, had no creeds or articles of faith or other forms of teaching that could be threatened by new discoveries in the natural sciences or the social or psychological sciences. Attracted by the prospect of a living tradition that had much of what I found so appealing in the ancient Greeks, I began to read an anthology of translations of Buddhist sūtras.

Reading about Buddhism proved to be both a little disappointing and a little fascinating. The simple and straightforward teachings that the Buddhist scientists had talked about were indeed to be found in

Buddhist literature, but one had to sift these little gems of wisdom out of mountains of barely comprehensible jargon. I enjoyed many of the Theravādin suttas, but the Mahāyāna sūtra material seemed hopelessly cluttered with inflated rhetoric and exaggerated claims, and I initially developed quite a distaste for it. The tantric material was even less appealing than the Mahāyāna sūtras, and even my self-congratulatory sense of open-mindedness could not withstand more than very brief exposures to the seemingly endless labyrinth of pointless fantasies that the Mahāyānists and Tantrics had devised. It was, however, quite intriguing that such a rich diversity of styles of teaching and literary tastes could coexist with no apparent animosity on the part of people who followed these widely divergent traditions. Being open to different ways of thinking and of seeing things was something that I greatly admired as an abstraction, but in practice I found it virtually impossible to develop even a minimal willingness to be patient with types of thinking and acting that were not obviously rooted in the rational scepticism that I so admired.

Learning to be tolerant of people with a radically different understanding of Buddhism was a matter of great importance and much frustration in the late 1960s and early 1970s in North America. In 1967, shortly after the seminar on Buddhism, I left the United States for Canada in the belief that I would never set foot in the country of my birth again. For the first eighteen months I lived in rural parts of the Western provinces and had little contact with other American exiles. Following the Stoic example, I cleansed myself of all my suburban sins by doing hard physical labour in the factories and on the farms of Manitoba, British Columbia, and Alberta. During those months I read several books on Buddhism and made efforts to piece together whatever instructions I could find in various sources on Buddhist meditation. Meditation became part of my daily routine, but I could find few people in rural Alberta with whom to talk about Buddhism or meditation. My only contact with people who understood meditation was with a group of Quakers, whose example of love and kindness made a deep impression on me. I sat with them regularly in silent meetings, but aside from this small group I found no one with an interest in meditation of any kind. My reflections on Buddhist teachings were therefore formed in solitude. While there was no one available to reinforce my interpretations of Buddhism, there was also no one available to challenge them.

This situation changed dramatically in September 1968, when I decided to enrol in Carleton University in Ottawa. Ottawa is not a large city, but it is the national capital and is located in a relatively populous and cosmopolitan region, and the ambient culture and prevailing attitudes there bore little resemblance to what I had experienced several thousand kilometres to the west. Among the important differences at that time was the fact that a relatively large community of young Americans had settled there, people who like me had left the United States in order to avoid military service. It was interesting to see how many of these people had picked up some familiarity with one or more of the forms of traditional Asian religions. Perhaps because a number of American conservative Christian ministers had been so vociferously patriotic and supportive of the American military involvement in Vietnam, it was natural for war resisters to develop a great mistrust of Christianity and look for alternative religious traditions that more actively favoured peace as a way of life. So people read whatever they could get their hands on about Hinduism, Buddhism, and Daoism. But at the same time that large numbers of people were rejecting American forms of Christianity and the tasteless values of 1950s American consumerism, while also rejecting the puritanical mentality that emphasized 'deferred gratification' and self-denial, people began to rediscover the joys of immediate pleasure.

Among the American war resisters in Canada, experimentation with drugs and alternative forms of sex were fairly common, and the majority of people that I knew who were interested in Buddhism were also interested in hallucinogenic drugs and free sex. Most of them seemed to like Buddhism because in their interpretation of the Buddha-dharma the whole purpose of life is to become free of obsessive guilt and open to all forms of experience; from this it seemed to follow that Buddhist teachings condoned the spontaneous and unpredictable actions of the free spirit who lived by the 1960s slogan 'Do your own thing' in complete disregard of the consequences. I was strongly opposed to the use of drugs, probably because I had done some experiments with peyote in 1964 and felt that drugs of that type did far more to confuse than to expand my mind, and I was particularly disturbed that people spoke of taking drugs as simply another form of Buddhist meditation. I got into many arguments over this matter. I pointed out that one of the five basic training precepts was to avoid the use of intoxicants that clouded the mind, and my friends replied that the precept only ruled out alcoholic beverages and not hallucinogenic drugs. Of course there were almost no real Buddhist teachers around, so when differences of opinion about the interpretation of Buddhist teaching and practice arose, there was no means of settling the issues to anyone's satisfaction. People just believed what they wanted to believe and called it what they wanted to call it. Some called it yoga, some called it Zen, some called it aboriginal shamanism and some called it witchcraft, but whatever they called it, it was in fact a spiritual stew made up of ingredients from all over the world and from every period of history, all randomly thrown together to be devoured by an undiscriminating generation that managed to retain the minds of children in the bodies of adults.

The 'Buddhism' of the North Americans of the Vietnam War generation was something with which I had very little patience. At the same time I felt a strong bond with many of my fellow war resisters. We had the same enemies: hypocrisy, injustice, blind intolerance, ignorance, and patriotic arrogance. And we had the same weaknesses, for we all had exactly the same faults as the society against which we were in rebellion; we too were hypocritical, unjust, intolerant, ignorant, and arrogant, because we were, after all, products of a society that had never really shown us how to be otherwise. Coming from similar backgrounds, having similar faults, and driven by similar hate-filled dreams, we therefore had much in common.

As should be clear from the tone of everything I have said so far, the problem that was greatest for me personally was that of coming to terms with the great arrogant anger and contempt I had for people who seemed to be wrong-headed. This was no trivial issue, and I struggled with it for years in many different forms. On the one hand it seemed quite obvious that human society in general is in very deep trouble. The people of the past two centuries have pursued technological growth to such an extent that humankind has obliterated thousands of other life forms from the planet, and we have done irreversible damage to the soil, the rivers and lakes and oceans, and to the atmosphere. We are like thieves who have stolen the means of livelihood from future generations in order to increase our own comfort and pleasure. This blind and selfish pursuit of comfort and pleasure increases daily, and despite the fact that the disastrous consequences are well documented, very few people are willing to take the step of simplifying their own lives and learning to be content with less. We now take it for granted that we can have fresh fruit and vegetables all year round, fine products made by inexpensive labour all over the world, warm dwellings in winter and cool air in summer regardless of what the weather may be like outdoors, personal luxuries and conveniences in unprecedented abundance, and a battery of sophisticated weapons that will destroy anyone who may try to take any of it away from us. When one contrasts the way we live with the crushing poverty and widespread starvation found in most other parts of the world, most of us Westerners live at a level of opulence that is well beyond being obscene, and we believe it is our natural right to do so.

Surely this is a matter about which one is justified in feeling outraged and ashamed. Surely it is a cause of legitimate concern that so many of the world's peoples seek to solve their problems by systematic violence against people who belong to different ethnic groups, different language families, different religions, and different nations. And surely one is justified in feeling alarmed at how much valuable time is wasted by people who live in a fantasy world of 'alternative spirituality', or New Age thought as it is sometimes called: the eclectic world of astrology, the occult, mysticism, and pseudo-science that is still, unfortunately, quite fashionable among many of the people of my generation. What all these alternative spiritual paths have in common is that they are perfectly incompetent to deal with the problems of modern man. It is heartbreaking to see people wasting time on them. And on the personal level it is a great struggle for me not to become a little impatient with the blindness of our times. The greatest problem of all is to learn to be patient without at the same time becoming altogether passive and indifferent, without shrugging off the problems of the planet and saying 'I no longer care.'

It is in this struggle that the teachings and practices of Buddhism have been a great friend. It would be impossible to cite all the passages from Buddhist suttas and academic works that have provided guidance in this struggle alone, but one group of verses from the Sutta Nipāta has been particularly useful to me in the fight against arrogance.

> A person who persists in opinions regards as a waste
> everything other than that which he regards as best in the

> world, thinking 'it is supreme!' Therefore he fails to get beyond disputes. Then grasping at just that which he sees as commendable to himself in rules of conduct and vows and in what is seen, heard, or thought, he regards everything else as a loss. The experts call that thing a shackle owing to which one considers all else a waste. Therefore the monk should not pursue rules of conduct and vows and what is seen, heard, or thought. Nor should he form an opinion of people either on the basis of knowledge or on the basis of rules of conduct and vows. Nor should he present himself as an equal, nor should he think of himself as lowly or excellent. Giving up assumptions and not taking them up again, he does not pursue even knowledge. Indeed he does not side with any party in controversies, nor does he believe any opinion whatsoever.[2]

Being attached to one's own way of looking at the world can easily lead to looking upon oneself as superior to those who see things differently. One can very easily fall into the trap of thinking of other people as worthless or even downright dangerous because of the views they hold or because of the actions they perform. And once one has deemed another person or another people as worthless, it is not a long step to feeling that one is justified in somehow being rid of them. Human history is one long tragic story of societies ridding themselves of unwelcome forms of nonconformity to their own preferred values. It takes the form of international wars, civil wars, revolutions, uprisings, riots, acts of terrorism, religious persecution, racism, genocide, incarceration, systematic torture, brainwashing, capital punishment, and dozens of other methods by which one part of the human population imposes its collective will upon another part of the population. But the root cause is deep attachment to a particular way of viewing the world and one's place within it.

> It is by oneself that evil is done, by oneself that one is afflicted. It is by oneself that evil is not done, by oneself that one is purified. Purity and impurity are individual matters; no one purifies another.[3]

> Let us live most happily, free from hatred in the midst of the hateful; let us remain free from hatred in the midst of people who hate. Let us live most happily, free from disease in the

> midst of the diseased; let us remain free from disease in the midst of diseased people. Let us live most happily, free from restlessness in the midst of the restless; let us remain free from restlessness in the midst of restlessness.[4]

> It is easy to see the fault of others, hard to see one's own. One sifts the faults of others like chaff, but covers up one's own, as a crafty cheater covers up a losing throw. In one who watches out for the faults of others, always ready to blame, compulsions arise; such a one is far from extinction of passions.[5]

The ability to live in peace among the war-makers is not a consequence of divine grace, nor is it the outcome solely of one's genetic make-up or social upbringing, rather is it an acquired skill. Developing the skill begins with the determination to forget about the shortcomings of others and simply to focus on one's own. As this skill is developed, one learns to be responsive to the basic humanity of all peoples and to be unmindful of the ideological, cultural, and national differences that separate people into artificial categories. In practical terms the skill can be achieved by some form of loving-kindness meditation (*mettā-bhāvanā*) as taught in classical Buddhism. There are various ways of doing this meditation, but the method I learned first was that in which one begins by cultivating a sense of loving care for oneself by wishing oneself to be free from physical and emotional pain, and continues by learning to transfer that same loving care to friends, casual acquaintances, and finally to enemies. The goal is to be able to wish as strongly for an enemy's happiness and freedom from pain and conflict as for one's own happiness and freedom from conflict. Since the characteristic in myself that caused most pain to myself and to those around me was my arrogance, impatience with stupidity, and tendency to let impatience grow into destructive anger, I made a habit of setting aside a little time every day to do this loving-kindness meditation. Eventually it began to have a positive effect.

It was made very clear to me how powerful the meditation on loving-kindness could be during my time as a graduate student at the University of Toronto. While at Carleton University in Ottawa I had made the decision, urged on by Professor Nalini Devdas who had guided me with great kindness through the study of Buddhism and Sanskrit, to pursue the study of classical Indian Buddhism as my academic specialty. So in 1972 I entered the MA programme in Sanskrit and Indian Studies, and in 1974 went on to enter the PhD programme there. During these hectic years of study I became rather lax in meditation practice, and the regular loving-kindness meditation was almost completely set aside. In 1976 a crisis arose in the Department that eventually resulted in the decision by the deans of the University of Toronto to close the Department. The details of the conflict were far too complex to discuss here. Essentially the problem was that factions had evolved in the faculty. These factions were not founded on intellectual issues but were the result almost solely of differences in personality among the professors. Several of the key professors had come to hate each other for reasons known only to themselves, and their mutual animosity grew so severe that they began putting obstacles in each other's paths and in the paths of the students of their rival professors. The bitterness became so intense that not a single student escaped having to undergo a great deal of pain and inconvenience. There were no victors, but every single person, whether student or professor, became a victim of this uncontrolled childish hatred. Being one of the many victims of this collective stupidity, I very naturally became angry, and in my anger got into the habit of mocking and ridiculing all the professors and speaking about their shortcomings constantly to other students. Such actions served in many ways to fan the flames of hatred. I made many people laugh as I mocked the professors, but the laughter was always at their expense. It was not my specific intention to increase hatred, but that was the outcome of my careless use of cruel and biting satire in the situation.

It did not become clear to me how destructive my own actions had been until two years later. After the crisis of 1976 I completely withdrew from the academic scene for eighteen months. So great was my disgust with the pettiness of the professors that I had lost all desire to pursue an academic life and chose instead to earn a living doing manual labour, my Stoic remedy for all psychological ills. During this time of self-imposed exile from the academic world, one of my former teachers came to Toronto for a visit. Dr Shoryu Katsura had taught me classical Tibetan and had been the instructor in many of the courses I had taken in Buddhist philosophy. While he was teaching me he was himself a senior PhD student, and when he finished his doctorate in 1974 he returned to Japan in order to help his ageing father take care of the family Jōdo Shinshū Temple. On his visit to

Toronto in 1977 he learned that I was no longer pursuing my studies but earning a livelihood doing manual labour, and he made an effort to find where I was. He invited me to dinner and asked me whether I would consider going to Japan to resume my studies. He urged me to apply for a scholarship from the Japanese Ministry of Education for foreign students to study in Japan. My feelings were very mixed at the time, for I was happy doing labour and saw the academic world as a source of endless frustration and pain. But Dr Katsura strongly urged me to realize that I had a responsibility to make better use of the education that society had given me, so in the end I agreed to apply for the scholarship. Within a few months I heard that the application had been accepted, and by the end of 1977 I was living in Hiroshima, feverishly trying to learn Japanese and to get back into the habit of being an intellectual again instead of an honest working man.

The sixteen months that I lived in Japan proved in many ways to be a major turning point in my life. In the first place I was overwhelmed with gratitude that someone had gone so far out of his way to help me. As I began to settle into the new routine I had many occasions to reflect on kindness and on hatred. One afternoon I went outside to play baseball with the students of the Indian Philosophy Department of Hiroshima University, and we played until dark. When we came back into the study room of the department, Professor Uno, the chairman of the department, was busy binding books for his students. I found it moving that he would care for his students in this way, because I had grown unaccustomed to professors doing such acts of kindness. Eventually I observed that he stayed late almost every evening to bind books or do other tasks that would make life easier for the students in his department. Once I mentioned Professor Uno's kindness to Professor Katsura, and he said simply 'Professor Uno has known suffering.' I went back to my apartment and sat down and spent several hours thinking about that simple statement. Tears came to my eyes as I thought about what a beautiful way had been found to deal with one's own personal suffering: to transform it into kindness towards others. Once again I made loving-kindness meditation part of my daily routine, and I made a special effort to feel kindly towards the Toronto professors at whose hands not only I but all my fellow students had suffered.

A second incident that had a very powerful effect on me in Japan was visiting the museum that chronicles the dropping of the first atomic bomb on Hiroshima. There is no point in even trying to describe the impact that it has on one to see the evidence of so much concentrated suffering. What so impressed me about the atomic bomb museum, however, was the way that the exhibits universalize the pain of Hiroshima. Rather than being a testimony exclusively to the sufferings of the victims of the atomic bomb, the museum manages to draw attention to the enormity of unnecessary suffering caused by war in general. Never once during my sixteen months in Hiroshima did I feel any sense of hostility towards the Americans for using the atomic bomb; rather I saw again and again a strong determination to get the message out to the world that war must not be allowed to happen. As someone once observed, war is the last resort of the incompetent. Never have I seen that message more forcefully and so tastefully made as in Hiroshima. The city as a whole was another example to me of the power of transforming personal tragedy into universal kindness. It was an example that I shall never forget.

A third aspect of the stay in Japan was that I encountered Buddhist temples and practising Buddhists on a daily basis and eventually came to see that, aside from students and professors in the universities, few people had any formal knowledge of Buddhist teachings. Repeatedly I encountered people who told me they felt that Buddhist philosophy and the sūtras were very deep and almost impossible for ordinary people to understand. But this did not deter people from chanting sūtras or copying them in beautiful calligraphy and paying homage in various other ways, and it also did not prevent them from trying to embody the spirit of compassion. Seeing this forced me to re-examine a number of the assumptions I had acquired through the purely scholarly approach to Buddhist ideas; in particular, practices that I had once been inclined to dismiss as peripheral to Buddhism proper began to seem like perfectly natural ways of cultivating the wisdom and compassion that lies at the heart of Buddhism. Chanting and burning incense, for example, had always struck me as completely frivolous activities that had no connection with the 'real' Buddha-dharma whatsoever. I associated these actions with magic and mechanical religion. My only experience with incense was that North American hippies had used it in great abundance to mask the odours of marijuana smoke, so it did not have particularly spiritual connotations to me. But when I actually saw Japanese Buddhists chanting and burning incense and bowing before Buddha images, it was evident that when done in the right frame of mind such activities were hardly different from the various other forms of self-cultivation and meditation that I found so respectable and effective.

On one occasion while on a side trip to Korea, I visited a temple on a scorching hot summer day, and there I saw a very elderly woman doing prostration rituals. Despite being soaked with sweat and obviously stiff with age, this woman simply did prostration after prostration with such serenity that she seemed wholly unconcerned with either the blistering heat or the inevitable pains of an aged body. Here was a practice that I could not quite fit into the theoretical framework I had of the Buddhist path, because quite frankly it had never once occurred to me that one might develop and strengthen one's resolve by performing prostrations. But as soon as I saw this woman doing her prostration exercises with such calm and single-mindedness, I said to myself, 'Look here, you arrogant and condescending Sanskrit scholar, doing a few prostrations might be just what you need to help yourself down to a more humble vantage point.' Before long prostrations became part of my practice.

Returning to Canada from Japan proved difficult. I had almost no money, and was trying to finish writing my PhD dissertation. I learned on getting back that my Department had been closed down owing to the personal feuds among the professors, but it would still be possible for me to submit a dissertation. Many of the professors were still working at the University. A fellow graduate student in that programme had spent eight years researching and writing a dissertation on Sanskrit dramaturgy, and after an intense summer of very hard work she managed to submit a manuscript over 700 pages long. As the time grew near for her to defend her work, signs began to emerge that the old feuds among the professors were still alive, despite the professors having been placed in different departments to keep them from seeing one another. It was also becoming increasingly clear that my colleague was going to be caught in the middle of the fights among the professors. The deans also sensed that trouble was brewing, so they sent observers to the thesis defence to ensure that nothing went wrong. Despite their very best efforts, things went terribly wrong. A very serious argument broke out before the defence even began, and the air was charged with hostility during the entire examination. When it was all over, there were not enough votes in favour of awarding my friend the PhD. The deans immediately ruled that the examination had not been properly conducted, so it was not put on her record that she had failed the examination, but she was also not awarded a PhD. Officially it was as if nothing had happened at all. It was as if she had simply never submitted her thesis and no one had ever read it. After so many years of dedicated work on a topic she dearly loved, this was a cruel turn of events. There was nothing that we could do, nor could the University do anything more than offer my friend a second chance to defend her work.

It is a terrible thing to see an innocent person victimized by someone else's carelessness or malice. It leaves one feeling helpless and incapable of finding any words that bring comfort to the victim. On such occasions I usually find a great conflict arising within myself. On the one hand I am usually inclined to view personal tragedy from a 'philosophical' perspective. Not getting a PhD is, after all, of no great importance in the greater scheme of things. The ill fortune of my friend's not getting what she had spent the better part of her adult life trying to get was a tragedy that had to be borne by her alone, for in the eyes of the world at large the event was quite simply of no consequence. It was simply an event like any other, of no greater moment than the falling of a leaf on an autumn day. But such a cold philosophical perspective on ill fortune provides little comfort to the victim. On the other hand, I am often inclined to try to have sympathetic feelings for the victim. But when the victim's feelings are intense anger, how can one encourage another to continue dwelling on the anger until it festers into an incurable emotional wound? Telling someone 'You have every right to be angry and full of thoughts of revenge, for you were treated badly by another's stupidity and cruelty' would in the long run be most harmful, but that is often precisely what the victim wishes to hear. Then again, there is no point in simply trying to divert the victim's attention from the ill fortune, because sooner or later the victim must come to terms with the tragedy. It seems that whatever one says or does, even doing or saying nothing, only makes matters worse. This state of affairs has often made me reflect on how very incompetent I am at helping others when help is most needed.

Perhaps one can even make the general point that most human beings are inadequate to the task of offering one another true help and comfort. Nowhere is this inadequacy more apparent than in all the many religions that humanity has devised. Our imaginations have populated the universe with gods and demons and all manner of spirits and forces on whom we can blame our misfortunes and in whom we can have false hope for our escape from suffering. Buddhism itself has taken on the myth of karma and rebirth to drive home the point that ultimately we have no one to blame for our afflictions but ourselves. The myth of karma is no less cruel, and no more likely to be true, than any of the other religious myths that humankind has devised to deal with its collective anguish. While it is possible that it may provide people with some small amount of comfort to believe in karma and rebirth, it is also possible that it does very little good in the long run to encourage people to believe stories that have no real grounding but can only be acknowledged in the final analysis as arbitrary fictions. Since the mandate of Buddhism is to help people to learn to be at ease in a world of impermanence and uncertainty, since this mandate cannot very well be fulfilled if all we can do is ask people to change dogmas rather than to give up dogma altogether, and since there is no better reason to accept the story of karma and rebirth than there is to believe any other mythology, it is one of the many outdated dogmas that may well be discarded as Buddhism moves into the modern world.

Speculating about what kind of Buddhism might emerge in the modern world is not in itself a very productive exercise, but there may be a point in expressing one's views about the kind of Buddhism that we need. In my opinion what humanity desperately needs is to face reality very directly and very squarely. A major part of human reality is that we simply do not know what reality as a whole is all about. We do not really know how the universe works, and we do not really know even how we ourselves work. Our understanding of the physical body is very impressive compared to, say, the Buddha's knowledge of the body, and our knowledge of the mind and the emotions has also made great progress since his time. But this should never blind us to the fact that we still know very little, and probably never can get more than curiosity-arousing glimpses into the overall picture. Moreover, to pretend that we do understand is often to take enormous risks with the very ability of this planet to sustain life. This is not at all to say that we should not be curious and try to learn as much as possible. Rather it is to be constantly aware of the fact that we can never learn more than a fraction of what we really must know. Life is, and always must be, a frightfully risky business. Religion and philosophy should enhance our awareness of the risks, not shield them from our eyes behind a veil of pretty stories and palliative rituals.

An exercise that I find very useful is to imagine the worst possible kind of universe. Imagine a universe in which events are almost perfectly random, making it virtually impossible for sentient beings to learn from their experiences. Imagine a universe in which there is absolutely no justice. Imagine that people who are cruel and vicious get away with their malicious actions, often without even feeling a twinge of guilt. Imagine that some people dedicate their lives, individually and collectively, to producing things of beauty and benefit only to have them destroyed either by natural circumstances or by the negligence or meanness of other human beings. Imagine that people who have great integrity and honesty and ability are often overlooked in favour of people who are deceitful and hungry for personal power. Imagine that many of the people who control human destiny are opinionated, ill-informed, and incompetent. Above all, imagine that there is no rhyme or reason to things happening as they do. And after imagining all this, begin to recognize that there is no reason to think that the world is otherwise. There is every reason to wish that it were otherwise, but there is no reason to think that it actually is otherwise. This first part of this exercise might be a little discouraging. But the second part of it is to think of the things that have gone well in one's own personal life, however few those things may be, and to feel grateful for them. Then think of the very small number of things that are within our understanding and control, and realize what a tremendous difference it can make to our own outlook on the otherwise bleak landscape if we choose, in those small areas where we can make a little difference, to be cheerful rather than bitter, kind rather than mean, co-operative rather than obstructive. We have absolutely no one anywhere to help us, so we can only help ourselves, even if only in these small ways. There will be no justice at all unless we make it. There will be no comfort unless we provide it. There will be no freedom unless we bestow it. Developing the habit of thinking something like this, I believe, is the only good means we human beings have of collectively beginning to pull out of the horrible downward spirals of retributive warfare and the technological rape of the planet.

Last year sometime I happened to be listening to a radio programme on important breakthroughs in medical research. A doctor was being interviewed about the part he had played in finding the causes of a certain fatal disease. The enthusiastic interviewer said, 'Can we expect that within another five years there will be a cure available for this disease and that people will no longer die from it?' The physician replied 'Yes. Ten years from now it may well be that no one will die from this disease. They will then, of course, only die of something else.' There is, I think, much to be learned from this doctor's attitude. Rooted in the realization that death neither can nor should ever be eliminated, the physician nevertheless strives to postpone each individual death for as long as possible. For every patient the overall treatment is, in the final analysis, going to be a failure, for the patient must die of something. This is no call to be bitter or full of despair or depressed, because looked at in another way, every day of life is almost a miracle. A very similar attitude must be cultivated by those who work for peace, justice, sanity, and ecological and economic reform. Ultimately, no matter how many battles we may win, we will inevitably lose the war. Ultimately, humanity will vanish from the universe, and so eventually will all forms of life and consciousness. Long after life is no longer even a memory, there being no mind left to have memories, the planet will crumble, and the sun will die. After that, who knows? Given the overwhelming odds against us, then, every day that we manage not to perish is a cause of great wonder and joy. Let us strive to have several more such days. Failing that, let us strive to live in harmony just for today, just for this very moment.

Attitudes such as these are, I hope, what Buddhism will foster in the West and in the modern world in general. Classical Buddhism is a way of approaching life that has a great capacity to be in tune with our times. There is even a sense in which it has a great capacity to fulfil many of the dreams that Europeans had when they bullied their way on to the North American continent. That there is something very Buddhist about the traditional concept of America struck me when I visited the United States a while ago. Two years ago it happened that I had some work to do in Washington DC, and I had a few hours of spare time in which to see some of the sights of the downtown area. The District of Columbia is a city full of monuments and memorials. The Lincoln Memorial and the obelisk dedicated to George Washington have become familiar to people around the world, if only because pictures of them appear on American currency. Less famous but to my mind the most beautiful of the memorials to heroes from the American past is the Jefferson Memorial. It is a stupa-shaped marble dome overlooking a beautifully placid body of water. Inside there is a large statue of Thomas Jefferson (1743–1826), third president of the United States and one of the authors of the Declaration of Independence. When I entered the memorial it happened to be nearing sunset, and few people were present. The atmosphere was deeply tranquil and serene, as inside a great temple, and I could not resist sitting on a stone bench and doing zazen for some time.

Afterwards I began to read some of the words inscribed inside the monument. My eye was caught in particular by one sentence carved in marble on the walls that encircle the statue of Jefferson: 'I have sworn upon the altar of God eternal hostility to every form of tyranny over the mind of man.' Tears came to my eyes as I read these words, and I found myself looking up at the face of Jefferson and saying aloud, 'Where now is that country you founded?'

Thoughts turned to my reason for being in Washington. I had been invited to be on a panel to adjudicate grant proposals made to the National Endowment for the Humanities, and the day had been spent looking at numerous research proposals by the nation's leading scholars. The process is a very painful one, because there are simply more excellent proposals than there is funding for them, and the result is that truly excellent research projects receive either no funding at all or too little funding to carry out the proposed research as well as it deserves. The Reagan administration did not place a high priority on academic research, and funding in this area reflects the low esteem scholarship has in the eyes of those who control how money is spent. In contemplating the effect that these people are having on the civilization not only of the North American continent but of the whole world, I am reminded of these words of the philosopher Kant, written in 1784:

> Although … our world rulers at present have no money left over for public education and for anything concerning what is best in the world, since all they have is already committed to

> future wars, they will still find it in their own interest at least not to hinder the weak and slow, independent efforts of their peoples in this work.[6]

There has been a strongly demoralizing undercurrent of fear on the part of people who work for the NEH and other agencies that fund research in science and the humanities – fear that the leadership of these agencies will be taken over more and more by Christian fundamentalists, ultra-nationalists, and other elements of the American right, people who certainly do not support and who might even be willing to hinder 'the weak and slow, independent efforts' of people who are striving for what is best in the world. The American right, for all its mawkish flag-waving sentimentality for the lost greatness of the past, does not have a strong record of honouring Jefferson's 'hostility to every form of tyranny over the mind of man'. Rather, its hostility is reserved only for those forms of tyranny, real or imagined, that are politically allied to the Soviet Union or Cuba. Tyranny that serves American political interests is easily accommodated. The American right has delivered to the world a nation that is a grotesque parody of the beautiful ideals upon which it was founded.

But that is a topic to be discussed in another forum. What I wish to pursue now is a thought that hit me very forcibly as I looked at the face of the statue of Jefferson: this was a very Dharma-centric man who tried to found a Dharma-centric nation. There is perhaps something to be learned from the failure of this noble experiment. I do not yet have a clear idea of what can be learned, but it seems a worthy thing to think about for a little while.

Let me begin by explaining what I mean by the expression 'Dharma-centric'. Christian theologians sometimes make a distinction between theocentric and Christocentric theology, depending on whether the principal focus is upon the universalistic concept of God that is at the centre of not only Christianity but also Judaism and Islam and some forms of Hinduism or whether the focus is upon Jesus Christ as unique saviour of unworthy sinners. Adapting that terminology somewhat, I think we could speak of various types of Buddhism as being Buddha-centric, Dharma-centric, or Sangha-centric, depending on which of the Three Jewels is held as the principal focus of one's practice. Some forms of Buddhism could even be described as Guru-centric, owing to the strong emphasis placed on devotion and loyalty to one's personal teacher. What it means to be Guru-centric, Buddha-centric, or Sangha-centric is perhaps self-explanatory, but 'Dharma' is a particularly elusive word and has acquired more than its share of mystification over the millennia. The principal meaning of 'dharma' according to Indian commentators was simply virtue (*guṇa*). The dharmas of a thing are the features and characteristics by which it is known and distinguished from other things. The dharma of the Buddha, then, is that characteristic by which he was distinguished from other mortals, because of which he stood out. What makes an awakened (*buddha*) person awakened, and therefore distinct from the masses of foolish people (*bāla-puthujjana*), is just his wisdom. Therefore the Buddha-dharma is the key virtue of the Buddha, and the key virtue of the Buddha is just his wisdom.

Wisdom is by its very nature difficult to codify. True wisdom is always subtle and dynamic and rooted in very particular and concrete situations. It can never be successfully captured in static words and phrases and rules and formulas and creeds, because words deal only with broad generalizations and not with concrete situations. Wisdom cannot possibly be institutionalized. It cannot be made into something formal. Human history, in so far as it is a history of human institutions, whether religious or political in nature, is a tragic testimony to the simple fact that wisdom defies formalization and formalization makes a mockery of wisdom. Wisdom is an outlook, an attitude characterized by open-mindedness, impartiality, and freedom from prejudice and dogma; wisdom is not doctrines or slogans or adherence to any sort of orthodoxy. Because wisdom can never successfully be codified or formalized, and because it is by its very nature expressed in openness, it follows that wisdom can never be the exclusive property of any one religious or philosophical system. This point is worth belabouring, even at the risk of becoming a little tedious, because it is common to find Buddhists who regard the Buddha-dharma as 'the teachings of the Buddha' or 'the doctrines of the Buddha' rather than as the essence of wisdom that Buddhist teachings try, sometimes rather awkwardly and clumsily, to convey. And it is even possible, unfortunately, to find Buddhists who feel that the institutions of the Buddhist religion embody more wisdom than do other formalized religions and who have a rather narrow-minded contempt for all forms of wisdom other than that which is found in some sūtra or spoken by some high-ranking member of the bhikṣu-sangha.

Being Dharma-centric, then, means making wisdom itself the very centre of one's life. It means being philosophical in the root sense of that word: in love with wisdom. It was because Jefferson came from a tradition that tried very hard to do just that – to make wisdom the centre of their lives – that I call him Dharma-centric. Jefferson was not a particularly religious man if being religious is measured by outward signs of piety. He was a Deist, a person who believed in the so-called 'philosopher's God'. The philosopher's God is a rather abstract and remote notion of the perfect goodness towards which all intelligence strives; the Deist's God was sometimes called an 'absentee lord', because most Deists did not believe in direct divine revelation. Jefferson compiled a book called *The Life and Morals of Jesus of Nazareth,* in which he took passages from the Gospels that reflected a strong sense of morality and excluded all those passages that seemed in violation of human reason and common sense. The essence of religion for Jefferson was morality, and the essence of morality was not formal adherence to rules and laws but rather to the single principle of thoughtfulness and kindness towards others. A product of his time, Jefferson was deeply influenced by Francis Bacon, Isaac Newton, and John Locke. From them he inherited a deep appreciation of the supremacy of direct empirical investigation over speculation, and of the concrete experience of life in this world over the vague metaphysical and often self-contradictory promises of life on other planes of existence. In the language of his time, Jefferson's interests were exclusively secular, that is, rooted in this world that can be experienced directly through the human senses rather than in mysterious other worlds that can be known only through revelation and occult methods.

These traits in Jefferson make him, I would argue, a man very much in accord with the attitudes that set Śākyamuni Buddha apart from other men of his time. For the Buddha too was secular in the sense described above. And I would also argue that there is a way in which both Thomas Jefferson and Śākyamuni Buddha failed in their missions of establishing wisdom among their fellow human beings. In neither case is the failure really theirs; the failure really lies with those who followed the formal expressions rather than the essence of wisdom. And here, I think, lies the most agonizingly difficult problem of the human condition. Wisdom cannot be transmitted. One person cannot make another wise. A person can at best act wisely and hope that others are wise enough to follow the good example. But the vast majority of people do not follow the good example. The masses of people, the *puthujjana*, are fools (*bāla*), who pursue immediate pleasures and gratification for themselves and their own immediate families and clans and nations and are willing to act for themselves with complete disregard for how their actions affect other beings. That is the way of the ordinary folks, the *loka*. The way of the sage, on the other hand, is superior (*uttara*) to that of ordinary folks (*loka*): it is *lokottara*, which is often translated, rather badly, as supramundane or even transcendental.

Because the common masses of people are self-centred rather than altruistic, because they are ego-centred rather than Dharma-centred, the religious institutions of the masses tend to be filled with rituals that are designed to achieve those very things that fools want: property, social success, prestige, influence over others, comfort, luxury, and a very long life in which to enjoy all these things, topped off by plenty of offspring to pass all these things on to. Appealing to magic to achieve such things when other means of gaining them have failed is what to most folk religion is all about, what most of life in general is all about. It is also what technology, the modern man's magic, is all about. The most serious implication of all this, of course, is that as soon as a movement that begins in wisdom becomes popular, it is destined to be undermined by the folk trends that people bring with them. And yet, without popular support, no human institution can long survive. In many Asian countries the price that the bhikṣu-sangha has paid for surviving for so long is that the spark of wisdom has been all but completely buried in a mass of folk superstitions: a haphazard assortment of benedictions, blessings, prayers for the dead, supplications for good fortune and prosperity, exorcisms of malicious forces, and awe-filled reverence for the supernatural accomplishments of saints.

One might well ask: has Buddhism in fact survived any better in Asia than Stoicism has done in Europe? Was the wisdom of Buddhism any less snuffed out in Asia than the wisdom of the Greeks was snuffed out by the folk superstitions of pagan and Christian Europe? How one answers that will, of course, depend entirely on what one thinks the essence of Buddhism is. Now that Buddhism is becoming a factor in North American life, it is an appropriate time not only for

North American Buddhists but also for Buddhists everywhere to give some thought to the question of what in Buddhism is essential and what can be discarded without harm.

Buddhism is now taking root in an environment that has been formed primarily by Jewish and Christian ways of thinking and behaving, and early Christianity itself was largely the product of the rich cultural diversity of Hellenistic civilization, which included Greek, Persian, and Middle Eastern elements. North American Christianity is even more diversified than the earlier forms of Christianity, for it also includes many elements from the various European tribes. The great strength of Buddhism historically has been its ability to take full advantage of the cultural richness of each environment into which it has been transplanted. There is no reason to suspect that it will be any different in the West. Buddhists stand to learn a great deal from the Judaic and Christian traditions, for both of these religious traditions have benefited considerably from their incessant struggle to reconcile time-honoured ways of thinking with the ever new demands of historical change, and to reconcile the fluid perspectives of empirical science and common sense with the relatively static doctrines based on what was believed to be revelation. As a result of this struggle, the Jewish and Christian theologians and philosophers have gradually developed a science of interpretation and criticism that incorporates within it the finest intellectual achievements of humanity. Western-trained scholars of Buddhism, as well as many Japanese scholars influenced by European scholarship, have applied the critical methods of Judeo-Christian theological scholarship to the study of Buddhist thought with results that may be very challenging and stimulating to traditional Buddhists whose approach to studying Buddhism has often been somewhat more naïve. During the past five hundred years Christians have had to learn to re-examine the very foundations of their traditional religious beliefs and to discard many teachings and attitudes that once were regarded as divinely sanctioned. They have repeatedly had to purge their institutions of the accidental by-products of human political interests and struggles for power and territory and domination.

To give just one concrete example of this process of getting rid of dangerously outmoded ways of thinking, since the tragedy of the genocide of European Jews in the first half of the twentieth century, Christians have had to come to terms with the fact that much of the classical Christian religion was built on a foundation that was anti-Jewish to the core. Realizing that this bigotry against Jews was inexcusably uncivilized, many Christian leaders have been forced to question the authority of two millennia of anti-Jewish theology, and they have had to question even the authority of the Christian Bible itself, much of which has an unambiguously anti-Jewish tone. Can a body of literature that places so much emphasis on the evil of one particular race of people really reflect the mind of God? To face such fundamental issues directly has taken enormous strength and courage on the part of all thinking Christians and has done much to strengthen Western society as a whole by making many Westerners have the courage to be far less sure of themselves and of the doctrines that their society has historically taken for granted. By learning from this example of self-criticism and self-transformation that the Christians have given us, Western Buddhists may be able to build a vital new tradition of Buddhism that comes close in spirit if not in form to the original way of Śākyamuni Buddha and his early followers, for that early Buddhism was also above all a movement of self-improvement through self-examination.

It has been many years since I last had a nightmare. Although I have not completely rooted out my impatience and intolerance of those who think differently, the practice of Buddhist forms of meditation has helped me make some progress towards a less childish mentality. As I meet other Buddhists in North America, I see many of them experiencing the same struggles with their intolerance and prejudices that I experienced with mine. I look forward to working with them in the task of helping our world become more mature through a Dharma-centric religion. Let us make the foundation of our religion the habit of constantly re-appraising the foundation of our religion. Let us make our central practice the incessantly critical re-examination of our central practice. By so doing, we may all be able eventually to penetrate the veil of successive dreams until we are, at last, fully and unmistakably awake.

2

BODHISATTVAS IN BLUE JEANS

Dharma in North America

This essay, written in 1989, was based on notes for two public talks given in July 1987 at the Zen Buddhist Temple, Ann Arbor, Michigan. In the years that have passed since I wrote this essay, I have developed a less petulant attitude towards the doctrine of karma and rebirth, which receives a rather scathing treatment here. If time permits, and a more gentle and patient muse visits me some day, I may eventually respond to some of the arguments presented here. Meanwhile, I leave the formulation of suitable replies as an exercise for the reader.

THE HOUSE THAT ZEN BUILT

THE ZEN BUDDHIST TEMPLE in Ann Arbor, like many Buddhist facilities in North America and Europe, is a large house that at one time must have been a dwelling for a large extended family. My father spent part of his youth in Hillsdale, Michigan, not far from Ann Arbor, in a house much like the one that has now become the Temple. Some of the memories I most cherish from my own childhood were of listening to my father tell stories of his childhood and trying to picture the house in which he grew up with three brothers and a variety of aunts and uncles and cousins and people who just seemed to end up staying for a while during the hard years of the depression and the Second World War. The stories my father told were not exciting or entertaining in themselves, and I can hardly recall any of them now, but they conjured up a picture in my mind of a place full of love and joy and not a little bit of sadness. But the times of tragedy were also times of great sharing within a large extended family. That's the way people used to live in America. Not many live that way any more.

Some years ago I finally got a chance to see the house in Hillsdale where my father had lived. It had become a fraternity house associated with Hillsdale College. Many of the large houses in the Midwestern United States and Canada that used to be the homes of extended clans are now boarding houses or office suites. The building in which the Zen Temple is now located was probably a big family dwelling a century ago. Then it was made into a rooming house of some kind, and I am told it was not much more than an abandoned shell when the founders of the Zen Buddhist Temple bought it. Just think of the history that an old house like that has. At one time a place full of people living together as a big family, sharing their love though all kinds of joyful and sorrowful experiences, helping each other in so many ways, then a place inhabited mostly by transients and lonely people down on their luck, and then once again made into a place where people live and work together almost as a family, get to know each other almost as intimately as family and sometimes a lot more intimately than family.

I see the buildings in which so many Buddhist groups have taken up residence as concrete symbols of what Buddhism itself has the potential for helping to do in North American society as a whole. Of course Buddhism is much too small a force to do much by itself; only about one out of every five hundred people in America is a Buddhist. I do think, however, that Buddhists form part of a larger movement on this continent, a movement of people who have grown tired of the shambles that our culture has become and are seeking an intelligent alternative to the unparalleled materialism of our society without falling into the many mindless alternatives to materialism that have arisen to provide people with an escape from what really is an untenable way of life. In the same way that the Zen people in Ann Arbor have taken a dilapidated house and through a great deal of hard work turned an already existing structure into a facility that is suited for meditation and leading a simple contemplative life, this movement of people in America and Europe is taking the already existing institutions of Western civilization and rejuvenating and sometimes revising them. By turning to Eastern religions we are rediscovering some of what was once great in Western culture.

The situation in the West as Buddhism takes root here, however tenuously, is somewhat similar to the situation in China almost two millennia ago when Buddhism migrated there. Unlike Tibet and Japan, where members of the ruling classes welcomed Buddhism as a vehicle of numerous technological, cultural, and political advantages to a relatively underdeveloped society, the Chinese already had a great civilization when Buddhism arrived. Already in possession of a profoundly workable philosophy of government and social ethics in the form of Confucianism, and already at home too with the delightful musings of Daoist sages such as Laozi and Zhuangzi, the Chinese apparently had little to gain by adopting Buddhism.[7] Perhaps its principal appeal at first was simply that it was new and exotic and reinforced traditional values in seemingly novel ways. The context of the modern pre-Buddhist West is rather more similar to the pre-Buddhist Chinese context than it is to the situations in pre-Buddhist Tibet, Vietnam, Korea, or Japan. Ours is a not a preliterate society hungry for the military and economic advantages of written language, but a dominant culture already past its cultural peak and well on the way to cultural decline. Soon, like the Chinese before us, we Westerners will be overwhelmed and exploited by the more energetic and productive emergent cultures that we used to dominate and exploit, but political and economic decline need not mean death. For us, as for the Chinese of two millennia ago, we may be able to revitalize our own greatest cultural strengths by adapting a philosophy that, in its first appearances at least, is quite foreign to us.

The West has had from very early times the potential for greatness, for we have seen some astonishingly great minds with great visions, but collectively my forefathers, and the forefathers of all my fellow human beings of European descent, have failed miserably to live up to the greatness of the minds that might have shaped our civilization. Symbolically the fate of Western civilization was presaged by the death of Socrates, a thinker of unparalleled excellence put to death by stupid and narrow-minded fellow citizens for the crime of examining, with a truly open mind, the most cherished beliefs of the day. Since his time it has always been the same in Western civilization: those who do not run with the crowd die by the crowd.

The tradition of Socrates, and after him of Aristotle, has long been beneath the surface of Western civilization. It is always there as a kind of subterranean counter-culture, testing the patience of the autocrats who have always had the upper hand by dint of sheer brute strength and that confidence and self-assurance that always attend those who never stop to think. The Socratic tradition is often suppressed, but it can never be entirely eradicated. It is always capable of re-emerging as a weak but steady voice that challenges the authoritarian, the occult, and the mystical (for these are all but different aspects of the same anti-philosophical mentality), questions the received opinions and presuppositions of society, and shows a readiness to discard the most deeply entrenched habits of thinking in favour of something a little more humane. The philosophical tradition of Socrates and Aristotle is always prepared to leave aside the haphazard dogmas that societies acquire by historical accident and replace them with hypotheses (never firm conclusions) founded on more methodical observation and more careful analysis of experience. The Western philosophical tradition is one that is concrete and practical in its goals. The search for truth is always done in order to improve the way we live with one another, here on this earth. It is a tradition based on a firm sense of publicly observable reality, a love of personal moral integrity coupled with a tolerance and forgiveness of those who are weak, and a spirit of restraint in both external habits of living and internal habits of thinking.

The Socratic philosophical tradition, brilliant in its beginnings, was made even more rich through its eventual contact with Hebraic culture in the wake of the conquests of Palestine by Macedonian and Roman imperialists. The Hebrews had a religion based on the belief that human history is a reflection of a much larger cosmic history, a history shaped by humanity's rebellion from God and God's attempts to save human beings from their own self-destructive tendencies. God, according to Hebrew belief, participates in human history, and therefore history bears studying very closely with an eye to interpreting the various signs of divine purpose in the events of the nations. The religious beliefs of the Hebrews were conducive to taking great care in the recording of events and in discerning patterns and trends in history. It was a tradition rich in scholarship and the contemplative arts, treasures that supplemented and reinforced the cultural riches of the Greeks.

Relatively modern descendants of the happy marriage of Greek and Hebrew traditions are the traditions of science and scientific technology – I say 'scientific' technology deliberately to contrast the technological expression of humanity's quest for knowledge and wisdom with humanity's quest for short-term advantages and profits, which we might call 'commercial' technology. Another modern descendant of the Greco-Hebraic union is to be seen in the anti-authoritarian spirit of Protestant Christianity, with its constitutional suspicion of all forms of over-centralized power. Protestantism fathered two children, one highly-prized legitimate heir and one despised bastard. The latter child, born out of wedlock through the illicit union of one Protestant and one Roman Catholic parent, grew wretched in the eyes of its parents. This child was named Secularism by its Roman Catholic parent. The secularist movement was one that began in the Catholic Church partly in reaction to the Protestant challenge of the Catholic preoccupation with storing up merit for the future life in heaven. Rather than focus only on these invisible heavenly merits, said the secularists, let us turn our attention to the poor, the hungry, the downtrodden, and the disadvantaged people of the present age, or *saecularis* as it was called in Latin. Everyone who has a concern with social activism and ecological issues owes a debt of gratitude to secularism, the bastard child of the incestuous union of Christian siblings.

Protestantism also begot a legitimate heir, of which it is justly proud. One of the descendants of this heir is Jeffersonian democracy, a political and social philosophy that advocates the universal availability of education without subscribing to the fallacy that human beings are universally educable. What this means is that no one who has ability should be excluded from developing that ability on account of race, religion, or social class; but at the same time it must be recognized that not everyone has ability and that formal training may very well be wasted on the naturally incompetent. What goes hand in hand with this intellectual élitism, though, is a doctrine of the grave responsibility that must be borne by those who do become educated. Those who are capable of being educated are not to be educated simply for their own social and economic advancement, but rather for the general welfare of society. Education implies service to the community. These ideals of Jeffersonian democracy, born immediately out of the Protestant rejection of centralized religious authority, actually have very deep roots in both the Greek and the Hebrew traditions. The original spirit of American democracy is not different from the spirit of Socratic philosophy.

But practitioners of the Socratic philosophical tradition have always been in the minority, and like all minority groups they have been under constant attack not only by the majority but by other minorities as well. In classical times the enemies of the philosophers were the many mystery religions and the various types of gnosticism that were built upon a sense of despairing of the capacity of human reason to solve human problems. When people stop believing in reason, they begin believing in everything else. Lacking any criterion by which to eliminate any opinion as false or without value, people must accept every belief as equally meritorious. Every statement, along with every statement's contradiction, must be accepted on an even footing. The only criterion by which a person might choose one belief over another is personal taste. What one would like to be true, or what is fun to think is true, becomes far more important than trying to determine what really is true. In so far as one feels compelled to justify one's beliefs in these circumstances, one turns to mystery, which literally means that which is hidden. By appealing to what is hidden from the light of reason, to the obscure, the occult, one gains immunity from any possible attack coming from a rational perspective. Those who disagree are, by the very fact that they disagree, proven incapable of making contact with the mysterious source of truth. The breakdown of confidence in reason turns people into enemies, often very bitter enemies, of philosophy, which threatens to restrict people's fanciful acceptance of whatever happens to please them at the moment. Perhaps there is no hatred deeper than that of the mystic for the rationalist.

Christianity, one of the many products of the breakdown of confidence in reason in Hellenistic society, also did its share to perpetuate a suspicion of reason. Christianity would probably have been no more than a dim memory by now, along with its other mystery-oriented rivals, Manicheism and Mithraism, had it not been for historical accidents. The result of these accidents was the gradual establishment of a religious institution, the medieval Roman Catholic Church, that managed to concentrate more political, economic, and military power than any other institution in recorded European history. This institution was an avowed enemy of philosophy. Although the Church has lost much of its former power, the effects live on, for she was the spiritual mother of all the power-hungry totalitarian states that have haunted Europe and the Americas. In much of the world that has come under the influence of this spirit there is no quicker way to death than to think and speak with a critical open mind and a heart filled with a love of justice. The systematic torture and extermination of those who would see things as they actually are in this world is the tragic legacy of the mystics who blacken our minds with pretended light.

It is not only in past aeons that one can find enemies of philosophy. On the contrary, we still live in the Dark Ages of 'sophiaphobia', the dread of wisdom. The Socratic tradition recognized four cardinal philosophical virtues: wisdom (sometimes called prudence), justice, patience, and moderation. Socrates, in fact, taught that there is really only one virtue, wisdom, of which all other virtues are expressions or manifestations. Wisdom for Socrates consisted in insight into what is truly good for human beings, insight into what is truly conducive to health, harmony, and happiness. Wisdom, said the philosopher, can be learned and therefore it can be taught.[8] But if wisdom can be acquired, so can the lack of wisdom. If one can build pathways to wisdom, one can also build obstacles to it. Western society is one in which the obstacles to wisdom are many. Let me elaborate just a few of those many obstacles.

Wisdom is not quite the same as the acquisition of accurate information, but wisdom is very difficult to acquire when accurate information is not available. For if wisdom is an insight into what is truly good for human beings, one must have access to accurate information about what effects various things have on human beings. Wisdom is inseparable from practical morality, and practical morality is inseparable from politics and economics. But in no arena of human life do we find more deliberate manipulation of information and dissemination of misinformation than among those who have vested political and economic interests. Our society in North America is founded on institutions that propagate all manner of misinformation, and in so doing reinforce all the prejudices of our age. Examples of these institutions of misinformation are the public school system, which can always be counted on in any given generation to indoctrinate children in whatever prejudices have become fashionable among the middle-aged, and the mass media, whose information services are driven almost exclusively by the engine of commercial interests. For in the first place, the gathering of information requires huge sums of money and therefore must be sponsored by those who control capital, and those who control capital cannot always be assumed to be impartial and disinterested in what the majority of people believe. But it is not only a matter of the commercial giants trying to manipulate the beliefs of the general public. If the public were to demand real information instead of sensationalism, spectacle, and entertainment, the corporate giants would provide it, for that is where their economic interests would then lie. There is not much point in blaming the industrialists as if they were outsiders inflicting damage on our society. For in so far as it is our tastes that the industrialists are in business to please, we ourselves are the industrialists.

The established interests that control the mass media and the public school systems are of course not the only forces in the business of propagating misinformation. There are also counter-cultural forces adding their share of predigested news and commentary. The alienated, the disenfranchised, and the powerless also have voices, and they also have newspapers and magazines and occasionally even television and radio programming. Examples of the kind of nonsense that they disseminate among us can be seen in tabloid newspapers that are filled with stories of people who have spent a weekend on a spaceship from Alpha Centauri and ducks that can speak Swahili; other kinds of escapism coming from the underground can be seen in the so-called New Age movement, about which I will have more to say later on, and in the electronic ministry of the born-again Christians. All these seemingly disparate sources of news and commentary have something in common: they are alienated from the mainstream society, and they are more interested in putting forward dogma than in promoting a truly open-minded search for truth. They represent an alternative to the particular madness enshrined in the establishment, but they offer no alternative to madness as such. The voice that is least heard in our society is the voice of wisdom. That voice has become little more than a hoarse whisper.

One of the most important manifestations of the virtue of wisdom is the virtue of justice, the determination to see that everyone gets what is due to him. The impediments to justice are naturally as plentiful as the sources of dogmatism. In the place of justice we have collectively developed the 'special interest' mentality. No one wishes to be the victim of injustice, but unfortunately relatively few people really strive to see injustice eliminated altogether for everyone. One of the most grotesque caricatures of justice that have been enshrined in our present age is the policy of what is usually called Affirmative Action, whereby one group of people that has been systematically disfavoured is systematically favoured. There are, for example, universities, government offices, and some corporations that have explicit policies of giving preference to women, members of minority groups, and other disadvantaged groups; presumably this systematic preference of one group over another is intended to correct an imbalance. But surely it cannot eliminate injustice.

The very nature of injustice is depriving persons of their rights on the grounds of no other factor than what subset of the human race they belong to. It is an injustice to deprive any person of a basic human right on the basis of race. But if discrimination on the basis of race is wrong, then discrimination on the basis of race is wrong. If it is wrong to prefer people with white skin simply because they have white skin, then it is equally wrong to prefer people with dark skin simply because they have dark skin. And of course the same principle applies to any number of other subsets of humanity based on gender, native language, ethnic background, religious affiliation, sexual orientation, and so forth. There is no end to how we can subdivide humanity. There is no end to how many groups could arise and claim that past abuses against them warrant preferential treatment in the future: being of a particular height or weight, being left-handed, having five letters in one's middle name, being vegetarian, having an IQ over 140 or under 60, being incapable of resisting yodelling while having sex, having an allergy to shrimp and dandelions, having been seven years old before learning to ride a bicycle, having a nauseating aroma, being insensitive to the difference between beauty and ugliness, having been conceived in the back seat of a Chevrolet at a drive-in movie theatre, and so on as far as the imagination can take us. Justice itself can be achieved in exactly one way: giving up the whole notion of making decisions on the sole basis of irrelevant criteria, and instead taking up examining each individual exactly on the basis of his own talents, skills, and character.

The third of the Socratic virtues that have been buried and forgotten in the ruins of Western society is patience. There is almost nothing in our society that is designed to promote patience, although many features of our society have the inadvertent consequence of giving us the opportunity to test it. Ours is a society that seeks fast and simple solutions to complex problems. We have almost succeeded in replacing the essay with the slogan, especially in political and economic matters. Confident that there is no problem the solution to which cannot fit on a banner pasted to the bumper of a car or inscribed on a lapel pin, or in extremely severe cases explored at depth in a half-hour dramatized television documentary, we have raised the most humble oaf to the level of pundit. And we have finally achieved full equality between the expert and the imbecile by means of the opinion poll and universal suffrage, although in our hearts we prefer the simpleton to the savant, for the former is so much easier to understand and less likely to confound us with subtleties. We have, especially in North America, founded nations, states, provinces, counties, cities, and villages to be governed by people whose principal skills are the ability to sound convincing and look sincere on television for ten seconds at a time. Even if by some queer accident a person is elected who does have the ability to think further into the future than the next election campaign, we have little interest in hearing about the long-range consequences of our present habits of living, aside from passing a few maudlin platitudes a couple of times a year about making the future safe for our grandchildren.

We are surrounded daily with commercial messages that cultivate an ethos of immediate gratification of all personal needs, to the exclusion of all other pursuits, and encourage us to despise not only ourselves but everyone around for not being twenty years old, slender, and provocatively attractive. We scoff at the mentality of the mass culture to which the advertisements pander, we laugh and feel sophisticated and cynical about it all, but to no avail. For we are the very mass culture we love to mock. Paradoxically we both despise ourselves and celebrate ourselves for being ordinary. We do everything but cultivate genuine patience, which is the ability to recognize evil for what it is but to have the strength of character to withstand it and not be corrupted by it.

About moderation, the fourth of the Socratic virtues, there is by now little to say in addition to what has already been said about the fate of the other virtues in the modern age. Our whole economy is built on the illusion of unlimited abundance. We are encouraged at every turn to consume as much as possible, and if possible to go into personal debt to buy as much as possible of the inexhaustible storehouse of goods. The question whether those particular commodities are necessary has become completely irrelevant. By widely accepted convention, whatever a person wants is by that very fact also what he needs. We are made to feel guilty if we deny our children what they are seduced into craving, and we are made to feel guilty ourselves if we fail to go into debt to the very limits of our credit ratings in order to help stimulate the economy. In such a climate as this, I expect that most people will have to go look up the word 'moderation' in their dictionaries.

If we leave a world for future generations, then I am confident they will laugh at us, even as we laugh at those who sought to cure the world's ills by burning witches at the stake and to cure personal ills by the letting of blood. Our descendants will shake their heads in amazement at a century that strove to bring an end to war by fighting wars, an end to injustice by creating injustices, and an end to stupidity by proliferating stupidity.

In speaking for myself I believe I am probably speaking for uncountable others when I say that it is only because I had very little choice in the matter of when I was born that I am not deeply ashamed to be part of this century. It was the sense of chagrin that I felt upon discovering with some horror that I was a human being on the planet Earth in the midst of the twentieth century that first turned me to Buddhism. Once within Buddhism I suppose it was the innate sense of irony, irreverence, and flippant candour that goes with being an American of New England Protestant ancestry that first drew me to Zen. In some odd way it was this Indian religion in Far Eastern dress that awoke in me a feeling that it might be possible to get back to my own cultural roots.

Let us speak plainly. Buddhism is antisocial, if by society you mean the collective mentality of the half-awake masses who stumble their ways unreflectively from cradle to grave, gaining nothing along the way but a superabundance of adipose tissue. Buddhism is a philosopher's religion, if by philosopher you mean (as I do) a person whose only real concern is with overcoming the laziness and self-centredness to which we are nearly all heir, acquiring wisdom and putting that wisdom to the service of all living beings. Much like the Puritanical and Pietistic values of the people who came to North America from Europe, the values of Buddhism (and perhaps especially Zen) are those of personal integrity, intellectual honesty, a sense of appreciation for all that is of fine quality and careful craftsmanship, and an awareness of the long-term implications of our present actions.

These are very simple values, rather unspectacular and unpretentious, whose only virtue lies in being uniquely attuned to the realities of the human condition. They happen to be the values of Zen Buddhism, but they are, needless to say, by no means unique to Zen, nor are they unique to Buddhism. They are also the values of every little pocket of humanity that has achieved civilization. At one time, so I was led to believe when I was a child, they used to be the values of North America. And so I can't help thinking that in much the same way that a bunch of Zen Buddhists got together and rebuilt a rundown house, these same people or people like them might be able get together and help rebuild a society.

THE BUDDHISM THAT AMERICANS ARE BUILDING

It is not particularly easy to think about rebuilding a society. It is a very large task, and one hardly knows where to begin. To make matters worse, it is not at all clear what the goal is; it is not clear exactly what kind of society we might like to rebuild. It is not even very likely that the sort of society we would like to see has ever existed in the past, so it is not a task of reconstructing a society that existed in some Golden Age.

Rather, the task of rebuilding a society is more like the task of 'rebuilding' a house into a temple, taking an existing structure as a basis, modifying parts of it, eliminating other parts altogether, and building some totally new parts. All of this sounds rather easy in principle, and so far it is probably not very controversial, unless there are people who wish to keep things exactly as they are or who do for some reason wish to take on the impossible task of reversing time and duplicating some former age. But let us assume that ours is a more practical plan, one of taking an existing society that already has a great deal of strength and making it even more strong by reducing the damage done by some of the weaknesses. So let me begin with an assessment of where some of the principal strengths and weaknesses of North American society are. Then let me turn to an assessment of what some of the strengths and weaknesses of Buddhism are as it comes to the West. Let me then suggest ways in which both Buddhism and North American society might become stronger by a process of interacting with each other.

There is a feature of North American society that I find extremely puzzling – not only puzzling but alarming. The characteristic that so puzzles me is our gullibility. We are a people ready to believe anything. Now that might seem to some people to be a positive characteristic. After all, a person who will believe anything must be pretty open-minded, and a person who is open-minded is less likely to be dogmatic. Surely, one might think, there is some value in being free of dogmas and dogmatism.

Now if the North American readiness to believe everything were indeed a manifestation of our open-mindedness and freedom from dogmatism, then I would rejoice and sing the praises of our virtues. There is, however, a big difference between being open-minded and being gullible. Being open-minded is a quality of being prepared to set aside views that we have held in the past if there should arise good reasons for doing so; more than that, it is a readiness to look impartially at reasons that are put forward against some view that we may have held or may still be holding. By a readiness to look impartially, I mean simply a willingness to consider new evidence regardless of whether it conforms to our already established beliefs and expectations, as opposed to discarding evidence that fails to confirm what we already believe. Being open-minded is also being prepared to suspend judgement when there is insufficient evidence to draw a conclusion or when different pieces of evidence point to conflicting conclusions. Gullibility, on the other hand, is the quality of being easily deceived, of being prepared to take up a belief despite a lack of compelling evidence or reasons.

North Americans, I maintain, are on the whole very gullible and not very open-minded. Ours is a society filled with people who are eager to embrace any new theory or idea that comes along, and for the brief time that we hold that theory before moving on, we hold it most tenaciously. The North American mind is a dogmatic mind, and the willingness that some people have to change dogmas regularly does not alter the basic nature of being dogmatic. Why this is so is a most puzzling thing. Despite being in possession of an enormously complex and powerful technology, and despite having a highly organized system of storing and transmitting information, we are as susceptible to fallacies and half-truths as the most technologically primitive of societies.

Let me cite a few examples to make my case, for it would be most lamentable if people took my word for it without demanding some evidence that North Americans are dogmatic. Let me begin with one very general characteristic: the tendency of Americans to believe that everyone is entitled to an opinion on everything. The philosopher Hegel (1770–1831) expressed his bemusement over an assumption that was prevalent in his day that everyone was suited to be a philosopher. No one, he pointed out, would consider himself a shoemaker simply because he possessed eyes, fingers, a piece of leather, and two feet; and yet everyone considers himself suited to pass judgement on philosophical matters simply because he possesses a mind. Why, he wondered, do we acknowledge that it takes years of training to be a craftsman and yet assume that it takes no special training or preparation or practice to be a thinker?[9] What on earth would Hegel have thought of North America in the twentieth century? In 1980 the people of the United States of America elected to the office of President, arguably the most important and complex elected office in the entire world and certainly the office that has the greatest potential impact on the lives of people all over the world, a 69-year-old man named Ronald Reagan, who had no training as a lawyer or economist or military officer, and no previous experience in national or international or professional military affairs. This man won the election on a simple platform of simplifying government, reducing taxes, and returning to traditional American values. Despite the fact that this man exasperated his top advisers in his first term of office with his short attention span and his inability to absorb the details of economic and political policy decisions, this man was elected President of the United States a second time in 1984, this time winning 59 per cent of the popular vote and getting all the electoral votes except those of Minnesota and District of Columbia. Now quite aside from how one feels about the administration of Ronald Reagan, it is remarkable that a nation would feel such confidence in a person who had such poor credentials for the job to which he was elected. That he could be taken seriously as a candidate at all indicates that the American people felt either that Reagan was, against all appearances to the contrary, suitably trained to take on the enormous responsibility of his job, or that the job really requires no special talents, skills, experience, or training.

Let me give another example. Please bear with some statistics. The population of the world in 1985 was estimated at 4,843,000,000. The people of North America accounted for 8.2% of the total world population. But the United States alone accounted for 25% of the world's total consumption of energy, while Canada accounted for another 3%. This means that less than one-twelfth of the world's people are consuming over one-quarter of the world's fuel resources. It has been estimated that Canada and the United States together possess less than 5% of the world's resources of petroleum, yet these two countries consume 28% of the world's oil and 36% of the world's natural gas. Canada, with 0.5% of the world's population, consumes 12% of the world's electrical power. In Ontario, Canada's most populous province, 39% of the electrical energy is generated by nuclear power facilities.[10]

Statistics are notoriously difficult to interpret, but I think we would be safe in concluding that the people of North America have come to rely on the availability of very large supplies of fuel resources. Most of these fuel resources are non-renewable. Once they are consumed, we will still have the dependency but no longer the supply. This state of affairs would suggest to a person given to thinking clearly that some dramatic changes will have to be made in the way we live within the next few years and certainly within the next few decades. We must find ways to consume far less energy, since it is unlikely that we will learn to develop safe ways of producing or channelling enough energy to match our present rates of consumption. However obvious it may seem that we must reduce consumption, one sees only a few people voluntarily living more moderately, reducing travel, using fewer energy-consuming tools, and so forth. This indicates to me that the rest of us are living in a dream world. It means that we are gullible enough to believe that fossil fuels are infinitely abundant, or that nuclear power can be generated at much higher levels without endangering the environment, or that engineers will find ways of channelling the energy of the sun, the tides, and the wind in sufficient amounts to meet all our needs. Or perhaps we believe there will be some kind of divine intervention. But rather than counting too much on these dreams that we have been gullible enough to base our lives upon, we have come to a point where we must begin the process of waking up to realities.

I have suggested that Buddhism has the potential to play a role in our society's process of coming to our senses. So far, however, this potential has not been realized very well. On the contrary, much of the Buddhism that has found its way into the hearts of the North American community has been more a perpetuation of the fantasy world in which we live, more just another form of escapism, than a means of deliverance from our slumber.

It is my feeling that the fault for this failure of Buddhism to develop a liberating form for us in North America is not solely the fault of the Asian Buddhists who have brought their religion to us but is more a reflection of the sorry state of our own folk culture as it stands at this time. The Asian Buddhist teachers themselves, from what I have been able to see of them, often have a feeling of helplessness as they have to deal with North Americans, many of whom display an almost incredible lack of maturity and wisdom. To give just a couple of examples, I know a Theravādin monk who has given a good deal of his time to teaching the Dharma in North America. He is a well-educated monk, both in the sciences and in the Buddha-dharma, and he speaks English quite well, so he believed he would be very well suited to talk to Westerners. When he first arrived in the United States, however, he was in for quite a shock. When he went to universities to give talks on the Dharma, he found that the people who came to his talks were not necessarily well versed in the sciences, nor did they know much about Western or Asian philosophy, nor were they particularly sophisticated in their thinking. When he invited questions after his talks, he found that mostly what people wanted to hear about were stories of people who had developed miraculous powers through meditation. He went to talk about mindfulness and loving-kindness, and his audience wanted to hear about people who could walk through walls, fly around in the air, and live for months at a time without breathing or taking food, and could survive for days at a time without sex.

One time this Sri Lankan monk told his audience that he was going to demonstrate to them the powers of meditation. So he told the audience to watch him very carefully while he went into deep *samādhi*. What he in fact did for the next fifteen minutes or so was just to sit quietly, making no particular effort to meditate. After a while he asked his audience what they had observed. People told him they had seen his aura change colour, and that his skin had taken on a translucent quality. Some saw lights emanate from his body, and one person even saw him rise off the floor and float suspended in mid-air! The monk listened to all these reports of the wonderful things he had done in his 'trance' state, then he explained to his audience that we very often see only what we expect or wish to see rather than what is really there to be seen. Meditation, he said, is a method of gradually purging ourselves of expectations and wishful thinking so that we can see things as they really are. The people in the audience seemed let down. The monk was not invited back to give another talk.

It is not only Theravādin teachers who experience frustration and disappointment in their dealings with Westerners. Some time ago a group of Tibetan tantric monks came to Toronto as part of their tour around North America. They performed a chanting ritual in a large auditorium that was filled well beyond capacity. The Toronto newspapers carried articles explaining how these monks got themselves into 'altered states of consciousness' before chanting, and they stayed in these altered states throughout the chanting. Judging from the air outside the auditorium, which was redolent with the heavy scent of marijuana smoke, not a few of the members of the audience had found ways to achieve altered states of their own, the better to appreciate the finer spiritual vibrations emanating from these great tantric masters from Tibet. The master of ceremonies who introduced the monks explained before they began the chanting that its purpose was to purify the earth. Perhaps, he said, the chanting would help clean up the environmental pollutants that have been causing acid rain and dying lakes. Was he joking? It was difficult to be sure. Some Buddhist leaders expressed disappointment that a greater attempt was not made to use the opportunity of the monks' visit to inform the public about the real nature of Buddhism rather than giving the impression that Buddhists would sooner avail themselves of chants than of more effective methods to fight environmental pollution. It is sad to see monks presented to the public as a form of entertainment, as if a religious ritual were just another kind of jazz concert or carnival side-show, and especially sad to see them presented in this way by entrepreneurs who are themselves Buddhists.

Why is it, given that Buddhism has such a good potential to help people think more clearly and more critically, that we find among North American Buddhists so many people who are lacking common sense and clarity of thinking? There are probably several factors at work here. One of them is the plain fact that Asian Buddhism has managed to absorb a great deal of the folk cultures of the places where it has taken root. Rather than trying to suppress beliefs and practices that are in conflict with the basic teachings of Buddhism, Buddhist teachers have always found a way to accommodate the beliefs of ordinary people, incorporating them as conventional truths but not as ultimate truths. Ordinary people, especially in cultures where people have little contact with the advances in knowledge made in other parts of the world, tend to cling to old patterns of belief and practice and to be suspicious of new ways of doing things. Such reluctance to adopt novelty undoubtedly has the beneficial effect of protecting societies from the mindless pursuit of the latest fashion, the vice to which more urbanized cultures such as that of North America tend to succumb; but being protected from novelty is not in itself a virtue, especially if the new ideas really are improvements over the older ones. But, whether with good effects in the long run or bad, the Buddhist teachers in most societies have been rather cautious about alienating people by challenging their folk customs, and the result for institutionalized Buddhism as a whole has been that it has acquired a great many elements that really have nothing whatsoever to do with the original teachings and intentions of Buddhism.

When Buddhism came to the West from Asia, therefore, it arrived not only with its philosophical traditions of critical reasoning and meditation practices, but also with a whole array of exotic folk remedies, myths, and legends. It stands to reason that it was principally these folk customs that caught the attention of Westerners and attracted them to look into Buddhism more carefully. After all, people whose main interest is in critical thinking and contemplative exercises can find plenty of interest in Western culture without having to turn to exotic traditions. In fact, one who is truly interested just in the philosophy and the meditation exercises might do better to avoid the inevitable obstacles posed by having to learn several very difficult languages just to gain access to the most basic teachings. When one considers the amount of excellent material on Western philosophy and meditation readily available to a person who reads English or French or German, and compares that with the amount of excellent material available on Buddhism in those languages, it seems almost like madness to turn to Buddhism for guidance rather than to one of the Western philosophical traditions. And indeed one finds that relatively few of the West's brightest intellects have had more than a passing curiosity in Eastern religions, unless they incorporated the interest in Buddhism in a much wider interest in the study of languages, literature, history, geography, or anthropology.

Who were the Western people who turned to Buddhism? First of all it should be obvious that, as a rule, people who turn to another culture for inspiration do so because they have grown emotionally alienated from their own mainstream culture. It would be interesting to see statistics on the backgrounds of North Americans who have become Buddhists. I have no firm evidence at my disposal, and so all I have are personal impressions formed after talking to quite a few North American Buddhists over the years. One impression I get is that quite a few Buddhists, myself included, had an interest in Marxism or Maoism before they became involved in Buddhism. There is nothing at all surprising in this to me, for I am convinced that Marxism shares with Buddhism a feeling that the mainstream social values of our times are profoundly unjust and have resulted in the prosperity and comfort of the few at the expense of the many. Other Buddhists, while not Marxists, were typically involved in the ecology movement, various forms of the peace and disarmament movement, or one of the many manifestations of the civil rights movement. Again, all of these movements had in common with Buddhism the underlying sense that there were systematic injustices built into our social system that had to be remedied. Some brought their social activism with them into Buddhism, and others left activism behind them. In any case, in answering the question of which North Americans turned to Buddhism, one can hazard the guess that the broadest class of people who became Buddhists were people who had become disenchanted with the ways of Western society.

A society, and especially a modern one, is unimaginably complex and multifaceted. There are many aspects of it from which one can become alienated, and so it is only rarely that people who have in common the mere fact of alienation from society really have much else in common. Those who were alienated from what they saw as social injustices made up one segment of North American Buddhists, but another group of new Buddhists included those who saw science, technology, secularism, and rationalism as the source of most modern evils. Being ill at ease with science, technology, and formal reasoning can have many different causes. Some people are just not very good at systematic thinking and tight reasoning, or at least they think they are not, and people rarely think it is absolutely necessary to have skills they do not believe themselves to have. The more a person who is not a very methodical thinker is confronted by people who feel that rigorous thinking is indispensable for the good life, the more such a person is likely to sing the praises of being a free spirit, emotionally whole and honest, untrammelled by the conventional forms of thinking and behaviour. The laws of logic come to be seen by such a person as mere artificial human conventions, like the fashions of dress or the norms of etiquette in polite society. Wishing to be free of all such bonds, many people in the history of Western civilization have disparaged logic and reason. A number of such people in this century have seen in Buddhism a haven from what they regard as the tyranny of reason. For most people of this free-spirited nature, the chief virtue of Buddhism is simply that it is not what the majority of people in their own society practise. If it had been their fate to be born in a society that was predominantly Buddhist, these people would most likely in their eagerness to avoid conformity have become Calvinists or Sufis.

Yet a third group of people who seek the exotic are those who for whatever reason are lacking in confidence in their own ability to succeed according to the canons of success accepted by the mainstream society. Rather than trying to compete with a large number of people in the areas of activity that most people choose, such people turn to something little known by the general populace so that they are unlikely to have to come into daily contact with people who have done better than they. These people are examples of the old adage: 'When among logicians, claim to be a grammarian. When among grammarians, claim to be a logician. When among those who are neither, claim to be both. And when among people who are both, remain silent.' North American society, particularly after the Second World War, was one in which the most highly prized areas of achievement were in mathematics, the natural sciences, and engineering. People who lacked the ability or the spirit of competitiveness necessary to excel in these areas often turned to other areas in which they could easily rise to the top of their discipline. It is my impression that a good many of the people who were interested in Buddhism in the past two or three decades fell into this class. In a society in which very few people knew what a Buddhist was supposed to be like, one could easily get away with claiming to be a Buddhist, even claiming to be quite a good one.

The exceptions to these general observations about North Americans who turned to Buddhism are those people who, essentially by accident, happened to meet with good meditation teachers in or from Asia and in following the instructions of a particular person came into Buddhism 'through the back door'; such people were not necessarily caught up in either a search for the exotic or a rejection of the familiar in order to bolster a sagging ego. But these exceptions really were, so far as I have been able to observe, quite rare. And so, if one is to be quite honest about it, one would have to admit that Buddhism in North America has not skimmed the cream off the top of society. On the contrary, it has largely been a catch-all for misfits and renegades. It is hardly surprising, therefore, that the form that Buddhism has taken so far in North America has been neither Buddhism at its best nor Western society at its best.

Despite the present realities of North American Buddhism, I have great hopes in the ideals of Buddhism as a means by which some people might realize the highest ideals of Western civilization. I believe this potential will never be realized, however, until the kind of Buddhism that is taught in the West is purged of some of the Asian habits it has acquired down through the millennia. It is not that the Asian habits have been unfit for people in the past, but that some of them are not particularly well suited to meet the crises that the human race is now facing. People who come from a society that has been Buddhist for many centuries sometimes forget the principal observation upon which all the teachings of the Buddha were founded: everything is impermanent. This includes the effectiveness of teachings. Doctrines that do very good service in one age can be most harmful to another. Any teaching is like a medicine that is an effective antidote for a particular disease. When medicines or teachings have outlived their usefulness, let them be discarded with gratitude for the utility they have served in the past, but let them be discarded without further apology. In the remainder of this essay, I shall explore one or two traditional teachings of Buddhism that have come to seem particularly useless and even counter-productive to us in our present circumstances.

Before discussing which teachings of Buddhism we might do well to discard, or at least de-emphasize, for the time being, let me first discuss some of the characteristics of the mentality of many North Americans in the late twentieth century. These characteristics should be borne in mind as the conditions under which I claim that some Buddhist teachings are not particularly well suited for North Americans; if the North American mentality changes, then the teachings that will help North Americans will change.

First of all, North Americans, particularly those of Protestant background, have a tendency to be somewhat literal-minded. We tend not to think symbolically or to interpret teachings in purely metaphorical terms. Therefore, when teaching North Americans it is better on the whole to speak quite straightforwardly with a minimum of subtlety, for otherwise we are almost sure to miss the point of the teaching altogether. Secondly, North Americans nowadays are going through a long and slow crisis of confidence in traditional values. We have witnessed two millennia of bloodshed and destruction, much of it instigated by people who claimed to be in possession of Truth. We have been ravaged by the armies of men who claimed to have a clear understanding of the overall state of the universe and the place of humanity within it. What we desperately need now is not simply another dogma or ideology to replace the old ones, but a release from the grips of dogmatism altogether.

On the one hand, we crave something sweet and simple and suited for the mind of a child, but on the other hand we have a deep dread of the effects of those who come forth and promise radical and simple solutions to complex problems. On the one hand we crave to understand everything around us, and on the other we are terrified of what we might do with our understanding, for we know our own terrible, confused motive all too well; from this fundamental ambivalence stems our love-hate relationship with technology and science and indeed all of rational thinking, which we love because it brings us constantly closer to a feeling of understanding the universe around us, and which we hate because we are too immature on the whole to use it for purposes other than entertaining ourselves and making ourselves temporarily more comfortable. In our discovery of highly sophisticated forms of technology that we only barely know how to use, we are like a pubescent boy who has just discovered his genitals but has not yet moved beyond the self-absorbed joys of masturbation. We must be treated with great caution and skill, for we have the bodies of powerful adults governed by the minds of children.

Having said that, let me specify four families of Buddhist teachings that in my experience serve more to impede Westerners than to help them acquire wisdom and become less self-centred. The first of these obstructive doctrines is that of rebirth and karma. It has been my personal experience that Westerners are almost hopelessly incapable of understanding the Buddhist concept of rebirth. There are various ways in which one can interpret the doctrine of rebirth. By far the most silly and inept is, unfortunately, also the most common. This view begins with the assumption that a person has an identity, that is, a core of personality that remains the same from conception to death; on death a person leaves the physical body behind and takes the personality to a new physical body, sometimes after wandering around in a bodiless state as a ghost or a *duende* or the deity of a tiny village in Burkina Faso for some period of time. Thus according to this view it might be legitimate to say, for example, that in a former life one was a specific person, such as Thomas Hobbes, and then died and was eventually reborn as Marie Antoinette, and then eventually as Karl Marx, and then as Kiri Te Kanawa. According to some versions of this account, one might spend quite some time between these human births being an earwig, a weevil, a crayfish, and a bearded tit, or even a highly evolved incorporeal life form on the seventh planet of an unnamed dwarf star not far from Arcturus. As a result of deeds done and views held and attitudes cultivated in all these different bodily and psychological states, one is what one is now, a haphazard collection of titbits of unfinished business left over from the infinitely deep past. No action goes without its consequence, no matter how long it may take for some deeds to ripen.

Now what harm could there possibly be in a view such as the one just outlined? If all one is doing is exercising the imagination and seeing how many possible forms of life one can imagine being, there is probably nothing in the least harmful in spending some time reflecting on such things as how it might feel to be a wolf spider. In fact, trying to see the world from the perspective of a spider or a cockroach might help us become much less fearful of and disgusted by forms of life that are not similar to our own. On the other hand, if there is something good to be gained from reflecting on what it might feel like to be a spotted tick or some such thing, then that purpose can be served far better by undertaking a careful study of biology and actually becoming a little more informed about the many fascinating forms of life on the planet. Or, if one wishes to restrict what one thinks about to human activities, then one could benefit far more by reading the works of Thomas Hobbes along with some biographical accounts of him and his contemporaries than by dredging up dim and probably less than wholly reliable personal memories of the years between 1588 and 1679. Most of us, it must be admitted, scarcely remember our childhood from the present life with anything like accuracy, so there is little reason to suppose we could recall much of worth from over three hundred years ago. So even when we see the exercise of thinking about past lives in its most positive light, I think the best we can say for it is that it has far less value than more prosaic forms of study, learning, and thinking.

There is, however, also a rather dark side to the whole matter of dwelling on the thought of past lives. It dulls the mind and impairs the faculty of reason. In the first place, if one is prepared really to believe that one was Thomas Hobbes in a former life, then it is hard to imagine what one might not be prepared to believe, for clearly one would be prepared in principle to accept a belief without grounds for believing it. But if one is prepared to accept statements or ideas without asking for the grounds, then one must be equally prepared to believe that the cause of one's belief in rebirth is that a computer programmer, who happens to be a goldfish in Helsinki, has found a clever way to transmit ideas into the minds of people, making them believe such things as that they used to be Thomas Hobbes.

The more thought I give to this matter, the more it actually seems to me far more reasonable to entertain the hypothesis that there might be a goldfish in Helsinki somehow causing one to believe one has memories of having been Thomas Hobbes than to entertain the hypothesis that one might actually have memories of having been Thomas Hobbes. For what does it mean to have been Thomas Hobbes in the first place? What was Thomas Hobbes? How can one even begin to go about the task of answering the question of what Thomas Hobbes was in the first place? I quite honestly do not know.

Let us begin, then, by thinking about the few things about Thomas Hobbes that immediately flood into the mind of the man on the street when he hears the name Thomas Hobbes. Well, he was born the son of a vicar in Malmesbury, Wiltshire, England at the time of the Spanish Armada and died ninety-one years later; in the intervening years he studied at Magdalen Hall in Oxford, where he earned a bachelor's degree at the age of nineteen; he travelled in Europe as tutor to the son of the Earl of Cavendish and was exposed there to the thought of Kepler and Galileo and came to believe that the study of human nature could be carried out in the same systematic and mathematically rigorous way as the study of astronomy was carried out; owing to political circumstances in England he fled to France at the age of fifty-two, and there he entered into a rather bitter debate with René Descartes; perhaps his best known work is *Leviathan*, a classic in political theory. That still tells us very little about what Thomas Hobbes was, but it is a modest beginning, enough of a beginning to enable us to ask a few further questions and to begin thinking seriously about what in fact it would mean to have been Thomas Hobbes in the first place.

What was Thomas Hobbes? Among other things, he was a pile of an extremely large multitude of living cells, each of which was made of an astonishingly large number of organic molecules. Of course he was not precisely the same set of cells when he was born in Malmesbury as he was fifty-two years later in France. In fact it is not clear what criteria we would have to establish to say that a single cell of Thomas Hobbes was the same cell when he was a suckling as when he was debating with Descartes, for the cells were all absorbing nutrients and releasing various substances. The point becomes very clear in a short time: Thomas Hobbes the pile of cells in 1588 was not precisely the same Thomas Hobbes as the Thomas Hobbes who was a pile of cells in 1679. If it is not easy to determine what the physical identity of Thomas Hobbes was even during what we intuitively take to be his life, it is even more difficult to figure out what sense there might be in saying that anyone is now the same physical person as Thomas Hobbes used to be three hundred years ago.

Surely this issue of the physical Thomas Hobbes is a red herring distracting us from the far more important question of what made Thomas Hobbes a living human being. What made him a living being as opposed to a mound of stones was surely the fact that he also consisted of thoughts and ideas and memories and bits of information and desires and inclinations and fears. So let us assume that Thomas Hobbes the person was a set of these mental events. But which set? Obviously Hobbes did not have the same memories in any one moment as he had in any of his previous moments, for the simple fact that each moment of recalling a former moment itself became a past moment to be recalled by yet another moment of thought. If we were to say that to be Thomas Hobbes was to be, say, all the memories that he had in the last moment of his life, it would follow that he was not yet Thomas Hobbes until the moment of his death. And of course it would also follow that none of us today is Thomas Hobbes, because none of us has exactly the set of memories that Hobbes had in the last moment of life. None of us speaks English or French in quite the same way that Hobbes did three hundred years ago, so surely the linguistic evidence alone would show how much difference there is between Hobbes and any modern person claiming to be his present incarnation.

Having thought about this matter of what Thomas Hobbes was in the seventeenth century has led so far to more puzzles than solutions. But perhaps we have been thinking of the whole matter in the wrong way. Perhaps we should think in much more abstract terms. Perhaps we should say that Hobbes was a set of tendencies to think and act in a particular way rather than that he was a set of particular concrete thoughts and actions. Perhaps he was nothing more than a tendency to be analytic, systematic, and methodical intellectually and a tendency to be honest and moderate of habit morally. If we make this move, though, then Hobbes becomes even more amorphous; in fact we should be very hard pressed to distinguish Hobbes from an incalculable number of other living beings who tended to be analytic, systematic, honest, and moderate. But we have now come a fair distance from the original allegation that someone might make of being a present incarnation of the late Thomas Hobbes. Unfortunately, I think the more thought one gives to this question of what it might mean to have the identity of a person who lived in some former time, the more the matter becomes confused and obscure. It does not hold up very well under any sort of literal interpretation. At best rebirth might be a vague metaphor of some kind, an acknowledgement that, for example, all or many or at least some people who have similar intellectual and moral tendencies have similar subjective experiences of life. The angry and the suspicious, for example, have less fun than the cheerful and the trusting. But if that is all we mean, then let us just say that and let it go at that. We literal-minded Westerners cannot handle anything much more subtle than the straightforward telling of things as they really are.

Supposing we now regard the story of karma and rebirth not as a telling of things as they are but rather as a myth for those who are sophisticated enough to handle well-turned fiction as well as narrative history. There might be some point in holding this myth in reserve for the extremely gifted, but if it is so held in reserve, it should be the most secret of all secret doctrines, never a mythology for the masses of people. Look at what the doctrine of rebirth does for the masses who are inclined to take it literally. It becomes a justification for complacent acceptance of the most cruel of realities. The Armenians, one might claim, deserved to be victims of genocide, either because of their collective karma or because each individual Armenian had done some dreadful event in the past to merit being made a victim of torture and execution without trial. Did the members of the Baha'i faith who had sharpened stakes hammered down their throats by the Iranian authorities in the nineteenth century deserve to be treated that way because they had been so stupid as to protest against injustice and intolerance, or was it because they had eaten human babies in some past incarnation? Do not the wealthy deserve to be comfortable, because of the good deeds they have done in past lives?

When someone kills a cow for food, does that release the consciousness of the cow so that it can seek a higher form of life? Before accusing me of dreaming up outlandish questions just to raise a smile, know that I have heard not only one but several Buddhists justify their eating of meat on just those grounds. If their premiss were granted, would it not follow that the more pain we inflict upon the cow in killing it, the more of its previous bad karma we burn off? Would it not generally be kinder to inflict the greatest possible suffering on everyone around us so that they can be freed from the prolonged agony of being a human being? Should we not, in fact, start up a nuclear war to help every living thing burn off a good deal of bad karma? It is somewhat amusing but ultimately pretty disgusting how many rationalizations for shoddy behaviour one can wring out of the doctrine of karma and rebirth. Let it remain in Asia. It is not a doctrine that will do us North Americans much good, and it may in fact do us more than a little harm.

Another doctrine, which finds home only in the wonderful and always interesting world of Mahāyāna Buddhism, is that of the transfer of merit. According to this doctrine, it is possible for one being to accumulate a great deal of excess merit through the performance of good works and then to transfer that merit to another being who needs it but has not been capable of earning it. It is a beautiful idea, and the ritual practices that attend it produce a good feeling. It is customary at the end of a Mahāyāna religious ceremony or at the end of a session of meditation to offer the merits that one has accumulated to the welfare of all beings. There is something very charming about this myth, and it has an immediate appeal to people like me who favour a socialized state. We North Americans could stand to cultivate the habit of greater generosity towards other beings, for given our affluence we are on the whole appallingly tightfisted with our money and stingy with our talents. A ritual act of giving merit is a good reminder of why we do religious practices at all: in order to benefit all beings. But despite its benefits, the doctrine of the transfer of merit and the ritual practices associated with it seem to confuse many Buddhists, who somehow get the feeling that it is sufficient to perform religious ceremonies and offer the merit of these ceremonies to other beings.

One example of confusion that I have heard about, and one hopes this example is quite extreme, was of a Buddhist teacher who grew ill as a result of living in a very damp basement apartment in a cold climate. His disciples, knowing that he was ill, came by daily to perform religious ceremonies and to offer the merit of their ceremonies for the recovery of their teacher's health. The most dedicated of these disciples happened to be a carpenter. The teacher took him aside one day and said, 'You are willing to come here every day and perform religious ceremonies for one hour. Would you be willing instead to spend one hour every day doing repairs in my apartment so that it would not be so draughty and damp?' The disciple replied that he was coming to the teacher to do spiritual practice, and doing extra carpentry work would interfere with this spiritual practice. He was apparently more willing to do a symbolic ritual action of helping another being than to do a real action that would in fact help another being. This sort of blindness may be rather rare, but more common is the tendency that one finds too frequently among North American Buddhists to regard only a period of time set aside during the day for formal meditation as real meditation. In fact it might be better to regard the fifteen or sixteen hours a day that one is active in the world as one's *real* meditation, while the thirty minutes or hour that one spends in sitting meditation (*zazen*) should be regarded as the warming-up callisthenics that one does before strenuous exercise; the way that one conducts one's daily life makes a great difference to the happiness and welfare of many beings, whereas the way one does one's sitting meditation makes very little difference to anything but one's own subjective states of mind.

Lest one get the idea that I am recommending against doing formal meditation or devotional exercises, let me emphasize that doing some kind of regular meditation practice can be as important for one's overall physical, intellectual, and emotional health as doing regular physical exercise, eating sensibly, and keeping the intellect supple through regular study and problem-solving. To a person who wishes to lead an effective life, it is very important to keep oneself physically and psychologically healthy. There are healthy and unhealthy motivations for doing work in the service of other beings. The healthy motivation is the genuine desire to see all beings be happy and peaceful. This desire is not innate in most people and must therefore usually be acquired through training. There is no form of training better than being surrounded in one's youth by caring and altruistic people who both provide a good example and offer encouragement when one occasionally grows discouraged and weary of trying to love others. But, sadly, such environments are rather rare, so most people must try to compensate for the imperfect circumstances of youth by doing specific exercises such as that of cultivating loving-kindness (*mettā-bhāvanā*). By doing this exercise regularly for a sufficient period of time, one can develop a true wish that all beings be happy and peaceful. This wish constitutes a healthy motivation for doing works of service to others.

Only rarely are people actually motivated by such healthy emotions. More typically people are driven by a nagging feeling of guilt, an uneasiness with the seemingly undeserved advantages that one has over others. Wanting to be liked and praised by others, they set out to do works that others admire – or at least pretend to admire because it is considered very bad social form not to seem to admire noble works, so even if one does not really admire such things, it is always prudent to put on a good show of admiring them. When people are driven by such motivations as guilt, fear, and a desire to be praised, they very rarely do more than a half-hearted job, because part of their attention is always diverted to seeing what others are thinking of them. They are a bit like a vain person at a social gathering in a room with a large mirror; he is always stealing a sidelong glance at his reflection and so fails to give full attention to his companions. We all know such people. Only by luck do they occasionally do a task thoroughly and well. Being of true service to others cannot easily be the outcome of these unhealthy motivations, nor can it be the outcome of a mawkish sentimentality. Rather, being effectively altruistic results from a combination of pure selflessness, concrete talents and skills, and a sense of realism about what can and should be done. The selflessness and the realism can be acquired by meditation. The skills can be acquired only through study and practical experience in the real world. No amount of religious exercise can provide them, and therefore doing more than the necessary amount of religious exercise simply wastes valuable time and renders one less effective in the service of others. Unfortunately, some people seem to think that if some meditation is good, a great deal of meditation must be excellent. But as in all things, too much is as damaging as too little.

The point to be made with respect to the doctrine of the transfer of merit is that the way 'merit' is actually transferred to other beings is by using one's acquired skills and sensible attitudes to help other beings directly. There is no other way to transfer merit, nor is there really any such thing as merit aside from the results of one's hard work in acquiring some set of skills. Ritual actions of transferring merit are purely symbolic and have no effect except to help one cultivate the proper sentiments. It is almost embarrassing to have to point out something so obvious, but it has been my experience in talking to North American Buddhists that many people are confused on these matters.

Another doctrine that has a great potential to confuse rather than to enlighten North Americans is one that is found in all schools of Buddhism but is particularly emphasized in Mahāyāna, where it also has acquired a rather odd interpretation. This is the notion that the Buddhist worker should acquire great tactical skill (*upāya-kauśalya*) in the overall strategy of leading beings to wisdom. In its original form this doctrine was perfectly innocuous and in fact quite useful. Based on the recognition that wisdom by itself is of little value unless it is put into practice, *upāya* came to mean all the practical manifestations of wisdom: purity of deed in body, speech, and mind; self-improvement through meditation; being generous, kind, and helpful to all others without playing favourites to anyone and without neglecting anyone; practising tolerance, forbearance, and forgiveness; working energetically for the welfare of all beings; promoting peace and harmony among beings and striving always to avoid factionalism;

and seeking always to find ways to help others avoid becoming bitter and hate-filled as a result of their frustrations. Tactics, in other words, consisted in nothing more than leading a life that demonstrated the advantages of loving wisdom above all else.

The notion of tactics took on a new sense, however, in the development of some forms of Mahāyāna Buddhism. According to this new interpretation, the doctrine of perfecting tactical skill came to imply that the end of bringing someone to the Dharma justified whatever means had to be employed to realize that end. Even this extended idea of *upāya* was originally based on the commonplace observation that very immature people cannot be brought to maturity if one offers them only the most mature ideas. Delivering a discourse on Aristotle's Nicomachean ethics to a five-year-old child would probably be at best a waste of breath and at worst might create such an atmosphere of boredom and resentment in the child as even to delay moral development. Telling stories and fables to teach basic lessons might be far more effective. Similarly, since many human beings in the bodies of adults have minds that have become arrested at an immature stage of moral and emotional development, it may make sense in certain contexts to speak to them otherwise than one might speak to a fellow philosopher.

Moreover, even as a child sometimes grows angry at the adult world for no other reason than that some childish impulse has been thwarted, an emotionally immature adult might feel resentment towards others when things fail to go as planned or hoped for. Since it is not always the case that a child wishes for what is best in the long run, it often happens that a child interprets the kind actions of an adult as if they were malicious actions done with the sole intention of causing irritation to the child. Similarly, sometimes a wise person may act in ways that are in fact for the welfare of the foolish, but the foolish will perceive those actions as evil. Having the courage to do what is right, even when others resent it, is one of the marks of a sage; the actions of a Bodhisattva are not always pleasing to others, but then they are not intended to be pleasing. They are aimed only at being beneficial. They are part of the tactics in the Bodhisattva's long-range strategy of bringing others to maturity.

If this matter-of-fact understanding of *upāya* that I have just outlined were widely understood, I should see no harm in the concept at all. But unfortunately it is often used as a pretext for justifying all manner of careless behaviour rather than as a constant reminder of the wise person's responsibility to the less mature. It is, needless to say, absurd to see Buddhist training principles as inflexible commandments that must invariably be followed to the letter, but neither are training principles to be flouted on the pretext that society at large might be repelled by someone who seems too pure in conduct. Buddhist teachers in North America have occasionally availed themselves of such reasoning to rationalize their fondness for alcohol and other intoxicants, eating meat, and being sexually irresponsible. If Buddhist leaders wish to use intoxicants, then let them at least have the integrity to admit that they are indulging themselves for their own pleasure rather than that they are doing it for the sake of others; if they wish to eat meat, let them at least admit that they do so because they like meat and lack the will to give up something they love despite the harm it does to other beings. People readily understand such weaknesses. We all have them, and only the extremely foolish expect perfection from human beings. One can forgive teachers who have bad habits. One usually has a much more difficult time, however, understanding and forgiving the abuse of good doctrines to mask a teacher's personal weaknesses. Knowing clearly that a piece of behaviour, whether it is one's own or that of one's teacher, falls short of the ideals embodied in the training precepts is essential to the process of getting under way on the long journey to improvement; being confused on this matter of what does and what does not live up to the spirit of the precepts can lead only to personal and social stagnation.

North Americans are on the whole in a great hurry. We are among the most impatient people on earth, and this impatience manifests itself constantly in our unwillingness to take the time necessary to learn anything well or really master it. In commercial areas the consequences are not very serious, for the only implications there are that we make shoddy products and must import goods if we want anything fine or something that functions properly. But in the area of religion, the consequences are rather more serious, for we tend to read a little bit here and a little bit there, listen to one teacher here and another teacher there, choosing what seems most pleasing to us at the moment, now practising kuṇḍalini yoga and tomorrow taking up zazen for a while, then dabbling in Sufi mysticism, then going into group therapy. There is an entire industry dedicated to selling us the concepts of self-improvement and self-acceptance and the gimmicks by which to trick ourselves into believing that we are gaining some benefit from them. In the great rush, we usually fail to learn any one discipline really well. Therefore we are not a people who should be entrusted just yet with subtle and sophisticated doctrines. Perhaps in another two to three hundred years North American society will be ready for such doctrines as emptiness, tactical skill, rebirth, and karma. For the present, however, we need much more basic teachings – teachings that are well designed to lead us towards a new respect for reason and morality.

3

A DIALOGUE ON REBIRTH

Lati Rimpoche, a high-ranking master within the Tibetan Gelug (dge-lugs) Order, visited North America in September 1986. During his week-long stay in Toronto he graciously made time in his very busy schedule for an interview with Spring Wind: Buddhist Cultural Forum. Not long after the interview was recorded, Spring Wind ceased publication, so the transcript of this interview was never published there. The following is an excerpt from that transcript.

INTRODUCTION

IN SOME OF the other essays in this collection I have raised questions concerning the traditional Buddhist teaching of rebirth. In 'Bodhisattvas in Blue Jeans' I outlined a position that made sense to me, and in various other essays I express misgivings about the teaching of rebirth. It is only fair, therefore, to present the case for rebirth as advanced by a highly trained spokesman of a traditional point of view. The following is part of an interview with Geshe Lati Rimpoche (*dge bshes bla ti rin po che*) in which I asked him some questions on the topic of rebirth as it is taught in his tradition.

Lati Rimpoche was born in 1922 in the eastern region of Tibet known as Kham. When he was still very young he entered the monastic life. He studied at Ganden (*dga'-ldan*) Monastery in Lhasa, where he eventually received the Geshe degree, the approximate equivalent of a Doctor of Divinity degree. After completing his degree, he attended the Tantric College of Upper Lhasa. After the Tibetan exodus in 1959,

Lati Rimpoche eventually settled in the region of South India called Karnataka, where the Tibetan community has established Ganden Monastery in exile. Lati Rimpoche is the abbot of Shardzay College within this re-established Ganden Monastic complex. He is the author of *Mind in Tibetan Buddhism*, which is Rimpoche's oral commentary on a classical Gelug treatise.[11]

The conversation, which took place on 15 September 1986, was conducted with the very capable help of Rimpoche's interpreter, Mr Lobsang Gyaltsen. Mr Gyaltsen not only proved to be fluently bilingual and to speak excellent English, but he also clearly had a command of all the issues being discussed and was able to clarify matters for both Lati Rimpoche and myself. We are much indebted to him for his invaluable aid. This transcription has been abridged somewhat to avoid repetition. Also, owing to technical difficulties, some parts of the tape recording of the original conversation were inaudible or unintelligible. Some of these portions have been deleted from the following transcription, and some have been reconstructed from notes. Every effort has been made to be faithful to the original meaning of what was said even if on occasion the actual words were lost.

INTERVIEW WITH LATI RIMPOCHE

HAYES: I understand that Rimpoche has travelled in the West on a number of occasions and given instruction in the Buddha-dharma.
RIMPOCHE: I have given quite a few talks. I don't know whether it is proper to say that I have given many talks, but from my point of view it has been a lot.

HAYES: In teaching the Buddha-dharma to the West has Rimpoche encountered any special problems?
RIMPOCHE: I haven't met with any special problems.

HAYES: When giving a talk to a group of Westerners, is it your experience that they ask the same kinds of questions that Tibetans would ask when you speak to them? Or are there issues that come up more frequently when you speak to Western audiences?
RIMPOCHE: Let me say that I have found that most of the people who have made up my audiences in the West come from a very good educational background. When they ask me questions, I find that

they tend to be very good questions. Of course I don't mean that everybody in the West asks brilliant questions, but for the most part the level of questions is very intelligent.

HAYES: A very important part of the training of most Western intellectuals is to develop an attitude of being critical and rather sceptical. Many Western intellectuals live by the dictum *sapiens nihil affirmat quod non probat*, which means 'a wise person says nothing is true that he has not proven.' What I am wondering is whether Rimpoche has ever encountered a resistance on the part of Western intellectuals to accepting things that are part of the doctrine of Buddhism.

RIMPOCHE: Whenever I talk, I try to talk with reason. I try to give strong evidence for all the claims I make. And for this reason very few intelligent people have much of a problem accepting anything that I have to say.

HAYES: Let me give one example of a teaching that occurs in Buddhism that poses a problem for many intellectuals. It is often said that we have lived before in the past and that what we are now is the consequence of actions that we have performed in previous lives. It is also said as a part of the teaching of Tibetan Buddhism in particular that the abbots of very important monasteries are the incarnations of the former abbots of those same monasteries. These claims are very difficult to believe without proof. I think the majority of Western intellectuals would feel that there is not sufficient evidence to justify believing those claims. Has Rimpoche ever encountered scepticism on this issue of rebirth and incarnate lamas? And if so, does Rimpoche have a way of explaining these teachings in such a way that Western intellectuals can find them acceptable?

RIMPOCHE: I can't reply in a way that all people would accept. Actually this teaching of rebirth is questionable, because there is no absolute proof that it is true. All we can do is to see whether the balance of reason weighs more for it or more against it. I think it is more reasonable to accept it than to reject it. I approach the question like this. If we look at the beings around us, we see that they all experience different amounts of happiness. Some are very intelligent, and some are not. Some experience great joy, and some are almost incapable of ever feeling happy no matter what circumstances they are in. Everything in my experience that I know about for certain has a cause. So I assume there must be a cause also for this great difference that we observe among sentient beings. The cause is not apparent in the circumstances of their present lives. So it must be that the cause is from something in their past before they began their present lives. If someone has a propensity to be intelligent, this is something that was acquired at birth. It must come from a cause before birth. We say a being is born intelligent if in past lives it used its mind for good purposes. I am not claiming that every Westerner who hears this kind of presentation is convinced, but they do tell me that they believe what I have to say.

HAYES: What is the most frequently encountered question when you are speaking to Western audiences?
RIMPOCHE: People always want to know why the ways of the world are as they are and who created these things. People want to know why there is so much pain and suffering in the world, and why there are so many thieves and other bad people causing so much suffering for others.

HAYES: That reminds me of a question that was once put to me when I was giving a public lecture about Buddhism. A Jewish person in the audience asked me how the Buddhists would explain why during the Second World War in Europe so many innocent Jewish children, who had never done anything wrong to deserve punishment, were put to death in Nazi concentration camps or were left as homeless orphans. That situation was completely lacking in any justice in that so many of the victims were apparently totally innocent. How would Rimpoche answer that question if it were put to him?
RIMPOCHE: The proper Buddhist answer to such a question is that the victims were experiencing the consequences of their actions performed in previous lives. The individual victims must have done something very bad in earlier lives that led to their being treated in this way. Also there is such a thing as collective karma.

HAYES: Do you mean that the Jewish people as a whole have a special karma?
RIMPOCHE: Yes. All groups have karma that is more than just the collection of the karma of the individuals in the group. For example, a group of people may decide collectively to start a war. If they act on that decision, then the group as a whole will experience the hardships of being at war. Karma is the result of making a decision to act in a

certain way. Decisions to act may be made by individuals or by groups. If the decision is made by a group, then the whole group will experience the collective consequences of their decision.

HAYES: What can an individual do to change the karma of the group that he or she belongs to?
RIMPOCHE: You can change all karma through practice. You can persuade the group to adopt pure attitudes and to develop pure practices.

HAYES: Is what constitutes purity of practice and purity of attitude the same for every group? Let's return to the example of the Jews. According to Jewish belief there are certain practices that Jewish people should perform in order to remain pure. Other groups do not have to follow these same laws of purity. Is your suggestion that the Jews may have suffered the humiliations of the holocaust because they failed to live up to Jewish standards of purity, or rather because they did not live up to Buddhist standards of purity?
RIMPOCHE: There are attitudes that all peoples regard as pure. Being kind to other people, for example. I don't know specifically about the history of the Jews.

HAYES: Then let's talk about the Tibetans. The Tibetans have as a group suffered a great humiliation for these past several decades. Is it Rimpoche's belief that this is the consequence of impurity of practice within Tibetan culture as a whole? Is there some lesson that the rest of mankind can learn from the tragedy of your people?
RIMPOCHE: I'm sure that those Tibetans who were left behind to suffer great hardships under the Chinese Communists must have done something very bad in previous lives to deserve such consequences. It could be that in former lives they tortured other people or were responsible for injustice. As a result they must now live under an unjust system.

HAYES: That might account for those individuals. But it still does not answer the question about the collective karma of the Tibetan people. I still cannot quite see how collective karma works. It would make sense to me perhaps if a person were reborn as a Tibetan in every life. Then if he participated in a group decision in one life as a Tibetan, he could experience the consequences of that group decision as a Tibetan in a future life.

RIMPOCHE: Collective karma just applies to group actions and group decisions, such as the decision to go to war. But it should not be understood as applying to individuals. For example it is not the case that a Tibetan in this life was a Tibetan in a previous life or will be a Tibetan in the future. That is not how group karma works at all. The way it works is that if a group of people decide to agree with each other and live together in harmony, then they will experience happiness. But if they decide to be in conflict with each other, then they will experience the hardships of conflict. For example, Toronto is a very beautiful city that has so many wonderful hospitals and beautiful parks and is very peaceful with very little crime. That is because the citizens of Toronto have decided collectively to be civilized people. They have made an effort in that direction. And it is because of what they have done as individuals in their past lives that the individual citizens of Toronto are so fortunate as to be able to live here.

HAYES: I see. So is it possible that the Tibetans made some collective decision to be hostile towards the Chinese and as a consequence of that group decision were overwhelmed? Or is there any way of knowing exactly why a group of people experiences the history that unfolds for them?

RIMPOCHE: It is not such a simple thing to determine all the factors involved in karma. Karmic roots are beginningless and may ripen at any time.

HAYES: Does that mean that there is no way that an individual or a group can discover what specific actions of the past have made the present turn out as it has? Can we learn something of value from history in order to change the shape of the future?

RIMPOCHE: We ordinary people cannot understand completely the great complexity of causes and conditions that are behind the consequences we feel in the present time, because they are really infinite. But what I can say is that there are patterns that we can observe. There is no certainty that the theory of karma is true. But if we impartially examine the evidence that we can observe, we see that events have causes. We see that beings who help others are happy, and we see that beings who hurt others are unhappy. So if you want to be happy, then it makes sense to help others be happy. You can look at this whole question like this. Of course there is no certainty that we lived in the past, and there is no certainty that we shall live again in the future.

These matters are beyond absolute proof. But suppose that you decide to act as if the theory of karma and consequence is true. You then decide to help other beings. This alone will make you feel very good. And it will make other beings love you. They will think highly of you, and they will be very willing to do things to make you happy and to help you when you are in distress. It may be that in addition to all these consequences of your decision to be helpful to others you may also be born into a beautiful pure land in the future life. There is no proof that this will happen, but you have nothing to lose if you act as if it will happen. On the other hand, if you choose to be very selfish and act in ways that harm others, you may run the risk of falling into hell in the future. But even if this is not what happens, it is still true that even in this very life, you will find that other beings fear you and hate you and will be unwilling to help you when you are in distress. So you see, you have nothing to lose by acting as if the theory of karma and rebirth is true. You definitely do have something to gain by acting as if it is true, even in this life. And it may even be that you have more to gain than you realize. So it is really the most intelligent thing to do to choose to be kind and compassionate and friendly to all beings and to act in the realization that all beings, just like you, want to be happy. To state the matter very briefly, it makes the most sense of all just to be civilized and to act in a civilized way.

REFLECTIONS ON LATI RIMPOCHE'S ARGUMENT

One cannot help being struck at the similarity between Lati Rimpoche's discussion of karma and rebirth and Blaise Pascal's famous 'wager'. Pascal argued that even though there is no definitive proof for the existence of God, the atonement of sin, and beatific vision, it is still not unreasonable to believe in these doctrines. If it turns out to be true that there really is a God and an afterlife, Pascal argued, then the believer will not be disappointed, and may even be rewarded for having had faith. On the other hand, if it turns out that death brings oblivion, then the believer will still not be disappointed, for in his oblivion he will never realize that he once held a false belief.

In saying that karma and rebirth are doctrines around which one can make decisions on how to act in the present life *as if* they were true, Lati Rimpoche seems to place these doctrines in a mythical space, as opposed to a historical or scientific framework. Access to this mythical space can be gained, not by logical proof or through a methodical empirical observation of the sensible world, but by exercising one's imagination and then having the courage of one's imaginings.

The suspension of one's disbelief, which amounts to a willingness to think of the world as if it were a certain way, is then very similar to what one does in reading a piece of fiction. If a reader were so lacking in imagination that he could not even entertain the possibility of a land called Middle Earth, inhabited by hobbits and elves and orcs, then he could never enter into the wonderful stories told in J.R.R. Tolkien's *The Lord of the Rings*; by not being able to enter into that story, such a reader would probably not derive much pleasure from the trilogy, and, worse, might not be able to benefit by reflecting on some of the profound observations of human nature conveyed through the vehicle of myth. Of course, such a reader might be able to arrive at similar observations of human nature by some means other than fiction, and he might experience great pleasure by some means other than fiction, but he would be relatively dead to the potential joys to be gained by reading *The Lord of the Rings* and would, to that extent, be more limited than someone with an imagination rich enough to enter into the world of myth. Similarly, a person insufficiently imaginative to enter into the myths of karma and rebirth might very well find another means of leading an ethical and fulfilling life; it is not, in other words, strictly necessary to enter into these myths in order to be ethical. Such a person might, however, have more difficulty gaining the full benefit of Buddhist stories, and even of many Buddhist practices, than a person more willing to suspend disbelief and enter into the imaginative world of myth.

My experience has been that many Westerners still balk at accepting the doctrines of karma and rebirth. The reason for this hesitation, it seems to me, is that they expect, or perhaps even fear, that the notion of rebirth is supposed to be accepted literally as historical facts or scientific hypotheses about the natural world and that they therefore must be supported by the same kind of evidence and precise reasoning that characterizes good historical scholarship or scientific investigation. If, however, karma and rebirth are presented to such people as myths, or as exercises in the imagination that may have the effect of enabling one to reflect on the consequences of one's actions and attitudes by imagining oneself in the situation of other people or other kinds of living being, the hesitation that such people have to talk in terms of karma and rebirth seems to diminish. Talking about the Buddha's (or even one's own) previous lives then becomes no more odious than, say, having an animated discussion about Sherlock Holmes's struggles with Moriarity or about Frodo's heroic efforts to overcome his resistance to disposing of the evil ring that gave him the power of becoming invisible. Out of such animated discussions comes much that is often surprisingly, and always immeasurably, beneficial and positive.

4

TEACHERS

This essay, written in the autumn of 1986, is an excerpt from a longer essay entitled 'Gleanings in the aftermath' on the Conference on Zen in North America, written originally for Spring Wind: Buddhist Cultural Forum. The issue for which the essay was originally written never appeared.

IN THE SUMMER of 1986 the Zen Buddhist Temple of Ann Arbor sponsored a conference on Zen Buddhism in North America. Invitations to read papers or give talks or lead discussions were extended to a number of Zen teachers, all of whom had in common that they were born and brought up in the United States or Canada, as well as to a number of academic specialists in Buddhism, all of whom had in common that they were also practising Zen Buddhists. One issue that repeatedly came up for discussion during the week-long conference was that of the role of teachers, an issue that was especially poignant for those who had witnessed situations in which Zen teachers had failed to set an example of humanity at its best. Particularly painful emotions arise when teachers let their students down; in such situations, pain itself becomes the teacher.

A couple of years ago someone asked me what I thought was missing in North American Buddhism, and without hesitation I found myself blurting out, 'What is missing? Why, the Buddhism itself!' The word 'Buddhism', of course, is mostly the invention of scholars of comparative religion, and it does not really have very much meaning at all except as a convenient label. What I really meant in giving my answer is that the Dharma is missing, or at least is not yet here in its fullness. Just before Gotama Buddha passed into *parinirvāṇa* he told the assembled monks that after his death they should let the Dharma, rather than any human authority figure, be their leader. How this is usually understood is that the Vinaya and the Sūtras set the standard of what is acceptable as conduct and the expression of ideals. Here in North America, as in Japan, the Vinaya is almost unknown except to a few scholars and a handful of monks, and consequently there are many misconceptions about it and little respect for it. As is to be expected, the absence of a strong Vinaya tradition in North America goes hand in hand with the lack of a prominent monastic Sangha. We are a *pariṣad*[12] made up almost exclusively of *upāsakas* and *upāsikas* (laymen and laywomen) who undertake only the five training rules of avoiding five kinds of mischief: injury to others, theft, careless sensuality, verbal misconduct, and intoxication.

Many North Americans undertake even these five training rules rather casually and find excuses for eating meat, being relatively casual in the pursuit of sensual pleasures, and using alcohol, tobacco, or marijuana, and in so doing they do not strictly speaking measure up to even the minimum standards of conduct that go along with being part of the fourfold *pariṣad* that comprises monks, nuns, lay brothers, and lay sisters. The very idea of a bhikṣu-bhikṣuṇi sangha in which the ordained members undertake some 250 training rules strikes many North American Buddhists as almost preposterous or fanatical. To suggest that North American Buddhism without a healthy respect for *śīla* (pure conduct) hardly qualifies as Buddhism at all is evidently something that threatens many North Americans' sense of identity as Buddhists. Moreover, the claim that there is no real Buddhism without monks would strike many North Americans as simply false. What I wish to do here is explore why these attitudes prevail.

Despite the ever-increasing numbers of Asians and Africans migrating to North America, the culture is still overwhelmingly influenced by European patterns of thought, and as a rule our attitudes are very much shaped by events in European history. Nowhere is this more true than in our attitudes towards religion. In particular, the Protestant Reformation, the Roman Catholic Counter-Reformation, and the advent of rationalism and humanism, have culminated in an irreversible loss of innocence in European culture and in its offspring cultures in North and South America, and to a large extent in the formerly colonized parts of Asia and Africa. Virtually every North American, even one who has never read the words or even heard the names of Martin Luther, John Calvin, or Erasmus, is nevertheless affected by their critiques of institutionalized religion and institutionalized religious authority.

When Martin Luther, who was a Roman Catholic monk and professor of theology, began to question practices that he felt were unhealthy for the spiritual well-being of Christians, he was silenced by papal authority. As an Augustinian monk he honoured the vows of poverty, chastity, and obedience. The Augustinian and Benedictine vows of obedience were founded on the principle that spiritually immature people are not the best judges of what they truly need for their own spiritual growth. Obedience to a higher authority is the first step in breaking down pride, self-centredness, and complacency, which are universally recognized as the principal obstacles to maturing into a fully functioning adult. Luther was an extremely serious monk, almost obsessed with his own sinfulness, so he did not take the matter of questioning the supreme authority of the pope at all lightly. It was an agonizingly difficult decision for him to make, whether to be openly critical of the pope or to remain obediently silent even in the face of practices whose spiritual value he seriously questioned. Luther ultimately decided to speak out, and eventually he came to publish his criticisms of the very institution of the papacy and the whole spiritual hierarchy of which it was the pinnacle.

In his criticisms of the institutionalized spiritual hierarchy of the Roman Catholic Church, Martin Luther argued that the pope had become immune from all criticism. While the pope was theoretically guided by his advisers, in fact he had the discretionary power to choose and dismiss the members of his advisory councils, with the result that he could just choose those advisers who agreed with him and remove those who disagreed. He had similar control over the courts that interpreted canon law, the result being that few decisions were made in canon courts that did not meet with full papal approval. In justifying their use of these powers, the popes appealed to the principle that to question a spiritual authority was merely a manifestation of pride and spiritual immaturity. All of this made it virtually impossible for anyone to offer the pope truly critical advice.

Luther argued that such a system could work only if the pope really were a nearly perfect spiritual being. But if he were subject to the same human failings as other men, then the pope's absolute authority would only prove to be a very dangerous and harmful thing. Luther's argument is quite reminiscent of Aristotle's claim that a totalitarian state is either the very best or the very worst of governments, depending on whether or not the absolute power resides in a truly just and wise leader. Since truly just and wise leaders are most uncommon, the least dangerous form of government is a democracy, which is so awkward and unwieldy that it impedes the carrying out of unwise and unjust decisions. In using essentially secular arguments from the domain of ordinary politics and applying them to spiritual institutions, Luther came to question whether there was in fact any difference at all between cleric and layperson and between the spiritual and the secular domains.

John Calvin took Martin Luther's arguments to their natural conclusions and argued strenuously that the very notion of spiritual hierarchy was a positive evil, because it allowed men who were in fact still weakened by sin to believe that their own thinking was divinely inspired. Since, he argued, mankind as a whole is overwhelmed by pride and disobedience, nobody is really in a position to make a reliable judgement as to what is divine and what is human. Therefore, said Calvin, to set up an institution in which a corruptible man can pass off his own thinking as the inspiration of an incorruptible supreme being is so dangerous to human spiritual welfare that it must be the work of Satan himself. Thus in Protestant circles that followed Calvinistic thinking, the pope came to be regarded as the very Prince of Darkness, the Antichrist.

Much of North America was colonized by English and Dutch Calvinists. Especially in the United States the very law under which its citizens live, the Constitution that is the backbone of the American legal system, is completely permeated with the Calvinist suspicion of misplaced authority. In both Canada and the United States the system of government and the whole way of life is founded upon checks and balances, that is, institutionalized controls on power and restraints against its abuse. In the English-speaking parts of North America this suspicion of authority extends to the spiritual as well as to the secular. When it comes to the fear of the abuse of power and authority, most

English-speaking North Americans make no distinction between the sacred realm and the secular realm.

Whatever one may think about the effects of Protestant culture on European and North American attitudes towards religious authority, one must, I think, acknowledge that even in these times when relatively few people consider themselves to be actively religious, Protestant values and attitudes make up the ocean on which the Buddhist boat must sail. As Buddhists we can reasonably expect to cross this ocean but not to replace it with an entirely different kind of water. Protestantism is as much a part of the basis of North American culture as Confucianism and Daoism were part of the basis of East Asian societies when Buddhism was introduced there. To ignore this fact will be to fail to establish Buddhism on this continent as anything more than the passing fancy of a few generations in the late twentieth century.

Now to be just a little more concrete, what can we expect a North American Sangha to be like, if indeed one ever emerges at all? In asking this question I am not interested in simply speculating about the future. Rather, I am interested in exploring ways whereby the Buddha-dharma with its long history might productively merge into the shorter but much more forceful historical momentum of Protestant North America.

First of all, given that outside the Spanish and French areas of North America there is very little history of monasticism here, it may be necessary to make the case for having a bhikṣu-sangha at all. The case for having a strong monastic community rests quite simply on the fact that it is this community that keeps the Dharma alive and pure by teaching it, devoting full time to studying it, and knowing its interpretations, translating it, and living completely in accordance with it. This does not mean that one must be a monk to appreciate, study, and practise the Dharma, or to realize the fruits of practice. Far from it. All it means is that the tasks of transmitting the Dharma in its purest form require a body of people who dedicate themselves full-time to those tasks and carry them out without the distractions and impediments of ordinary family life. Monks provide a model of selfless service to the Dharma that can be a source of unparalleled inspiration to those who are caught up in the complicated business of rearing families and financing a household, enterprises in which ideals nearly always must be compromised somewhat by pragmatic concerns. Ideals are precious things and should be kept alive in communities especially designed to uphold them as purely as humanly possible. I personally feel that keeping noble ideals alive is of especial importance in the cynical and tough-minded milieu of modern North America.

If it may be granted that a monastic Sangha is something to be desired in North America, the question that now arises is which model of a Sangha we should try to follow. What I personally would be inclined to argue here is that, rather than copying any Sangha as it actually exists in Asia, the model to be followed should be the original blueprint as contained in the Vinaya. Comparative studies of all available Vinaya collections would be most useful in this connection, as would be studies of concrete descriptions of how Buddhist monastic communities actually functioned. The more comprehensive such comparative studies could be, the better. It would be most agreeable to have a group of male and female scholars, practitioners, and monks convene to study the extant Vinayas and their major commentarial traditions and to work on ways of implementing them in our present circumstances. Of all the branches of Buddha-dharma, the Vinaya has proven to be least prone to proliferating sectarian differences, so a careful study of it could easily serve to bind together the many forms of Buddhism that have come to North America, whether they be Theravāda, Pure Land, Zen, or Vajrayāna.

The original blueprint for an ideal Buddhist society is one for which most North Americans, given the Calvinistic mistrust of absolute authority that permeates our culture, should have a natural affinity. The original Sangha was non-centralized, non-authoritarian, and non-absolutist. It was non-centralized in that each monastery (*vihāra*) was autonomous in the matters of setting up its own administrative structures, its own programmes of teaching and practice, and its own form of relationship to the lay community that supported it. Despite this lack of centralized authority and power, however, the Sangha communities were bound together by their recognition of common rules for ordination. A monk or novice could take vows in one vihāra which would be acknowledged in another vihāra, so a Sangha member was in effect at home wherever there were Buddhist monasteries or centres. A monk's seniority, calculated from the exact time of taking full ordination, was portable to anywhere in the Buddhist world, as were the official recognitions of his accomplishments in whatever specialized training had been undertaken. Therefore a monk could travel rather freely and take advantage of the different strengths of a number of different training environments, thereby getting a well-rounded education.

Moreover, as large numbers of monks went from place to place, they were in a good position to compare the practices and the standards of conduct at one place with what they had observed elsewhere. If any one vihāra developed unacceptable or substandard practices, news of it got around to the rest of the Buddhist world and informal steps could be taken to help the ailing community re-establish a more healthy practice. Some system such as this, in which quality of training is kept in check by the consensus of a community guided by the Dharma and the Vinaya itself but in which there is no centralized institutional authority, seems ideal for the North American setting. The original Sangha blueprint is an idea that could prove very timely for Buddhists on this continent, for our society feels at home with the idea of a democracy in which the powers of the leaders are limited by the consensus of the community at large.

The question of institutional authority in the Zen tradition in particular has been complicated somewhat by the mythology of enlightenment. A similar mythology occurs within all the various forms of Hinduism and Buddhism in which a central place is given to a guru who is supposed to have achieved a higher spiritual state than his disciples have achieved. In Tibetan Buddhism, for example, a lama (the Tibetan translation for the Sanskrit word 'guru') is usually regarded either as a person who has achieved an extraordinarily high state of spiritual evolution through training in this lifetime or is an incarnation of a person who made such achievements through training in previous lives and has returned for the benefit of all sentient beings. In Tibetan ritual, therefore, it is common for the disciple to take refuge in his lama even before taking refuge in the Three Jewels of ordinary Buddhism. The lama is seen as a living concrete manifestation of the somewhat more abstract and remote Buddha, Dharma, and Sangha. The lama is present here and now for the disciple and is therefore in all practical respects even more precious than the Three Jewels themselves.

The Zen master is in a number of important respects similar to the Tibetan lama in that he is surrounded with a certain mystique due to the claim of enlightenment. By the very fact that he or she is supposed to be an enlightened being, the Zen master can claim a degree of immunity from the criticisms of disciples, who by the very fact of being disciples acknowledge their spiritual inferiority. The mythology of enlightenment is one that invites abuse for the simple reason that it is much easier to claim to be enlightened than it is actually to be enlightened. It is even easier to be perceived by disciples as an enlightened teacher than it is actually to be an enlightened teacher. Events in Zen and other guru-oriented traditions in North America have made this painfully clear. What makes these situations so alarming is not simply that one individual is allowed to receive more respect than his behaviour would normally warrant, but rather that his behaviour is allowed to bring so much pain and confusion into the lives of so many other people, many of whom have sacrificed a great deal in order to undergo Zen training in the first place.

The tragedies of abused leadership that some North American Zen centres have experienced were not necessarily isolated incidents but may rather be reflections of the dangers inherent in the very mythology of spiritual hierarchy based upon the claims of enlightened leadership. But it is a kind of tragedy that need not be repeated in Buddhist circles. The Buddhist Sangha, after its founder died, was not an institutional hierarchy. Even the relationship between a student and his teacher was not founded on the assumption of the teacher's spiritual superiority. Since this is a very important matter, let us take a closer look at the ideal student-teacher relationship as it is described in the Vinaya texts.

The question of the duties of teachers and students towards one another comes up for discussion in the chapters beginning with the twenty-fifth of the first section of the Mahāvagga of the Pāli Vinaya.[13] Here it is noted that, at a time when the Sangha was still young, a number of monks were given to churlish behaviour when they went out on their begging rounds. They were sloppy in their dress, they asked for seconds and requested certain types of food rather than graciously accepting what was offered, and they were loud and noisy. As a result, people mistook them for Hindu priests! Monks who were serious about their training and who wished for the Sangha to have a better reputation among the general public approached the Buddha on how to keep the rowdy monks under control. He suggested that newly-ordained and novice monks be given teachers and preceptors who would be responsible for overseeing the training of newer members of the Sangha.

The senior monk who was chosen to be a teacher to a younger monk was to regard the younger monk as his son, and the younger was to regard the older as his father. If the two monks regard each other in this way, say the texts, then both of them 'united by mutual reverence, confidence, and communion of life, will progress, advance, and reach a high stage in this Dharma and discipline'. Both the teacher and his student stand to gain by their relationship if they approach it with the proper attitudes. The student is expected to help take care of the teacher's basic articles of clothing, utensils, and health-care requisites. He is also expected to help the teacher keep his living quarters clean and to see that his teacher is reasonably comfortable. And if the teacher becomes ill, then of course the student is expected to attend to his needs.

But in addition to all these duties of service to the teacher's physical person, the student is also responsible for helping the teacher live up to the Dharma! If the teacher becomes angry or depressed, or if he commits a serious wrongdoing, then the student should give the teacher an uplifting talk on the Dharma. The student, in other words, has precisely the same duties towards the teacher as the teacher has towards the student: to set an example of good conduct, to teach in words to reinforce the teaching by example, and to offer constant encouragement to help the other live by the Dharma. There is never any assumption made that the older monk is in any less need than the younger of training and encouragement. It is the duty of the teacher graciously to accept criticism and admonishment from his disciple as much as it is the duty of the disciple to accept criticism and admonishment from the teacher.

Given that the teacher and the student have the same basic duties of training and helping one another, and given that neither is regarded as the spiritual superior of the other, we may ask what the difference is between a teacher and a disciple. The answer is quite simple: the teacher has expertise in some area in which the student lacks it. Thus a monk might have several teachers, one who was a master in Vinaya, another who was a master of Sūtras, another who was a master of commentaries and philosophical treatises, and yet another who was a master of meditation. It was from this last kind of teacher, the *dhyāna ācārya*, that the Zen master evolved.

The original *dhyāna ācārya* was a person who had mastered the skills of meditation and who had acquired sufficient judgement of human character to be able to prescribe meditation practices for other people. Meditation was regarded as a medicine; for each kind of defect in character there was a corresponding therapeutic meditation, and as in medicine it was recognized that a therapy that cures a patient suffering from one kind of illness might very well kill a patient suffering from some other illness. This basic metaphor of meditation as medicine runs throughout Buddhist sūtra literature, both Theravāda and Mahāyāna. In the Indian languages the word for physical disease is the same as the word for defect in character: *doṣa*. The three basic defects of character recognized in Buddhism (greed, hostility, and delusion) were viewed almost as organic diseases that could be cured through the proper application of the appropriate treatments.

What is particularly interesting about this therapeutic metaphor is that there is no underlying assumption that the therapist is any more healthy than the patient. A good meditation master was someone who knew how to teach suitable meditation exercises to other people, just as a good physician was one who knew which herbs to prescribe to cure a fever or how to apply a splint to set a broken limb. But it does not follow that a person who knows how to apply a splint to a broken arm does not himself have a broken arm. Nor does it follow that a good meditation master is free of the character disorders that befall all sentient beings. It is only when we forget this bit of common sense that we begin to run the risks of experiencing the kinds of breakdown of basic Dharma that have occurred in North American Zen establishments and that can so easily occur anywhere where students and teachers begin to lose sight of the vulnerability and fallibility of all human beings, whether their roles happen to be that of the master or that of the disciple.

Part of what this Conference on Zen in North America made very clear to me was that we in the North American Zen movement must all make up our minds as individuals whether our first loyalties are to the Buddha-dharma or to the institution of Zen. The two are by no means one and the same. If we come to feel that our greater loyalty is to the Buddha-dharma, to the wisdom that it embodies, and to the way of life that follows from accepting that wisdom, then we are free and indeed obliged to study what the Buddha-dharma really includes and what it does not include. We are free to acknowledge that the authoritarian structures of patriarchal Zen are more the products of

Confucian society than aspects of the Way of Buddhism itself. In fact, the whole notion of the Zen master as it has evolved in East Asia is arguably as foreign to the original Buddha-dharma as it is to those of us who live in Protestant North America. If we come to feel that the prospects of spiritual growth through the methods of Patriarchal Zen are not worth the risk of the abuse of authority, it is at least good to realize that there is an alternative: the Dharma and the Sangha as originally conceived.

I have been ruminating in the aftermath of the Conference on Zen Buddhism in North America for long enough. I personally left the Conference with a much clearer idea in my mind of what exactly I expect of anyone who claims to be a representative of the Buddha-dharma. Such a person must conform as closely as possible to the descriptions of enlightened behaviour that we read about in the Buddhist sūtras. Let me end by citing just two such descriptions out of the many that exist in Buddhist literature. One is from the Pāli Sutta Nipāta, the other from the Mahāyāna collection called the Ratnakūṭa, a word meaning a pile of gems.

A theme that comes up for frequent discussion in the literature of early Buddhism is that of which kind of religious leader is most worthy of respect. The Hindu priests, the brahmans, claimed to be born with qualities that made them automatically uniquely qualified not only to serve as priests but also to be the objects of popular respect. The Buddha, on the other hand, never tired of arguing that the only true warrant for a person's receiving respect is the quality of that person's conduct. That and that alone is what makes a person a genuine religious figure. And what kind of conduct is it that marks the true religious leader? It is described in lines from the Sutta Nipāta, verses 513–17. In this text the story is told of how the Buddha has been approached by a wandering ascetic named Sabhiya, who has gone to see many different people 'who have orders of monks, have groups, are teachers of groups, are well known, famous, founders of sects, and well thought of by the general public'. Sabhiya approaches Gotama the Buddha, who invites him to ask any question he wishes to ask. Sabhiya is astonished at this invitation, for his experience with all other religious leaders had been that they 'showed anger, hatred, and ill-will' when they were asked questions about their teachings and their practices. Sabhiya then asks the following question:

> 'What must one obtain in order to be called a bhikṣu?' asked Sabhiya. 'On account of what qualities do people call a person gentle and restrained? What must one have in order to be called awake? Please answer these questions for me.'
>
> 'He who has become calm by the path that he himself has practised, who has got beyond doubt, who has abandoned both birth and death, who has lived the proper life, and whose future existence is destroyed, is called a bhikṣu.
>
> 'He who is even-minded on all occasions, mindful, a recluse who does not harm anyone in the whole world, who has crossed over [the flood of life and death], is not agitated, and has no arrogance, is called gentle.
>
> 'He whose external and internal faculties are developed, who has understood this world and the next, and who maturely awaits the time of his own death, is called restrained.
>
> 'And he who is free of defilements after investigating saṁsāra both as death and as being born through all the ages, and who is pure and clear-minded, and has come to the end of rebirth, is called awake.'[14]

The tone of this passage from the Sutta Nipāta is to be found throughout the Pāli literature. But these sentiments are by no means confined to Theravādin suttas, for very similar sentiments occur throughout Mahāyāna sūtras. Compare, for example, this following description of the paradigm of Mahāyāna practice, the Bodhisattva.

> 'Furthermore, Kāśyapa, a Bodhisattva is not a Bodhisattva in name only. One who can practise wholesome dharmas and has a mind of equality is called a Bodhisattva. Briefly speaking, one who accomplishes thirty-two things is called a Bodhisattva. What are the thirty-two? (1) To aspire to bring sentient beings peace and happiness; (2) to enable all sentient beings to abide in all-knowing wisdom; (3) not to resent another's wisdom; (4) to shatter one's own haughtiness and arrogance; (5) to take deep pleasure in the Buddha's path; (6) to love and respect all sentient beings sincerely; (7) to remain thoroughly kind to friends and foes alike up to one's attainment of nirvāṇa; (8) always to speak with a smile and be the first to offer greetings; (9) never to stop halfway through in performing a task; (10) to extend great compassion equally to all sentient

> beings; (11) to seek extensive learning untiringly and insatiably; (12) to look for one's own faults, but not to speak of others' shortcomings; (13) to be inspired by *bodhicitta* [the desire to attain enlightenment in order to benefit others] in every aspect of one's behaviour; (14) to practise giving without expecting anything in return; (15) to observe the discipline, but not for the sake of a higher rebirth; (16) to practise patience with an unimpeded mind among sentient beings; (17) to strive with vigour to cultivate all good roots; (18) to practise meditation without aspiring to rebirth in the realm of formlessness; (19) to apply the wisdom of skilful means; (20) to practise the four inducements [unbounded generosity, pleasant speech, useful livelihood, indifference to one's own state of comfort]; (21) to be equally kind to both good and evil sentient beings; (22) to listen to the Dharma single-mindedly; (23) to remain detached in mind; (24) not to indulge in worldly affairs; (25) not to enjoy the inferior mode of progress, but always to see great benefit in the great mode of progress; (26) to avoid bad friends and associate with good ones; (27) to accomplish the four immeasurables [unlimited friendship, compassion, joy at the happiness of others, and impartiality] and achieve total command of the five powers [the powers arising from faith, vigour, mindfulness, concentration, and wisdom]; (28) always to rely on the true wisdom; (29) not to forsake any sentient beings, whether their actions are right or wrong; (30) always to discourse with decisiveness; (31) to value the true Dharma; and (32) to dedicate all one's deeds to awakening. Kāśyapa, a person who fulfils these thirty-two things is called a Bodhisattva.'[15]

North American Buddhists who let themselves be guided by the study of sūtras such as those quoted above and who use their meditation practices as a means of achieving the ideals constantly depicted in these sūtras – and Buddhists who take the time to learn the standards of conduct described in the Vinaya texts – should be well equipped to judge for themselves whether the conduct of any Zen master or Tibetan lama matches up to the standards universally recognized within the Buddha-dharma. If, on the other hand, we allow ourselves to remain ignorant of the Buddha-dharma, and if we cling to the mythology of a transmission of the enlightened mind outside the teachings without really understanding just what that mythology implies, then we really cannot blame anyone but ourselves if there continues to be an abuse of spiritual authority of which we are the unhappy victims.

BIBLIOGRAPHICAL NOTE

The bibliography gives details of translations and studies of the Buddhist Vinaya texts for anyone wishing to learn more about this area of traditional Buddhist doctrine and practice.

5

DR AMBEDKAR'S SOCIAL REFORM THROUGH BUDDHISM

The short items that follow are reflections on Buddhist thought that have been inspired by Dr Ambedkar and by Darshan Chaudhary and other members of the Ambedkar Mission in Toronto, from whom I have received the benefits of a most warm friendship over the years. The section called 'The Buddha's teachings on birth and social position' is the text of a talk delivered on the occasion of the 95th Birthday celebration of Dr B.R. Ambedkar on Sunday, 11 May 1986 at Toronto Buddhist Church. Various versions of the section called 'The religious politics of eating meat' have been read in several academic settings, including at a symposium on Buddhism and Human Rights held at the University of Toronto in 1993. The other sections, in somewhat different form, have appeared in talks given at the Ambedkar Mission in Toronto.

A YOUTH IN SEARCH OF HEROES

THERE IS SOMETHING in the Anglo-American psychology that gives the people of this background a tendency to love underdogs who struggle heroically against all odds to achieve some great moral victory over the dark forces of poverty, bigotry, or injustice. Probably all societies love myths of white knights who vanquish evil, but Anglo-Americans especially love their white knights to have lived as children and young adults in states of such deprivation that their characters were thoroughly tested by situations that would have driven anyone else to depravity. And so it was that as schoolboys the young men of my generation were nurtured on the heroic biographies of the likes of Benjamin Franklin, Abraham Lincoln, Booker T. Washington, and George Washington Carver.

When adulthood could be delayed no longer and I was forced to give serious thought to the questions of how to deal with the human condition, the one issue that most troubled me was how to achieve social and economic justice in a world that has come to take it as almost axiomatic that the struggle between rich and poor must eventually express itself in the form of armed confrontation. Deeply opposed to the use of violence, both against people and against property, I sought as a young adult to find inspiration in the words of people who had fought injustices through purely non-violent means. I found much that moved me in the diaries of John Woolman, the American Quaker who spent much of his life fighting slavery, and in the sermons of Martin Luther King, Jr. I also turned to one of the men who had done much to inspire Rev. King: Mohandas Karamchand Gandhi, called Mahatma.

Gandhi was one of the heroes of a good many of my friends during the turbulent days of the civil rights campaigns of the early 1960s and the anti-war movement of the later 1960s and early 1970s. But for some reason that I could never quite articulate, I myself never liked Gandhi's autohagiography very much and never found much in his life that struck me as inspirational. Trying to express what made me uneasy about Gandhi, I always hit upon three points. First, he seemed obsessed with matters of spiritual purity, especially in his concerns with sexuality but also in the manner in which he approached dietary restrictions and fasting, which struck me as sanctimonious. Second, his methods of non-violence did not seem to me to be truly non-violent at all; his threats to fast to death in order to achieve political goals seemed to me a form of spiritual blackmail implicit in which was the real risk, in case he should die, of severe bloodshed and mob violence. And third, he refused to renounce the Hindu caste system, and in fact endorsed the practice of caste duty as the backbone of the Hindu Dharma. None of these points made me seriously question Gandhi's personal character or integrity, but they did make it impossible for me to look to him as a person whose example I felt comfortable trying to follow.

In the days when Gandhi was a hero of young Americans involved in the non-violent struggle for social change, not many of them had heard of Bhimrao Ramji Ambedkar, another leader who, like Gandhi, was involved in the movement towards India's independence from the British. Like Gandhi, Ambedkar had received a British higher education, which he took after completing his studies at Columbia University in New York City. But, unlike Gandhi, Ambedkar was concerned not only with the campaign to gain self-rule for India, but also with a campaign to free his own people, the so-called Untouchable classes of India, from the invidious yoke of the Hindu caste system. At first working with Gandhi, Nehru, and the Congress Party, Ambedkar grew increasingly disillusioned at the reluctance of caste Hindus to consider making any fundamental reforms in the Hindu religious law according to which a person's place in society is determined by the person's birth. Himself an Untouchable who had suffered, even after he had earned a PhD degree, the deep humiliations of being treated with far less respect than the cows and monkeys venerated by the Hindus, Dr Ambedkar was also a profound scholar of constitutional law and had absorbed the best principles contained in all the national charters and constitutions of the European and American states.

Convinced that an independent India could flourish as a state in the modern world only if it abandoned the religious customs of hereditary inequality rooted in the ancient past, Dr Ambedkar proposed social reforms that Hindu religious leaders such as Gandhi simply could not accept. Following Gandhi's own example of leading non-violent demonstrations to prove his point, Ambedkar led groups of Untouchables into Hindu temples and into bathing facilities from which Untouchables were excluded by Hindu religious law and custom. He also fought for the right of Untouchables to have, like the Muslims, Sikhs, and Christians, their own representatives in the parliamentary government. In 1932 when the Untouchables won this battle for a separate electorate, Gandhi reacted by announcing that he would fast to the death unless this new provision was retracted. So great was the popularity of Gandhi that public opinion turned bitterly against the Untouchable cause, and Ambedkar, perceived as the man who was responsible for causing Gandhi to risk his life by fasting, received threats against his own life. He went back to the negotiating table and eventually reached a new compromise with the Hindus, whereupon Gandhi abandoned his fast.

Eventually, when India won her independence from Great Britain in 1947, Ambedkar was chosen by Prime Minister Jawaharlal Nehru to serve in his cabinet as the first Minister of Law, and not long afterwards he was elected chairman of the committee that drafted India's constitution. And so it was that a man who as a boy was forbidden because of the status of his birth to drink water from the public wells and to sit in the same classroom with caste Hindu children, came to be celebrated as the father of the Indian Constitution. Justly hailed as a most remarkable man who had risen to prominence against some of the most staggering odds that anyone must face anywhere in the world, Ambedkar was not interested in his own personal success. His chief concern continued to be the liberation of the 60,000,000 people who inherit lifelong membership of the oppressed Untouchable classes of India. In the Indian Constitution the institution of Untouchability was officially outlawed, but no one was so naïve as to believe that some two thousand years of Hindu custom would come to an abrupt end by the passage of a new law. The task of improving the lot of the former Untouchables was just beginning.

Throughout the 1930s and 1940s Ambedkar fought to improve the standard of education for his people and to win for them greater political power, for he knew that without educational reforms his people could never rise from the bottom of Indian society. But Ambedkar's experiences with Gandhi and with the Congress Party also convinced him that the Hindus would never be ready for fundamental religious reforms and that the fate of the former Untouchables would therefore never be improved unless they renounced Hinduism and took up a new religion in which there was no systematic inequality. He began an intensive study of the major religious traditions of the world, and after some two decades of research made the decision to become a Buddhist. When Dr Ambedkar took the simple vows of becoming a Buddhist layperson in October 1956, he was joined in his conversion by some 400,000 of his fellow ex-Untouchables.

Even in his conversion to Buddhism, Ambedkar was a reformer at heart. He was not a man to do anything in half measures, and he chose Buddhism as his religion only after very thoroughly studying the fundamental texts of Buddhist theory and practice and meeting with Buddhist leaders from all over the world. Not entirely content with any tradition of Buddhism as it now existed in Asia, Ambedkar had dreams of founding for his people a pure Buddhism, free of the influences of Hinduism and other Asian folk religions that it has acquired during the past 2,500 years. In this respect, Ambedkar serves as a model that many Western Buddhists find worthy of emulating.

One Western Buddhist who has found inspiration in the writings of Bhimrao Ramji Ambedkar is Sangharakshita, who has consistently been one of the most prolific and intelligent Buddhist authors in the English-speaking world. Founder of the Friends of the Western Buddhist Order, a Buddhist community with headquarters in Great Britain that has been engaged for many years in work with the formerly Untouchable classes in India through its Karuna Trust (formerly Aid For India) programme, Sangharakshita has written a fine account of Ambedkar's life and his thoughts on Buddhism.[16] It should be on the required reading list of every North American Buddhist.

THE RELIGIOUS POLITICS OF EATING MEAT

Among the many topics to which Dr Ambedkar turned his research skills and his fine reasoning abilities, one of particular personal interest to him and to tens of millions of other Indians like him, was the topic of how the institution of hereditary Untouchability began. Ambedkar recognized that the answers traditionally given to this question are pretty obviously false when examined in the light of historical evidence. One of the two standard hypotheses that have been put forward is that the Untouchables were originally a distinct race of people who came to be discriminated against by the mainstream society. But this is unlikely, because whatever part of India one examines, the Untouchables in that area belong – according to the criteria that anthropologists use to distinguish races and ethnic groups – to the same race as the mainstream society in the area.

The second hypothesis is that the Untouchable classes were made up of those people who performed unclean tasks, an unclean task being one that involves habitual contact with death or waste products; thus hunters, butchers, fishermen, leather workers, and so forth came to be regarded as in a state of perpetual ritual uncleanliness. But this hypothesis, which is the one usually advanced by Hindus, also has its problems. Firstly, it turns out that many Unouchables do not perform tasks that are ritually unclean at all. Secondly, one often finds that the people who do perform the unclean tasks do not thereby become Untouchables. So Untouchability is certainly not now a consequence of ritual impurity, and there is no decisive evidence to show that it ever was.

So who were the original Untouchables, and how did they come to be so despised by the caste Hindus? This was the question to which Ambedkar turned his scholarly attention in *The Untouchables*, published in 1948. The arguments provided there are long and complex, and since they have been very neatly summarized in Sangharakshita's excellent book, *Ambedkar and Buddhism*, I shall not recapitulate them all here. Rather, let me state the bare outline of Ambedkar's conclusion and part of how he arrived at it. The basic hypothesis that Ambedkar advanced was that the first Untouchables were Buddhists who were not reabsorbed into mainstream Hindu society at the time that the previously Buddhist kingdoms of India came under the political domination of the Hindu Gupta dynasty in the fourth century of the Common Era. Not all Buddhists met this fate of becoming Untouchable, suggested Ambedkar, but only those who habitually ate beef.

The historical background was somewhat as follows. At the time of the Buddha, in the sixth century BCE, the most common form of public religion was the practice of animal sacrifices in which various kinds of animals, but especially cows, were ritually killed by brahman priests and then eaten by the whole community. The form of religious community founded by the Buddha, in which the emphasis was solely on morality and personal integrity, was an alternative to this sacrificial religion. The Buddha and his followers were sharply critical of animal sacrifice, but because there were never more than just over a thousand Buddhist monks during the Buddha's lifetime, they had little impact on the religious practices of the mainstream society. Some centuries later, however, when the mighty emperor Aśoka become a patron of Buddhism, the sacrificial form of religion came into disfavour, and the brahman priests lost influence. The principal form of religious practice in India came to be individual and family-centred worship, in which the central practices were pilgrimage, making offerings, and chanting before statues and relics of the Buddha and other great personalities of Buddhism. The brahman priests, having lost their power as priests of the great public sacrifices, adopted a set of religious practices similar to the Buddhist ones, and so began the evolution of what would eventually become the temple-oriented religion that modern scholars usually call Hinduism. Since the name

Hinduism is usually reserved for this temple religion that evolved many centuries after the time of the Buddha, incidentally, it is not correct to say, as some people still do, that the Buddha was a Hindu; rather Hinduism evolved out of the ancient Brahmanic religion in reaction to Buddhist reforms. The story that has been told up to this point is widely accepted by most historians of the religions of early India. But now we begin to see the special features of Ambedkar's version of the story.

The brahman priests, says Ambedkar, were not content merely to copy the patterns of worship of the Buddhists and to adapt those patterns to the worship of such gods as Śiva and Viṣṇu. If they were to regain popular support, the brahmans had to make people believe they were more pure of conduct than the Buddhists. And so began a series of moves in which the Buddhists and the brahmans each tried to demonstrate their spiritual superiority over the other. As the stakes got higher, the criterion of what it means to become spiritually pure became more stringent. First, animal sacrifice was abolished. Next, many monks and priests began to give up the eating of animal flesh altogether, and vegetarianism came to be seen as a sign of great spiritual purity. Finally, when the Hindu Gupta dynasty came to power, they took the further step of protecting cows by making them objects of such veneration that killing one became a crime punishable by death.

Of course not everyone participated in this game of trying to surpass others in being spiritual, and the issue of vegetarianism came to be very controversial among Buddhists. As a rule the Mahāyāna community adopted the new fashion of vegetarianism, while the orthodox Buddhists continued to eat meat. But under the new laws protecting cows, even those people who still ate meat had to give up the eating of beef or else face severe social stigma. A large part of the Buddhist population, however, came from the segment of society that lived outside the villages and tended cows for a living, and it was their custom to eat the flesh of cows that had died. Since their whole economy was based on cows, and beef was their principal source of food, they could not easily feed themselves if they abandoned beef-eating. And so they were branded as Untouchables, altogether beyond the pale of Hindu society. So long as there were still Buddhist monks around, the beef-eating Buddhist laypeople did not suffer being spiritually alienated from the Hindu brahman priests, but when

Buddhism eventually died out in India, the beef-eaters had nowhere to turn. No longer able to practise Buddhism, they were also excluded by birth from Hindu society. Many eventually converted to Islam, but those who did not become Muslims have become a class of people despised by Hindu and Muslim alike. And they still eat beef.

Whether or not Ambedkar's hypothesis of the origins of Untouchability will stand up to close historical investigation remains to be seen. Ambedkar himself was very much aware how speculative his hypothesis was, since it deals with a set of circumstances the details of which may be lost for ever to historical researchers. On the surface, at least, this hypothesis seems much more likely to be near the truth than the hypotheses that Untouchability was based primarily on race or occupation; it does seem more likely that Ambedkar was right in suggesting that Untouchability was a result of a very complex set of causes that included religious, economic, and political factors, and in suggesting also that the institution of Untouchability began as a deliberate policy of persecution of one group by another. Whether or not the whole story as Ambedkar told it proves to be accurate, it does raise some very interesting observations about the origins of vegetarianism in India in general and in Buddhism in particular.

Since the issue of whether or not it is suitable for Buddhists to eat meat is a matter about which many Buddhists in the West can be rather strongly opinionated, and since a number of historical claims are made in defence of one side or the other in this issue, this seems like an area where an impartial look at the evidence would do none of us any great harm. The purpose of the following paragraphs, then, is simply to look at the evidence provided by the vegetarian sūtras and to try to interpret what conclusions that evidence seems to support.

The *Laṅkāvatāra Sūtra* is one of the principal sources for Buddhist – and more specifically Mahāyāna – arguments against the advisability of eating meat. An entire chapter is dedicated to the question of whether eating meat is a merit or a vice. The question is hardly raised before it is decided that eating meat is vicious. Next it is observed that even non-Buddhists who hold and teach false views avoid and prohibit the eating of meat; therefore, Buddhists who make compassion for others their main teaching should do likewise. The exercise then becomes one of producing arguments to persuade meat-eating people to change their ways so that they might better approach the Buddha-dharma. The arguments produced are as follows:

All beings now alive have been reborn countless times in the past, and therefore each living being has been at some time or other one's mother or father. Realizing that, the Bodhisattva reckons that all living beings are relatives who should be loved and respected. That being the case, how can one eat the flesh of one's relatives?

Even rākṣasas, the terrifying carnivorous fiends who appear in many Indian stories, abandon meat-eating when they hear the Buddha-dharma. So it stands to reason that a benevolent Bodhisattva, who is much more pure and kind-hearted than a rākṣasa, would avoid eating flesh.

Meat is sold by the roadside for money so should not be eaten.

Meat is impure, since it arises from the mixing of blood and semen, which are impure substances.

All animals, even carnivorous ones, are terrified when they detect the odour of someone who eats meat, and they run and hide. One who has undertaken a vow to bring comfort to all beings cannot do so by so terrifying them.

The smell of meat on one's breath is very foul, and no wise person will approach a person with foul breath to hear his teaching.

Villagers expect holy men and priests to renounce meat. If Buddhist monks eat meat, the villagers will not consider them holy and will lose respect for the Buddha's teachings.

The flesh of corpses burning in the cremation grounds has a nauseating stench. The burned flesh of dead animals smells and tastes equally obnoxious.

People who eat meat cannot develop magical powers against demons who haunt the wilderness.

Those who eat meat cannot conquer their sensual desires.

People who eat meat have great difficulty sleeping, and when they do sleep they are prone to having nightmares. Even while awake meat-eaters frequently suffer attacks of sudden terror for no apparent reason.

Meat-eating causes gluttony, because the appetite of those who eat meat is never satisfied.

Meat-eating causes one to get intestinal worms and leprosy.

One who eats meat becomes insensitive to all health hazards and therefore runs a much greater risk of getting diseases.

People who acquire a taste for animal flesh are very likely to become cannibals.

Buddhist monks who develop a fondness for meat are likely to develop shameless habits of twisting logic in every conceivable way in order to justify their evil practice; and they are likely to invent teachings and attribute them to the Buddha, just to make others believe their practices have the approval of the Buddha. But if they will distort logic and invent teachings to justify their own craving for meat, they cannot possibly be trusted to teach the Buddhadharma in its purest form.

Many of the same arguments that are made in this sūtra about the unpleasant effects of eating meat are then made about the effects of consuming garlic, onions, leeks, and alcohol. Meat, garlic, onions, leeks, and alcohol all cause bad breath; all are considered impure so are forbidden to holy men and priests, with the result that villagers will not regard monks who eat such things as holy and pure; all prevent the acquisition of magical powers against demons; all cause rebirth in hells or into the wombs of cats; and all have been most strictly forbidden by the Buddha from the very outset, and those who say otherwise are guilty of lying and distorting the Buddha-dharma in order to rationalize their own craving for forbidden foods.

One thing that is striking about these arguments is what an emphasis is placed on the offensive odours of people who eat meat. What is striking about this observation is that people who all eat the same diet do not normally smell offensive to one another, and in fact only rarely notice one another's odours at all. In a society where meat-eating is the norm, a meat-eater is not likely to be conspicuous by the odour of his breath and perspiration, and similar observations can be said about the odour of garlic-eaters in garlic-eating cultures, the odours of tobacco-smokers in tobacco-using societies and so on. Odour becomes an issue in societies in which different people have different dietary habits and therefore can be distinguished by bodily odours. All this suggests that the *Laṅkāvatāra Sūtra* was probably written at a time when meat-eating people and vegetarian people were both present, but vegetarianism was becoming the norm, at least the norm of the élite classes. It is fairly likely, then, that the *Laṅkāvatāra Sūtra* was written at a time when meat-eating, which had once been the norm of the ruling classes in India, was coming to be seen as a mark of the lower classes and of the religiously impure classes, and the Buddhists could not afford to be associated with the lower and less pure classes.

Another observation that catches one's attention is that the sūtra is as vehement about the evils of garlic, onions, leeks, and alcohol as it is about the evils of meat. Given that in Hindu works we find that garlic, onions, leeks, and alcohol are classified as impure foods unfit to be consumed by both brahman priests and those who practise yoga, it is tempting to conclude that the principal concern of the *Laṅkāvatāra Sūtra* is just to show that if Buddhist monks are to be perceived as being as religiously pure and therefore as worthy of being supported by villagers as are brahmans and yogins, then Buddhist monks must adopt the same dietary habits that the brahmans follow. What is especially telling is that the claim is made in the *Laṅkāvatāra Sūtra* that these dietary restrictions have been in effect in Buddhism *from the very beginning* and that the passages in Buddhist scriptures that suggest otherwise must have been inserted by untrustworthy monks who had been carried away by their excessive fondness for meat and garlic.

Another Mahāyāna sūtra that accuses depraved monks of having inserted passages allowing the eating of meat into the Buddha's teachings is the *Śūraṁgama Sūtra*. Towards the end of this long sūtra, the Buddha explains to Ānanda and the gathered assembly of monks that it is impossible to become enlightened without concentrating the mind, impossible to concentrate the mind without keeping the precepts, and impossible to keep the precepts without concentrating the mind. Therefore, keeping the precepts and concentrating the mind are inseparable requirements for those who wish to become enlightened. There are some habits, says the sūtra, that, being violations of the precepts, make it impossible for one to concentrate the mind through the practice of *dhyāna*. The single most important obstacle to enlightenment is sexual intercourse, says the Buddha, because the desire for sexual fulfilment is the most fundamental of our desires and the most persistent of our attachments; people who cannot overcome their desire for sex are therefore destined to remain stuck in the vicious cycle of attachment and frustration. The Buddha of the *Śūraṁgama Sūtra* then predicts that after his death many evil spirits will circulate among men, and these demons will take the form of wise and learned men, who will teach that there is nothing impure in sex, and by teaching this doctrine they will lure countless people into leading impure lives, making enlightenment impossible for them to attain.

Second in importance only to lustful thoughts as an obstacle to enlightenment, says the *Śūraṁgama Sūtra,* is pride. It is pride that drives people into being unkind, unjust, and cruel towards other living beings and towards non-human life forms. If the purpose of seeking wisdom and enlightenment is to become free of sorrow and to free others from sorrow, nothing can do more to defeat this purpose than to inflict pain and death on others. Once again the prediction is made that after the Buddha's death, evil spirits will disguise themselves as wise and learned teachers and will teach people that it is possible to eat meat and still become enlightened. They will also teach that there is no harm in wearing silk and leather clothing, despite the fact that these products cannot be made without taking life. And they will also teach that one can use dairy products, despite the fact that milk can be used by people only by depriving the young animals for whose sake the mother animals produced it in the first place. In fact, says the sūtra, no one can become enlightened if they eat meat or dairy products, or wear silk or leather, and no one can be considered a true follower of the Buddha if they eat or use products made of dead animals.

Having made this point, the sūtra goes on to discuss various forms of theft, and it says the most serious form of theft is to steal a person's chances of gaining enlightenment; and once again the point is made that goblins and fiends will circulate among men in the form of wise teachers and enlightened masters and teach false doctrines such as the doctrine that Buddhists may eat meat, and by teaching these things they will steal people's chances of becoming enlightened.

What is noteworthy in both the *Laṅkāvatāra* and *Śūraṁgama Sūtras* is the great effort that is being made to show that true Buddhists have been vegetarians from the very beginning of the Sangha and that all evidence to the contrary has been planted by evil demons or corrupt monks. The fact that it requires so much effort to discredit the teaching that Buddhists may eat meat suggests that it was widely accepted in the Buddhist community that there was nothing at all wrong with eating meat. The pro-vegetarian propaganda, in other words, bears the marks of being an attempt to reform the Sangha by introducing moral guidelines different from those that were commonly accepted.

Such a conclusion is supported by modern scholarship. All the evidence available to modern scholars suggests that the *Laṅkāvatāra Sūtra* first appeared some time around the fourth century of the Common Era, that is, about a thousand years after the time of the Buddha. The *Śūraṁgama Sūtra* was probably slightly later than even the *Laṅkāvatāra*, which makes it one of the last Mahāyāna works in India to be given the status of a sūtra, that is, an authentic teaching of the Buddha. It is known that a good many Buddhists in India rejected both the *Laṅkāvatāra* and the *Śūraṁgama Sūtras*, considering them to be 'forgeries', that is, new works that some factions were trying to pass off as authentic teachings of the classical Buddhist tradition. But both of the works apparently enjoyed unchallenged popularity in China. The unanimous verdict of scholars nowadays is that these two works were indeed 'forgeries' and could not possibly have been part of the first thousand years of Buddhist tradition. Indeed, it is virtually certain that they were composed during the time of the Gupta dynasty, at just the time when laws were being passed by the Hindu kings making the killing of cows a crime punishable by death. Perhaps Ambedkar's view of history is not so far off the mark when he argues that the issue of vegetarianism had become such an emotionally charged political issue that the Buddhists, who had lost political power, simply could not afford to be perceived as evil meat-eaters by the Hindu brahmans whose criteria of purity of conduct had newly come to include a taboo against the eating of meat.

Let us recapitulate some of what we can infer from the historical evidence. There is absolutely no doubt that at the time of the Buddha the majority of Indians ate beef, and there is also no doubt that eating beef did eventually become a very strong taboo in India and that in Gupta India the killing of cows was punishable by death; therefore, there is no escaping the conclusion that somehow and at some time a dietary reform of Indian society took place. There is also no doubt that the Untouchables are a persecuted people. What remains in doubt is whether the persecution of the Untouchable classes is in any way connected to the politico-religious reforms of the Indian diet.

Does the question of how Hindus and some schools of Buddhism first came to adopt vegetarianism have any relevance to the issue of how modern Buddhists in the West should view vegetarianism? In a way, it has no relevance at all. Whether one is willing to eat the flesh of animals is a matter of conscience. The question of whether it is morally acceptable to kill animals for clothing or food is a purely moral and hence a philosophical question, and no philosophical question can or should be decided by historical methods. The study of history can at best show us when people discovered that some things are morally wrong, in much the same way that it can show us when people discovered that the earth revolves around the sun; in other words, when and how people discover truth has no bearing at all on the truth being the truth. To state the matter in another way, if eating meat is morally wrong, then it is morally wrong, and its being wrong is not altered one iota by an appeal to the words or conduct of the Buddha or anyone else. Once it is determined what is morally correct, a discussion of what the Buddha taught by word or by example can prove nothing except that what the Buddha taught was or was not in keeping with what is known to be morally correct.

In one other respect, however, the historical questions around vegetarianism are of great importance to us. Even if it should turn out that Ambedkar was wrong in his hypothesis that Buddhists who ate meat became the Untouchables so despised by Hindu society, the fact remains that his hypothesis is still an account of a series of events that we have no trouble believing could have happened. One does not have to read much history at all to realize how often a social reform turns into the social persecution of those people who do not accept the reform. Nearly always when a reform is successful, one of the first things the reformers do is neutralize the people who most strongly opposed the reform. The opposition may be neutralized by indoctrinating them, discrediting them, exiling them, putting them into prison, or killing them, but whatever method is used, the opposition is always neutralized. More often than not, neutralizing the opposition turns into a brutal affair.

Dr Ambedkar has given us a great deal to ponder. Any Buddhist who takes social reform seriously (and I believe every Buddhist ought to take social reform seriously) needs to pause to think about the possible outcome of the methods used to achieve reform. There is much to learn from the mistakes of the Indian Mahāyāna Buddhists who tried to achieve reform within Buddhism at the unacceptably high price of verbally abusing those Buddhists of the 'degraded path' (*hīna-yāna*) who, 'under the influence of fiends and demonic spirits', thought reform was unnecessary. There is something chilling in the very possibility that an attempt to protect animals by introducing a dietary reform could have the inadvertent consequence of turning an entire class of people into despised Untouchables. Let us, in our eagerness to achieve justice through social reforms, be most cautious, lest the dictates of our own conscience result in condemning others to such a level of degradation that our attempts to establish justice end up making a mockery of justice.

THE BUDDHA'S TEACHINGS ON BIRTH AND SOCIAL POSITION

When one considers the present social conditions in India, it is both surprising and painful to recall that a formula for a more just society was set down over 2,500 years ago by Gotama Buddha and has not been realized to this very day. The question of birth was an important one in India at the time of the Buddha, as two social classes were struggling to hold the top position in a society that was already decidedly hierarchical. In many ways the struggle for control of society in ancient India was similar to struggles that have happened all over the world throughout recorded history. It was a classic struggle between the military classes and the intellectuals. The military classes always have a relatively easy time gaining control of society, because they have the force necessary to overpower those who resist their authority. When a military regime is unable to remain in control, it is usually because struggles for power within the military regime itself weaken the military force. The intellectual classes rarely have direct control of force, so their claims to authority have traditionally been based on the control of essential information. The more successfully intellectuals can restrict the flow of information to the society at large, the more indispensable they make themselves to the smooth running of society and the more power they have.

Power is easy to abuse, and too few people in the history of humanity have been able to resist the temptation to use power and authority for personal goals rather than for the good of humanity. The past two centuries have seen the collapse of many once-strong governments that had failed to use power for the general welfare. In many places the fall of traditional power has resulted partly from a weakening of authority by men who have selfishly used their authority. In numerous cases, when the intellectuals of a society have been irresponsible in their use of power, the resentment of the people has grown so strong that large numbers of intellectuals have been systematically tortured, killed, or imprisoned. We have seen this pattern repeatedly, often with tragic consequences, in nations that have experienced violent revolutions. When a society's intellectuals are killed or taken out of effective circulation, the society invariably suffers a loss of essential expertise in the very areas that are important to the functioning of a modern society.

It is a most important matter for people in the present century to learn how to share power and responsibility and to realize that all members of society – intellectuals, workers, agriculturists, managers, armed forces, and merchants – need all other members of society. We cannot afford the solutions that people so often sought to use in the past – solutions such as genocide, racism, and other forms of prejudice in which entire classes of men and women were systematically abused and used as pawns in the power struggles of a privileged few. Therefore it may be useful to study how people in the past have attempted to control society and why their attempts have alienated the general population. And it will be useful to examine the advice of the Buddha and to see how it can be put to use in the society of the present day.

We can gain some insight into how intellectuals of ancient India tried to gain control by studying how the ancient brahmans are described in the Pāli suttas. In the *Sāmaññaphala Sutta* of the *Dīgha-Nikāya*, for example, the story is related that Ajātasattu (494–62BCE), king of Magadhā, desires to call upon a recluse or brahman during the Uposatha day. His minister Jīvaka suggests they visit Gotama the recluse, better known to us of course as the historical Buddha. The king agrees to visit the Buddha. On meeting him, Ajātasattu asks the

Buddha whether he might question him on a certain matter, and when permission is granted, he asks this question:

> [Various craftsmen] enjoy here and now the visible fruits of their skills, they themselves are delighted and pleased with this, as are their parents, children and colleagues and friends, they maintain and support ascetics and Brahmins, thus assuring for themselves a heavenly, happy reward tending towards paradise. Can you, Lord, point to such a reward visible here and now as a fruit of the homeless life?[17]

One is struck by the practical concerns of the king. It is obvious to him that people with trades and crafts and skills perform a useful social function, for they provide livelihoods for themselves, their families, and their elderly parents. Not only do they provide livelihoods for their families, but they also support the brahman intellectuals. And what services do those who work for a living get in return for supporting the intellectuals? Rebirth in heaven! What we see, in other words, is that the brahmans at the time of the Buddha had managed to convince society at large that they possessed the secret of a power far greater and more important than any power on earth; they claimed to have the secret of gaining entrance into a good existence after the present life is over. In a way they had managed to make a livelihood out of people's natural fear of disasters, sickness, and ultimately their fear of death.

In his many sermons and dialogues the Buddha makes it abundantly clear that no one knows for certain what happens after death. No one can guarantee entry into paradise, and no one can even offer us assurance that we will exist in any form at all after death. All we can know for certain is that we will die, and that all we have come to love will also die. This is a very unpleasant truth, and it is difficult for many people to face. Many people would rather believe in heaven, even when there is absolutely no evidence for it, and there is never a shortage of self-proclaimed holy men to sell us our own dreams. But the constant advice of the Buddha is to learn to live with the truth, no matter how unpleasant it might at first seem to us. And this means learning to judge when intellectuals are talking good sense and when they are talking nonsense. Speaking nonsense is rather easy for some people, and if one is crafty he can manage to talk only about those things, such as heaven and religious merit, that no one can disprove.

But we should never let people get away with speaking utter nonsense. The truth may at first frighten us, for it is alien and opposed to what we would wish. But like all things that are strange and frightening at first, the truth is something that we can feel most at home with when it becomes familiar to us. Learning to be comfortable and at home with reality and learning to let go of our unrealistic and fantastic dreams is the main purpose of most Buddhist meditations. A firm friendship with solid realities is our best defence against the clever schemes of charlatans who would make a livelihood out of our fears and delusions.

The importance to a brahman intellectual of appearing wise and full of knowledge in the eyes of other people is shown in an anecdote in the *Soṇadaṇḍa Sutta* of the *Dīgha-Nikāya*. In this sutta it is told that the people of Campā, when they hear that the Buddha is in town, go to see him in large numbers. The doorkeeper of Soṇadaṇḍa the brahman tells his employer of all these masses of people going to see the Buddha, and Soṇadaṇḍa announces that he too would like to see the Buddha. A group of five hundred brahmans, hearing that Soṇadaṇḍa is planning to make such a visit, try to talk him out of going. They claim that since the Buddha is not a brahman and Soṇadaṇḍa is a highly respected brahman teacher who has many disciples, it would be socially acceptable only for the Buddha to come to him, not for him to go to the Buddha. Soṇadaṇḍa, however, offers a series of arguments that demonstrate that the Buddha is the social equal of brahmans. The brahmans of Campā are convinced by Soṇadaṇḍa's arguments, so they all go together to visit the Buddha. As they are on the way, Soṇadaṇḍa becomes fearful that he might ask a foolish question and thus be embarrassed in front of all the other brahmans, or that he might be asked a question by the Buddha and give a foolish answer and thus be embarrassed. Moreover, he might suffer a decrease in reputation and therefore a decrease in income if he makes a fool of himself. On the other hand, he realizes that if he turns back, the others will think him a coward and a fool, and his income will decrease. It is clear that Soṇadaṇḍa represents a segment of society that can no longer afford to be too open-minded. To be open-minded always involves the risk of being shown to be wrong in one's beliefs and teachings. When one is making a livelihood on the basis of one's superior knowledge, the risk of being shown to be wrong may involve a risk of losing one's livelihood.

The brahmans of ancient India based their power on the carefully controlled knowledge of the Vedic mantras and the rituals to be performed on various occasions. Sometimes this knowledge made them arrogant and proud, as we see in the *Ambaṭṭha Sutta* of the *Dīgha-Nikāya*. This sutta tells the story of the time that Pokkharasādi the brahman hears of Gotama the recluse and urges his disciple Ambaṭṭha to go and listen to this sage that everyone is talking about. Ambaṭṭha, who is very knowledgeable about the three Vedas, the rituals, grammar, and philosophy, goes to meet the Buddha. But when he does so he remains standing and paces about while the Buddha is seated. Gotama asks him whether it is considered good manners among brahmans to remain standing while a venerable brahman is seated or reclining. Ambaṭṭha replies that good manners among brahmans is to stand when an elder stands, sit while an elder is seated, and recline while an elder is reclining. The Buddha then suggests that Ambaṭṭha is being rude to remain standing and to pace about when he has come to seek an interview with Gotama Buddha. Ambaṭṭha becomes angry at the suggestion that he is being rude. He replies that he has no respect for Sākyas, the race to which the Buddha belongs. Ambaṭṭha's reasons for disliking the Sākyas is a classical expression of racial and cultural prejudice. The reason he gives for disliking the Buddha is that he once went to visit a group of Sākyas in Kapilavatthu, and they were very ill-behaved, being given to poking one another in the ribs and making jokes. The Buddha suggests that since the Sākyas were in their own home city, and Ambaṭṭha was a guest there, the Sākyas were entitled to behave as they were accustomed to behave, and Ambaṭṭha was somewhat petty in passing judgement on their conduct. Ambaṭṭha replies that it is the duty of all classes of men to pay honour to brahmans and to give them gifts and pay them respect, so it was really the Sākyas who were being ill-behaved in this matter.

On hearing Ambaṭṭha's reasons for disliking Sākyas and therefore being disrespectful of Sākyamuni, the Buddha teaches him a lesson. Gotama asks Ambaṭṭha what his family name is and learns that it is Kaṇhāyana. He then tells Ambaṭṭha the ancestral legend of the Sākyas, and adds that the Kaṇhāyanas were descended from one Kaṇha (Kṛṣṇa), who was the son of a slave of Okkāka, the patriarchal king of the Sākya clan; he was called Kaṇha (Black) because he was black at birth and his mother thought he was a demon. So the Kaṇhāyanas have no reason to be proud of their lineage, since they are descendants of a slave girl of the Sākya royal family. Gotama asks whether he has ever heard this story, and Ambaṭṭha admits that this is the story of his lineage even as his own clan tells it. The other brahmans in the party then begin to hoot and jeer at Ambaṭṭha, accusing him of being of very low birth. Gotama, seeing that his story has brought humiliation to Ambaṭṭha, then tells the brahmans not to be so hasty in passing judgement on the descendants of Kaṇha, for he went on to become a great sage who travelled in the south and became very learned in magical lore. So despite an apparently humble birth, Kaṇha became a great sage and married into the royal family and produced a line of noble descendants. Therefore, it is unsuitable for the brahmans to chide Ambaṭṭha Kaṇhāyana on the matter of his birth.

In fact, says the Buddha, it is altogether inappropriate for anyone to judge anyone on the basis of birth. The human race is a natural species, and as such it is one and undivided. All divisions into race, caste, ethnic group, social class, religious group, language group, and so on are unnatural and man-made. Trying to live on the basis of such divisions is living a lie. And living a lie inevitably has disastrous consequences, not only for a given society but for all of humanity. The lie of artificial divisions in the oneness of humanity is responsible for war, for the mistrust and misunderstanding that leads nations to prepare constantly for war rather than using limited and diminishing resources for the health and welfare of the people, and for the crippling breakdown of co-operation. Given that co-operation is the only real hope that humanity has in this complex world, the breakdown of co-operation is not only a social and political tragedy, but it could even be fatal to our species. Any religious system that is built upon the justification of social inequality on the basis of birth can only be regarded as an obstacle to civilization. Buddhism, being a philosophical system that lays a stress on equality, positive moral guidelines that are valid for all men and women without exception, and intellectual honesty, has a unique potential to help humankind find its way past the obstacles of essentially racist forms of religion.

In all his dialogues with brahmans and kings, the Buddha lays greatest importance on leading an ethical life. In his dialogue with Soṇadaṇḍa, for example, the Buddha asks the great brahman teacher what characteristics a person must have in order to be called a brahman. Soṇadaṇḍa answers that a man must have five things in order to be called a brahman: (1) pure descent on both sides of the family for seven generations back, (2) knowing the sacred verses by heart along with the attendant rituals and exegesis, (3) being handsome and of fair complexion, (4) being virtuous in conduct, and (5) being learned and wise. The Buddha then asks whether all five of these attributes are indeed necessary, or whether one might fail to have one of them and still be considered a brahman. Soṇadaṇḍa replies that one could fail to be handsome and of fair complexion without losing his status as a brahman. The Buddha then asks whether all the four remaining attributes are necessary, and Soṇadaṇḍa replies that one could lack the knowledge of sacred verses and still be a brahman. The Buddha then asks whether all three of the remaining attributes are necessary; Soṇadaṇḍa replies that one could fail to have pure birth and still be a brahman. The other brahmans get agitated at this point and tell Soṇadaṇḍa that he is giving a false answer and that he is underestimating the value of birth, colour, and knowledge of the Vedas. So Soṇadaṇḍa turns the attention of the brahmans to his nephew Aṅgaka, who is acknowledged by all to be of pure lineage, of beautiful colour, and expert in the Vedas and all their accompanying lore. He asks 'What if this Aṅgaka were to commit murder, theft, or adultery, or tell lies or take strong drink. Then surely his good lineage, good colour, and Vedic knowledge would do him no good.' Therefore, he argues, it is virtue rather than the other attributes that make a man a brahman.

The Buddha then asks Soṇadaṇḍa whether both of the two characteristics, virtue and wisdom, are essential for one to be correctly called a brahman, or could one fail to have one of them and still be a brahman. The brahmans all agree that both these two attributes and these two alone make a man a brahman. They admit, however, that they are not very sure exactly what virtue and wisdom are. So the Buddha outlines his guidelines for a morally pure life. The morally pure life for a religious teacher consists in: being kind and merciful to every living thing; being honest; being chaste; being truthful, peaceful, courteous, and sensible in speaking; avoiding harm to plants or seeds; eating only once a day; avoiding entertainments and ornamented clothing; avoiding luxury; accepting no precious metals; accepting no raw grains or meats; accepting no women or slaves as gifts; accepting no domesticated animals or fowl; accepting no farmland; avoiding commercial transactions; refraining from bribery and committing no violence; not speaking about pointless things, such as tales of kings, robbers, government officials, war, horrors, battles, food, drink, clothing, beds, garlands, perfumes, relationships, possessions, villages, towns, cities, countries, women, heroes, street matters, wells, ghosts, speculative concerns such as how the land or the sea was created, existence and non-existence; not bullying disciples or speaking obscurely of important matters; not acting as a go-between or matchmaker; not chanting, casting spells, making charms, or performing exorcisms; not practising augury, divination, fortune telling, or the oracular crafts; not predicting the future, making prophecies, arranging marriages, or worshipping gods.

Anyone who has observed the behaviour of modern Buddhist monks, priests, and lamas must find the above account of morality rather surprising. It has, unfortunately, become common in many Asian countries for Buddhist monks to make their livelihoods by practising many of the things that the Buddha repeatedly said had no place in the truly moral and religious life. It is sad to see that many Buddhist religious leaders spend a great deal of their time chanting and conducting rituals of various kinds, telling fortunes, and casting out evil spirits. And when they teach, they too often appeal to the authority of tradition, failing to examine the tradition afresh in the light of reason and their own personal experience. In this respect a good many Buddhist leaders have become rather similar to the brahmans that the Buddha criticized for failing to live according to the fine example set by the great poet-sages (*rishis*) of the past. It was for this reason that Dr Ambedkar felt that reform within the Buddhist Sangha was important if Buddhism was to be of any benefit to the ex-Untouchables of modern India.

The moral weakness of the brahmans in the Buddha's time is discussed in the *Ambaṭṭha Sutta.* In this sutta the Buddha explains to Ambaṭṭha that a servant of the king might overhear the king and then repeat the king's words to others, but simply repeating what the king says would not make the servant himself a king. Similarly, he says, a man might repeat what wise men have said, but just repeating it does not make him wise. But many teachers do just that: they merely repeat what genuinely wise people have taught. This is, for example, what brahmans do in their repetition of the words of the maharishis. Knowing the words of these great poet-sages by heart hardly makes one a poet-sage. The great poet-sages, the Buddha reminds his brahman friends, did not parade around in white cloth with garlands on their bodies and perfume in their hair chanting memorized verses, nor did they live on the very finest of rice and beans and sauces, nor were they waited upon by the most beautiful of women clad in the finest of clothes, nor did they drive the finest of chariots and dwell in heavily guarded palaces full of riches as brahmans do. Brahmans who simply recite the words of these poets and fail to live a life in imitation of them are not in any sense wise or righteous as the rishis themselves were. Unfortunately, one could today make very similar observations about the conduct of modern Buddhist leaders; simply reciting the words of the Buddha from memory does not make a person wise and virtuous.

Buddhism is rapidly attracting the attention of Westerners, who see in the teachings of Gotama Buddha a path of great moral strength and social responsibility that is based purely on reason rather than on authority and superstition. Buddhism has the advantage of any great tradition coming to us from the past; it is a rich storehouse of the accumulated wisdom of scores of generations of men and women from countless nations and occupations. And, unlike so many of the other religious traditions of humankind, Buddhism has the added advantage of being compatible with the methods of modern science. The method of science is critical thinking, which is based on a constant willingness to abandon old ways of viewing the world in favour of new discoveries. This is also the principal method of Buddhism. Buddhism, like science, acknowledges at the outset that our understanding of the world is very limited, and insists that we must admit our ignorance and set out to learn rather than pretending that we already know the secrets of the universe.

Few people of modern times have been as deeply aware of the potentials of Buddhism for establishing social justice and wisdom as Dr Ambedkar. Being a victim of cruel and persistent injustice and prejudice during his whole life, Ambedkar knew at first hand how vitally important it is for us to achieve a society in which men and women are allowed to realize their full human potentials through education and meaningful employment. It is only in a society of this kind that all people, and not merely those in places of privilege, can enjoy a decent livelihood. Ambedkar saw clearly that the social structures of classical Hinduism can only impede the establishment of a truly just and well-ordered society. But he also clearly realized that the system of classical Hinduism must be replaced by peaceful means rather than by armed struggle. A patient who is suffering from a disease must be cured, not killed. India, like so many other traditional societies in the modern world, must learn to heal itself of such crippling diseases as racism and caste discrimination, but the population must not be destroyed in the process. And for this reason Dr Ambedkar turned to the teachings of the Buddha, who taught that hatred can never be eliminated by hatred, and war can never be eliminated by war; hatred can be removed only by love, and war can be removed only by peace.

Buddhists in the West tend to have a strong sense of social consciousness. Consequently, many of them become actively involved in the movement for nuclear disarmament and international peace and social justice. Western Buddhists believe that these are the concerns of classical Buddhism as it was first taught by the Buddha himself. Many changes have occurred in human society since the Buddha's time, but the struggles for power between military forces, economic interests, and intellectuals still continue with far more devastating effects today than they had 2,500 years ago. The time to bring about effective change through general education and responsible leadership is long overdue. For this reason, the example of Dr Ambedkar has been a source of great inspiration to Western Buddhists, and as more people hear of the achievements of this great man, his example of wisdom, courage, and steadfast determination to help not only his own people but all people will serve to inspire countless more.

THE CLASSICAL BACKGROUND TO AMBEDKAR'S PHILOSOPHY

As Dr Ambedkar frequently pointed out in his many writings on the Buddha-dharma, Gotama Buddha completely rejected the doctrine that there are natural divisions within the human race. On the contrary, all of humanity has a single nature. This means that all divisions of human beings into groups arise because of social or political factors but never because of factors that belong to human beings through birth alone. All divisions within the human race are artificial, whether they be divisions into ethnic groups, language groups, or caste. Similarly, nations are artificial, and so are organized religious institutions.

Despite the artificiality of dividing the human race into groups and factions, every society seems to make such divisions. And many cultures in history have justified these divisions by developing a dogma or ideology according to which some groups are born to rule while other groups are born to serve the needs of the rulers. Ever since the time of the Buddha, Buddhist teachers of every culture have challenged the dogma that some people are born to be masters while others are born to be slaves. This challenge has not gone unanswered. In India, for example, there was a very long and bitter debate. Followers of the Buddha pointed out that no social group has special claim by birth on the qualities that rulers should have. No group has a monopoly on intelligence or physical strength or talent or moral integrity. On the contrary, an individual may possess these qualities or lack these qualities regardless of which family or clan or nation or caste he or she belongs to. Therefore, social achievement should be a purely individual matter and not a result of accidental membership of an artificial group.

Reacting to this Buddhist challenge, many Brahmanic and Hindu teachers insisted that a person's social group was a fact of natural birth. The Sanskrit word for birth is *jāti*, usually translated into English as 'caste'. Just as some animals are elephants by birth and some are rabbits, and there is no way that an individual animal can change from one species to another, so also some men are brahmans by birth (*jāti*) and some are princes or merchants or workers or outcastes, and no person can change from one *jāti* to another. Of course the Hindu teachers had to admit that it is possible to observe the characteristics that make elephants different from rabbits, but we cannot so easily see what makes a brahman different from the Untouchable outcaste. But this is no problem, says the Hindu philosopher; we do not need to see these differences, because we can know them by consulting the revealed word contained in the Vedas. The Vedas are supposed to be eternal, according to some Hindu philosophers, or composed by an all-knowing and compassionate god, according to other Hindu thinkers. But while brahmans disagree on the origin of the Vedas, they agree on this: not everyone may hear the Vedas. Only members of higher birth may hear the scripture, and only the brahmans may study it and interpret its meaning for the rest of society. As a consequence, those members of society who are born into families who cannot study the very rules by which society is run have no opportunity to improve their individual lots. Nor do they have access to the instruments by which social change might be achieved. The system is beautifully designed to remain just as it is.

The Buddhist teachers rejected these Hindu dogmas altogether. According to the Buddhist teaching, no idea or opinion can be accepted as a truth unless it is supported by direct observation, and no theory can be accepted as truth if it violates the basic laws of logic. The brahmanical theory of society, however, cannot be supported by direct observation. On the contrary, we can easily observe that some (but not all) brahmans are not very intelligent, and some brahmans are morally corrupt, and some brahmans are confused, agitated, perplexed, and completely unsuited to learn or teach or set good examples for the rest of society. And one can also observe that some Śūdras and Cāṇḍalas are intelligent, have moral integrity, and are calm and clear-thinking, and so would be, if given the opportunity, brilliant teachers and social leaders. The Buddha gives the example of an outcaste named Mātaṅga, who reached the heights of fame and was served by brahmans and warriors.[18] One splendid example of an Untouchable in modern times who was given a chance and proved to be brilliant and honest and effective was of course Dr Ambedkar himself. Who knows how many others like him there might be? Therefore, observation and experience alone show us that there is no correlation between the circumstances of a person's birth and their potential for leadership and social accomplishment.

Of course, even the Hindu acknowledges that the Hindu social hierarchy and the rigid system of caste cannot be supported by observation. That is precisely why the Hindu must appeal to a source of information that is allegedly higher than the authority of science and logic. This supposedly higher authority is the Veda, and all Hindu writings that do not directly contradict the Vedas, such as the many Purāṇas, the Rāmāyaṇa, the Mahābhārata, and the Manusmṛti. It was this appeal to an authority supposedly higher than human experience and logic that Gotama Buddha and all subsequent Buddhists absolutely rejected. Like the materialist Cārvāka philosophers and the Jaina teachers, the Buddhists were very suspicious of any priest or teacher who taught doctrines that could never be verified. And especially when the priest or teacher benefits personally from widespread acceptance of unprovable dogmas, his teaching must be regarded with utmost suspicion. And so it is little wonder that we read of

Cārvākas and Buddhists dismissing the Hindu scriptures as 'nothing more than the gibberish of charlatans' kept alive by 'crafty hypocrites who proclaim themselves to be holy'. The appeal to superhuman authority, to divine revelation, is the act of a coward who is afraid to let his ideas be put to the test of logic and experience. The truly courageous teacher, according to the Buddhists, is the person who has the courage to invite a careful scrutiny and rigorous criticism of their teachings by impartial judges.

What kind of teacher has the courage to invite criticism? According to Buddhism, it is only the person who has mastered the practice of self-renunciation and renunciation of the concerns of popular culture. The popular culture is based upon the preoccupations of the masses of ordinary people, who care most of all for acquiring money, gaining social status, living in comfort, and enjoying the approval of others. The goal of all Buddhist practice is to rise above these popular concerns and to develop the courage to seek the truth and live according to the truth, and to do so with total disregard for money, social status, comfort, and approval. This most emphatically does not mean that we should glorify poverty, but rather that we should never let greed for possessions take priority over our respect for truth and integrity. Similarly, let us never glorify being despised and rejected by the rest of society, but at the same time let us never lose the heart to act in accordance with what we know is right and just, even if that does result in our being despised by those who fear justice and truth.

The Buddha spoke on this theme incessantly. We must not, he said, be in the least concerned with our own social status. We must not be concerned whether we are higher than others, lower than others, or equal to others. We must not worry whether we are morally superior to others or morally inferior. Having no mind of distinctions of high and low based on comparing ourselves with others, we must be concerned only with whether we are doing the best we can, right at this very moment, to eliminate behaviour and attitudes that are harmful to ourselves and to others.

Perhaps the most difficult attitude to renounce is anger. Yet no emotion is more destructive of ourselves and harmful to others. When we are the victim of some stupid and mindless injustice, or when we see others made victims of injustice and intolerance, our sense of outrage and indignation and anger inevitably builds up and boils over. Our world is full of examples of such reactions to injustice. Daily we hear of innocent individuals whose lives are disrupted or brought to an end in wars and disputes between angry and hate-driven factions. We see it today in the tensions between Hindus and Sikhs in India, between Tamils and Sinhalese in Sri Lanka, and between different social, religious, and political factions in Ethiopia, Nicaragua, Iran, Ireland, Cambodia, Vietnam, the Middle East, and South Africa. In each of these areas, the situation can do nothing but get worse until people begin to understand these words of the Bhagavant Arhant Samyak-sambuddha, who said in the *Dhammapada*:

> In those who dwell on such thoughts as 'He abused me, he beat me, he conquered me, he robbed me', the hatred will never cease. Only in those who give up such thoughts will the hatred come to an end. For never is hatred eliminated by hatred. Hatred is eliminated only by love. This is the eternal Dharma.

The members of the Ambedkar Mission, and other Indian Buddhists who have followed Ambedkar's example, are a people who have been deeply wronged by a grotesquely unjust social system. And yet by becoming Buddhists they have all pledged to renounce the memory of such injustices. They have vowed to forget the times when they and their families have been abused, beaten, conquered, and robbed. If they can succeed in forgetting these abuses, and if they can turn around and show love and compassion to the very Hindus who have wronged them, they will set an example that all other Buddhists around the world will be most proud to follow. The Ambedkar Mission is in a position to show the rest of us the truth of the Buddha-dharma, which tells us that injustice and hatred always have two victims. The more obvious victim is the person who is hated or treated badly; the less obvious victim is the person who hates or treats others badly. Both deserve our love. Both deserve our compassion. Our wisdom must help us to find the way to free both the person who hates and the person who is hated from the shackles of hatred itself.

6

CHRISTIANITY AND BUDDHISM

Dialogue or Debate?

This is an updated version of a paper first read at an event entitled 'A Buddhist-Christian Dialogue: recognizing differences and changing attitudes', held on 21 November 1987 at Hung Fa Temple in Toronto and sponsored by the United Church of Canada and the Buddhist Council of Canada. I am most grateful to the comments of Sister Benedetta of St Mark's Anglican Church in Hamilton, Ontario. A contemplative nun who has participated for many years in Buddhist-Christian meditation workshops and whom I have long admired, Sister Benedetta responded to the paper and led a most thoughtful discussion of it. In the light of some of her comments and the comments of members of the audience, I revised and expanded the original paper into its present form.

THE MAIN QUESTION that I wish to consider in this essay is that of how important the differences are between Christianity and Buddhism. But this question, once asked, seems to undermine the very ground on which it is based. For no sooner do I ask how important the differences between Christianity and Buddhism are than I begin to wonder why it is that I should bother to compare these two systems of thought and action at all. I begin to wonder whether they have enough in common to warrant taking the time to distinguish them. Aside from the rather obvious fact that both Buddhism and Christianity are systems of thought – using 'thought' in the widest sense of the term – and that as systems of thought they both serve to determine the activities of the people who subscribe to them, it is not entirely clear why one should mention them both in the same breath.

The fact remains, however, that in the past several decades there has been an increasing interest among Christians and Buddhists in talking to one another and sharing their views, experiences, and practices in ways that have been fulfilling to participants from both traditions. So part of what I must set out to do in this essay is to try to explain two things. Firstly, I must try to explain why it is that comparing and contrasting Christianity and Buddhism seems a rather odd way to be spending our time. Secondly, I must try to give an account of why it is that, despite its being rather odd, we do in fact spend our time in this way.

Let me turn first to the question of why comparing Christianity and Buddhism seems a somewhat misdirected use of our energies. The answer in its simplest form is just that if one looks at these two great religions historically and examines their earliest forms, it is quite obvious that they had quite different concerns. They were as different from each other in the sorts of issues about which they were concerned as, say, chemistry and mathematics. In defending this claim, let me offer a brief sketch of how each of these religions stood in the first generation or so of its founding.

At the risk of oversimplification, one might describe Christianity as the product of a Jewish society that perceived itself as being under the intolerable yoke of a foreign power. The desire to be free of this oppressive foreign domination was expressed in a feverish hope for the return of a messiah, a Jewish king who would, with the help of God, rid the homeland of the alien presence and re-establish Jewish home rule under divinely inspired law. Jesus of Nazareth was one among several people in the history of the Jews who stood for a while as a candidate for the messiah, the anointed one, or *christos* as the Hebrew word *māshīaḥ* was translated into Greek. By virtue of his untimely death, Jesus was disqualified as a messiah by the majority of the Jews, for a messiah must above all be a living leader. Those who were dedicated to following Jesus even after his death, however, came to reinterpret the traditional concept of messiah, and in so doing came to discard much of the very tradition from which that concept emerged. And so we find that a considerable amount of the writing of early Christianity reveals a preoccupation with showing the inadequacies, and even the wickedness, of those Jews who did not endorse the new interpretation of a messiah as put forward by the followers of Jesus. This task required a new interpretation of virtually the entirety of recorded human history as it was known to the Jews of the time. But more importantly, the principal architect of the new Christian religion, St Paul, the man who more than any other gave this new movement its distinctive shape and transformed an essentially local political movement into a universal religion, had to supplement the divinely revealed scriptures of the Jews with a new revelation. The Old Covenant with God was replaced with a New Covenant, and the Old Israel was replaced by the New Israel in the form of the Christian community. The keystone of this new edifice, therefore, was this new revelation from the God of Israel. To be a Christian was to place this new revelation above all other possible sources of knowledge. Not surprisingly, the new Nazarite faith did not gain very many converts among the traditional Jews in Palestine, but it did gain a respectable following in the wider Hellenistic world, where it came into contact with the descendants of the philosophical traditions of classical Greece.

Studying the character of the encounter between Christianity and Hellenistic philosophies offers us a fairly firm foundation for speculating about how the early Christian community probably would have regarded Buddhists. For in most essential points early Buddhism was simply one of the many variations of a widespread pattern found in the chaotic world of the centuries following the career of Alexander the Great. One of the most important human issues that thinkers had to deal with at that time was the problem of how to secure happiness in an insecure and unpredictable world. Alexander's calculated attempt to break down the barriers between ethnic groups and to make people cosmopolitans, or citizens of the world, was welcomed by many, but it also ushered in an age of great uncertainty and moral relativism. Whereas the pre-Alexandrian world had had the luxury of taking it for granted that the code of conduct of the local tribe or village was valid for all places and all times, the citizens of the multicultural Hellenistic world were exposed on a daily basis to the fact that human societies with widely different customs and institutions and forms of government could all function very well. Life itself in the cosmopolitan Hellenistic world was evidence to the philosophers that there is no one form of correct government, no one set of social conventions, and no one true religion.

The kind of philosophical system that the Hellenistic thinkers tended to develop was one that placed emphasis on individual reason as opposed to received and transmitted authority; they strove to think about and live according to moral principles that were so basic and universal in nature that they could be found at the root of all particular systems of social conduct, no matter how diverse. Given the fundamental incompatibility between a religious system that founded itself upon a very particular revelation, and a set of philosophical systems that based themselves on reason alone to the exclusion of authority and revelation, it is not at all surprising that there was a rather deep-seated conflict between the Christians and the philosophers. The Christian solution to this conflict was to identify reason itself with Christ. The new Christian revelation could not be unreasonable, according to the Christians, because its very source was reason or logos personified. The philosophers who remained unconvinced by this approach tended not to be held in much higher regard by the Christians than the Jews.

Now Buddhism, of course, was not a product of Hellenistic culture, but it did evolve in a social milieu that was characterized by many of the same kinds of uncertainties deriving from the clash of radically different cultures as was found in the Hellenistic world. Moreover, if we apply the principles of textual and historical criticism to the Buddhist sources, it is difficult to escape the conclusion that much of what we know of early Buddhism was probably written during the time of the Emperor Aśoka and therefore reflects the climate of post-Alexandrian India more than the climate of the India of the time of the Buddha, some two centuries earlier. But even if we set these historical matters aside and focus on just the basic teachings of Buddhism as found in the earliest sources, it is clear that Buddhism was in temperament very similar to the Hellenistic philosophical schools. In virtually every one of the dialogues attributed to the Buddha the point is made that each individual human being must work out their own disentanglement from the root causes of sorrow. Neither the Buddha nor anyone else can help another in any other way than by offering advice and encouragement to individuals undergoing the lonely task of building their own storehouse of moral character and wisdom. The Buddha and the community that followed him were uncompromising in their insistence that there is no divine help for anyone in this task of building character and wisdom;

those people such as the Hindus who believed in revealed wisdom were, according to the Buddhists, plainly mistaken in their beliefs. Belief in a creator god or in a god who revealed superhuman gnosis to humanity was seen as one of the most serious obstacles to the Buddhist philosopher's career. Had this anti-mystical and anti-authoritarian community of Buddhists come into contact with Christians, there would almost surely have been a fairly strong feeling on both sides that neither movement had much to learn from the experiences of the other. The prospects for any kind of fruitful dialogue between Christians and Buddhists in the early centuries of the Common Era would have been very poor indeed.

This raises the very interesting question of why the prospects for fruitful communication between Buddhists and Christians have dramatically improved in the past century. At the risk of offending anyone's intelligence with an oversimplified answer, I would suggest that dialogue has become possible because both Christians and Buddhists have almost entirely lost their way in the epistemological wilderness and the moral wasteland of modern life. Christians and Buddhists alike have long since lost the courage to take a firm stand against the silliness and shallowness of the childish populism that has come to replace civilization. We no longer have the stomach to be élitist, to preach the obligation of wisdom to provide firm leadership for the morally feeble and intellectually immature. Christians and Buddhists have both lost the heart to take the unfashionable stand that there is a vast difference between truth and falsity, and between moral right and moral wrong.

We have even lost the courage to disagree with one another. When we meet we rarely debate such issues as whether any scripture can really be the word of God, or whether it makes sense to say that God or any other intelligent source outside of humanity can communicate intelligible and relevant ideas to human beings, or whether any being can atone for another's sins, or whether there is really such a thing as sin at all, not to mention original sin. And yet it is how we stand on these issues that is the very basis of what makes Buddhists Buddhist and Christians Christian. We both believe that truth is absolutely vital, since it is untruth that lies at the root of all pain; we both agree that it is the truth that shall set us free, and yet when it gets down to important details, we could not be more in disagreement about what the truth really is. Even more fundamental, we cannot agree on the methods whereby we must seek to find the truth, for Buddhists discard all forms of revelation and celebrate reason above all else, while Christians place great importance on God's communication to humanity through the agency of the Holy Spirit.[19] How could we disagree more? We now live in a time when people think that questions of truth can all be reduced to matters of personal taste or culturally determined customs or fashionable trends. But let us speak clearly. What separates Christian from Buddhist is not culture or fashion or taste. Rather, it is truth itself. It is reality that stands between us. We cannot both be correct in our beliefs. And if we value and love truth, we must lament falsehood. If we really feel that our religion is one that we have chosen, not because we mindlessly accepted it when it was handed to us by our parents, but because it strikes us as *true*, then we must feel saddened that others follow ways that seem to us to be *false*. We must see those who purvey falsehood as somewhat unwelcome intruders in a territory that can be set free only by truth. And yet, when we Christians and Buddhists meet together, rather than squaring off against each other like two lions trying to protect their territories from unwelcome intruders, we huddle together in the dark like a couple of senile pussy cats, purring and licking each other's ears. Why is this so?

Lest my feline imagery be taken too literally as a call to Holy War between Buddhists and Christians, let me add that the kind of combat I wish to see is strictly of the intellectual and philosophical sort. We all grow weak for want of worthy philosophical opponents, and we become complacent; we have paid a very heavy price for shying away from questions of truth. Nothing could do us both more good, I think, than to learn to disagree and disagree strongly from the depths of our being, but to do so without feeling the slightest malice towards each other. Let us fight like lions, who hiss and growl and snarl but rarely draw blood. Let us not fight like human beings, who kill and mutilate and devastate but rarely draw back.

I have said that we grow weak and complacent for lack of worthy opposition to keep us sharp and alert. Let me pursue that thought just a little further. Let me leave it to Christians to analyse their own situation, for it would be offensive for me to arrogate to myself the role of critic of a tradition to which I have never belonged and to which I have in fact chosen, after a certain amount of study and thought, not to belong. Let me focus my attention rather on the ways that we modern Buddhists have, in my opinion, lost sight of the Middle Path to which we so predictably and tediously pay lip service. First of all, let us remind ourselves that the middle path in the early teachings of Buddhism was described as a mode of life that avoided the one extreme of unreflective participation in the vulgar pursuits of possessions, comfort, fame, and influence over others. To follow the middle path was also to avoid the other extreme of self-mortification and losing all concerns with the affairs of this world. Seen in positive terms, the Buddhist path was a way of life in which the whole of one's concern was with the realities of this world rather than with any kind of afterlife. The renunciation of society that monks underwent was a retreat from the many distractions and bad influences of companionship with the childish masses (*bāla-puthujjana*) and a retreat to the simplicity and sanity of life among those few people of any generation who are genuinely concerned with wisdom and the cultivation of better character. The monk's life was seen as a retirement from the madness of the world but not a retirement from social responsibility. On the contrary, the monk had an obligation first to become cultivated through systematic training and meditation and then to infuse the rest of society with the benefits of that methodical training by coming into contact with laypersons. Like Nietzsche's celebrated *Übermensch*, the Buddhist monk was to become superhuman (*lokottara*), not in the sense of being like other human beings but to a greater degree, but rather in the sense of being morally superior to them. Whereas ordinary human beings would concern themselves with asserting their power and control over one another and over nature, the superhuman monks were to concern themselves with gaining control over their own aggressive tendencies and developing the courage to be gentle, harmless, and non-acquisitive.

Living in the modern world as a modern human being requires the daily violation of all five of the moral guidelines by which Buddhists are supposed to live. The kind of life we commonly lead by participation in ordinary society is responsible for massive destruction of many forms of life, so we cannot be said to be doing very well at following the precept to cherish all life. And being content to tolerate vast disparities between rich and poor, we participate in socially acceptable modes of institutionalized theft in which the poor are robbed of the very means of dignified survival. Self-indulgent and pleasure-oriented to an extent rarely seen before in human history, we daily violate the precept encouraging moderation in sensual pleasures. Refusing to acknowledge the devastation that the North American lifestyle is bringing to the whole planet, we violate the precept to be truthful and honest. Addicted to every kind of stimulus and excitement, we violate the precept to maintain an even and sober mind. It is little wonder, then, that the kinds of Buddhism that North Americans are attracted to in the largest numbers are those forms that belittle the pure life of the precepts as the obsession of petty-minded rule-bound Hīnayānists. If we took the precepts at all seriously, we would be obliged to die of shame.

Let me dwell for a moment on the sheer madness of our lives in a modern world. We modern human beings have learned to take it for granted that we are entitled to eat fresh vegetables all year round, forgetting the cumulative environmental damage done by the aeroplanes and trucks that rush us our fresh fruits and vegetables from the south in December. Similarly we have learned to take it for granted that we ourselves are entitled to travel great distances in the shortest possible amount of time; we cannot even think of selling our cars, or refusing to take aeroplanes or refusing to travel altogether unless absolutely required to do so. In our daily lives we have grown accustomed to taking it for granted that we are entitled to heat in the dead of winter, light in the dark of night, and cool refreshing air in the midst of summer. We shake our fists at the wicked and greedy industrialists for sending us acid rain from their smokestacks and dumping deadly toxins into the soil and the waters, but it is we who consume their products. It is we, who are afraid of the dark of night and the cold of winter, who place such a strain on our planet that we kill thousands of species of life-forms every single day, because they can no longer sustain life on the planet that we have created. It is our consumption of unprecedented amounts of artificially produced energy that is murdering the planet. The conduct of daily life in the modern world is obscene and offensive to reason. It is positively evil. In Christian terms it is a world that only Satan could have devised. In Buddhist terms it is the dominion of Māra, personification of Death and uncontrolled lust, of which we have all become loyal citizens.

Our Buddhist leaders should be outraged at the state of affairs in which we now find ourselves. They should be screaming at us about the selfish greed that drives us to demand lives of unprecedented comfort and luxury; they should be scolding us for the contempt for the poor and the downtrodden human beings and for all other forms of life that is implicit in our realization of our selfish demands; and they should be forcing us to confront the blind stupidity that makes us somehow believe that our ways of living are acceptable. But instead of risking the certain unpopularity that would come of providing true leadership, our Buddhist leaders are themselves flying around the world and participating in the very life that they should be warning us to abandon. They have lost the skill of plain speech and independent critical thinking, and few of them can explain such basic concepts as emptiness and non-dualism without making them sound like incomprehensible gibberish. They teach us to chant idiotic mantras and dhāraṇīs, and fill our heads with fantastic tales of other worlds and of imaginary states of being between one life and another. Lacking the courage to truly question whether the Buddha's teachings might have been mistaken, they are daily reminders of the truth of the Buddha's prediction about the fate of the movement he had founded. 'After five hundred years,' he said, 'people will still be mouthing the words that I have spoken. But they will have entirely forgotten the wisdom that those words convey.'[20]

And that is why we Buddhists find ourselves talking to our Christian sisters and brothers, talking about all we have in common and occasionally daring to whisper about our differences. Nowadays there are not many differences to discuss. Whether we are Buddhists or Christians, we are all part of that vulgar mentality of the masses that Nietzsche called the time of the Last Man. God is dead. The Dharma is dead. Whether we pretend to be in the family of Christ or the family of the Buddha, we have both come so far from our respective homelands that we meet in the wasteland, where religion exists hardly at all. The only real basis of friendship is that we have both become alienated from our original purpose. But now that we are here, we have no real choice but to strive to help one another develop the courage to become the superhuman, the *Übermensch*. We need to encourage one another to rediscover the vitality of the superhumans of our respective traditions in the early days of their existence, before they had given way to the fat and complacent house slaves of the teeming multitudes. We need to help each other in the struggle for civilization. We need to recognize that our common task is not to preserve civilization as we know it, for we have not yet known civilization at all. Rather, our common task is to bring civilization to the world, despite the deafening groaning and the screaming that will issue from those who resist adulthood and would postpone it for ever if they could. To establish civilization in an uncivilized world was, I claim, the principal agenda of both the Christian fathers and the early Buddhist Sangha. Where they have failed it is imperative that we succeed, simply because we cannot afford much more barbarism. Our planet will not sustain it. Therefore, we must teach each other not to flinch when the fools in the market place heap abuse upon us and accuse us of the filthiest sin of which they know: not being one of them.

It is at this point that I must come back to a discussion of the differences between us, for they are differences that could very well stand in the way of our working effectively together. As a Buddhist I am supposed not to have very rigid opinions about things, and I am supposed to be able to avoid giving offence to others through what I say. So let me confess at this point that in these matters I am not a very good Buddhist at all, for I do strongly believe that the only basis upon which civilization can be built is the foundation of reason. It is my belief that the only means by which we can become superhuman is to abandon all thought of the supernatural and the transcendental[21] and to focus all our attention and energy on the concrete and particular problems of that which we can observe and understand in this world. We must reject the mystical, the spiritual, the gnostic, and the mysterious, and discipline ourselves to think and speak plainly about only those things that can be spoken and thought about plainly, and on all other matters to remain silent and unknowing. We must not take refuge in the false securities of the pretended certainty that comes with unexaminable authority. We must rediscover the spirit of the earliest form of Buddhism as taught by the Buddha himself, whose often-quoted words of advice to his followers were:

> Live as islands unto yourselves, as refuges unto yourselves, taking no other as your refuge; live with Wisdom as your island, with Wisdom as your only refuge, taking no other as your refuge.[22]

It has been my experience that some Christians have some difficulty understanding Buddhist atheism, and because of this difficulty they waste a good deal of valuable time trying to think of us as people who really do believe in God without quite realizing that it is indeed God that we believe in. To avoid further misunderstandings, therefore, let me state as simply as possible exactly what aspects of the doctrine of God it is that Buddhists reject and why.

First of all, Buddhists are encouraged to avoid speculating on the origin of the universe; ideally, we should have no opinion at all on how or why the universe is here. We are not, therefore, predisposed to believe that the world was created by God for any definite purpose. While Buddhists are encouraged to suspend judgement on the question of how the universe got here, they are also encouraged to think critically and to reject hypotheses that seem either obviously false or very unlikely to be true. And so, when Buddhist philosophers of past ages, especially in classical India, were invited to consider the hypothesis that the universe was created by a single intelligent force, they rejected it. There is, they said, no reason to assume that the universe is in fact a single, uniform product with a single cause rather than an essentially random collection of products each having its own separate cause. Rather than being like a finely crafted piece of pottery or a skilfully woven carpet, said the Buddhist philosophers of India, the universe as a whole is much more like a huge sprawling city that has grown large without the benefits of central planning. It is not obvious that there is really much pattern or design in nature, and it is just as easy to see the universe as the accidental outcome of thousands or millions of minds, each having a slightly different purpose, as to see it as the product of a single mind. It is just as easy to see unresolved and unresolvable conflicts among the forces of nature as to see harmony and singleness of purpose. And so, since harmony in nature is not an obvious given and is itself controversial, it cannot be used as evidence that the universe had a single creator.

Secondly, even if it is granted that the universe had a single cause at some point in history, there is no compelling reason to suppose that that single cause was intelligent and had a benign purpose. It is especially difficult to accept the doctrine, advanced by some monotheists, that the creator might have been a perfect being who had no motive to create the world save to bring pleasure to his creatures. On the contrary, it is impossible to imagine why any being who was supposed to be benevolent would have created a world in which every being, including those who are supposedly the closest to God, experiences intense suffering. It seems rather unlikely that God allows us to suffer for our own good, for if the Supreme Being were all-compassionate and all-powerful, then our good could have been secured without any suffering whatsoever. Even if one accepts the explanation given by many theists, namely, that our misery stems from our disobedience to God rather than from anything that God has inflicted upon us, the question still remains why God, being all-powerful, failed to create us in such a way that we could not harm ourselves by being disobedient. Why did God need to test us, when it would have been possible to accept us without testing? According to some, God puts us through adversities to help us develop patience and other virtues, but surely patience is a virtue only in the face of adversity and would have been completely unnecessary if God had not visited so many hardships upon us. When faced with these problems, the believer in God usually resorts to saying that God is benevolent but that his benevolence works in mysterious ways. The Buddhist rejoinder to such a claim is that there is no obvious reason why we should prefer the hypothesis that God works in mysterious ways over the hypothesis that God is a cruel and brutal bully who delights only in seeing us suffer, or over the hypothesis that God means well but is somehow incompetent to help us out of our miseries.

A third aspect of the question of the existence of God that has come up for discussion is the question of whether God communicates with human beings. It is very common for theists in various parts of the world to believe that God has communicated to humanity through the agency of prophets or other inspired people. The central problem that we face, however, is that too many people claim to be speaking not their own ideas but God's ideas, and these many people are not all saying the same thing. Virtually every religion claims to be founded on principles delivered to humanity by God or gods through the mouths of prophets or oracles, but no two religions agree on the details of what God has said. So how are we to know who is really speaking the ideas of God and who is really speaking ideas of purely human origin? It is, after all, possible that someone might be mistaken in believing that God had spoken directly to him, and it is also possible that one might deliberately deceive other people into believing that one's ideas were of divine and not of human origin. Indeed, when we look at the sort of things that God has allegedly commanded people to do, it is easy to suspect that people were mistaken in their belief that it was God who ordered the actions. Could it really have been God who commanded people to butcher animals and burn them in temples, sent nations to war with one another, and sanctioned social hierarchies in which the powerful enslaved the weak? Every conceivable outrage that human beings perpetrate on one another has at one time or another been justified on the grounds that it was ordered or approved by God. So how can we know who is truly a prophet for the divine will?

The only criteria that we have to distinguish the true prophet from the false, say most theologians, are the criteria of the internal consistency of the message itself and the personal integrity of the putative prophet. But neither of these criteria is adequate. For while logical consistency is a necessary condition for a set of statements to be true, it is not sufficient; in other words, if a set of statements is not logically coherent, then we can be certain that some of the statements in the set are false, but even if there is no contradiction among a set of statements, we cannot be certain that any of them are true. As for the criterion of integrity, there is no invariable correlation between personal integrity and being correct in one's beliefs, so even if we are assured that a person is not deliberately lying, we cannot be assured that the person is not simply in error. In fact, experience shows that a person can be a paragon of honesty and still be mistaken in a great many beliefs. Indeed, there appears to be no area in which people are not subject to error, and so no obvious reason why a person should not be mistaken in the belief that some of their ideas come from God and not from any human source. Therefore, every idea, regardless of who said it or who is supposed to have said it, must be examined on its own merits, and no idea should ever be believed and no rule of conduct should ever be followed for the simple reason that it is supposed to be the word of God.

It is important to realize that Buddhists are atheists only in so far as they reject the hypothesis that the world had a single benevolent intelligent creator, and the hypothesis that any transcendent source communicates directly to human beings individually or collectively.[23] In rejecting these hypotheses, however, the Buddhist does not reject the virtues that are usually attributed to God. The Buddhist believes, for example, in the power of love and in trust and forgiveness and patience and compassion. But rather than saying that God is love, we prefer to say that love is love; in this way, even if it should be proven that God does not exist, the ideal of love would remain unimpaired. Similarly, rather than saying, as St Thomas Aquinas and other theologians said, that God is the greatest good and the highest standard of beauty and the principle of perfect justice, we Buddhists prefer to say that good is simply good and beauty is simply beauty and justice is simply justice, and there is no need to confuse these principles with the bewildering and controversial concept of divinity.

Not only is there no need to confuse the concept of justice with the concept of God, but there is good reason not to associate these two concepts. For if we say that God is justice, and if we think of God as a person instead of as an abstract philosophical principle, then we are inclined to begin thinking that justice is that which God wills. But this invites the question: what exactly does God will? This question admits of no uncontroversial answer, for all the reasons outlined above when the topic of revelation was under discussion, so defining justice in terms of God's will leads at best to a dead end. At worst, associating justice with divinity leads to a false sense of security in the correctness of one's own opinions about justice. Human history is filled with accounts of individuals and nations who were convinced that their thinking about what is just was in conformity with divine will; only rarely does this sense of irrecusable correctness manifest itself as tolerance for what is judged to be contrary to divine will. Far better than seeing justice as having any connection with divinity, says the Buddhist, is seeing justice as a purely human concept that, like all human concepts, is never complete and is always subject to revision upon further reflection. Justice, beauty, and rectitude are matters to be discussed by human philosophers, not decided by supposed prophets or messengers of God.

There is not a single argument for the existence of God that has not been carefully considered and ultimately rejected by philosophers of the Buddhist tradition. Buddhism has been, therefore, invariably atheistic and will probably always remain so, at least so long as Buddhists continue to think and to reject doctrines for which there is inadequate support. In so far as the Christian community can learn to feel at ease with us Buddhists whose thinking is similar to what I have outlined above, there need be no important differences between us. But in so far as Christians feel uncomfortable with these ways of thinking, the abyss between us can never be bridged. Time alone will tell how well we can work together.

7

SOME REFLECTIONS ON WORDS

Part of this essay is a revised version of a short item entitled 'A Lotus by Any Other Name ...' which appeared in 1986 in Spring Wind: Buddhist Cultural Forum vol.6, nos.1–3.

PRATIBHĀNA

WHENEVER PEOPLE have to deal with harsh realities, one of the most successful means of dealing with them is to create fantasies of times and places in which these harsh realities have no place. Whenever people feel weak and helpless, they love to create fantasies of heroes who have managed to remove all the obstacles and overcome all the limitations that people in the real world have to face. Buddhist literature abounds in examples of wonderful fantasies about heroes with unlimited abilities. The Bodhisattvas and Buddhas of *The Flower Ornament Scripture* are particularly vivid examples of fantastic heroes with almost unlimited ability and talent.

One talent that Mahāyāna Bodhisattvas are frequently depicted as having is *pratibhāna*, the gift of eloquence and readiness of wit, the ability always to say the right thing at the right time. Closely related to this talent is the talent of dhāraṇīs. The word *dhāraṇī* means support or maintenance, and a good Bodhisattva cultivates four types of dhāraṇī: self-support, Dharma-support, meaning-support, and mantra-support. Of these, two bear directly upon the gift of eloquence. Dharma-support is explained as the ability to memorize the exact words of enormously long speeches or sūtras, even speeches in foreign languages, after hearing them only once. And meaning-support is the ability to understand the meaning, as opposed to the exact words, of whatever is heard, regardless of what language it is in, and to be able to recall and convey that meaning in one's own words in a way suited for one's audience. What student or teacher of the Dharma, who has had to struggle for hours with tedious studying and memorizing, or has had to cope with learning a number of unfamiliar languages, would not long to be in possession of these dhāraṇīs! It is a relief from the tedium of struggling with languages even to imagine that someone somewhere copes with foreign languages with perfect effortlessness.

That the Buddhists had fantasies of linguistic superheroes reflects one of the most formidable realities of life in Buddhist Asia, namely, that nearly everyone who took on the task of transmitting the Dharma eventually had to acquire at least one alternative language, and usually several. In India the sūtras were preserved in Pāli and Sanskrit, scholarly languages that no one learned as mother tongues. Whichever one of the hundreds of languages and dialects of India a Buddhist teacher might have learned from mother, it was necessary to acquire at least some familiarity with one of these scriptural languages, in addition to any number of vernaculars of areas away from home. When Buddhism was carried by merchants into Central Asia, it entered into another sphere of tremendous linguistic complexity, and the same can be said of the migration into South-east Asia, the Chinese heartland, and the eastern outposts such as Korea and Japan. And in the twentieth century history repeats itself as countless man-hours are spent translating the vast corpus of Buddhist literature from Sanskrit, Pāli, Apabhramsa, Tokharian, Sogdian, Tibetan, Mongol, Chinese, and Japanese into Danish, Dutch, English, French, German, Italian, Polish, Russian, Spanish, and Swedish.

With all this transmission from one language to another going on, one cannot help wondering how much is being lost in the translation. This is not by any means a uniquely modern concern. On the contrary, the Buddhists of the past had a regard for linguistic precision that might seem almost obsessive to our present age, in which mass communications and the uncontrollable explosion of technical jargons have all but obliterated our sensitivities to nuance. An illustration of the careful reflection on language that many Buddhists went through is found in the story of how Buddhist literature was translated into Chinese. At the peak of activity of translation, which lasted for several hundred years, committees of scholars compiled large lexicons and used them to determine the most suitable expressions that would convey the message of Buddhism with a minimum of confusion to the readers of Chinese.

That situation is one from which we have a great deal to learn, for there we find the mentality of one great civilization, that of the Indian subcontinent, meeting head on with the already highly developed mentality of another great civilization, that of the Chinese peoples. The problems of translation were enormous, precisely because both civilizations were so highly developed. The Chinese peoples already had a rich literature, a deep philosophical heritage, and a highly evolved language in which to express their thoughts, and this very richness made it difficult to find suitable expressions for the translation of the new Buddhist ideas. If translators used familiar expressions from Chinese Confucian and Daoist philosophy, the message of Buddhism was lost in that it ended up sounding like nothing more than another version of the already familiar Daoism and Confucianism. But if translators used new expressions, the message of Buddhism sounded too exotic and mysterious and ended up losing much of its down-to-earth common sense. These are exactly the same kinds of problems we face today as translators struggle to find ways of expressing the essential wisdom of Buddhism into languages that are replete with the technical vocabularies of Greek philosophy, Christian and Jewish spirituality, and the post-Enlightenment scientific traditions.

As with all problems, the first step towards the solution of the accurate presentation of Buddhism to speakers of modern European languages is the cultivation of a deeper awareness of the many dimensions of the task. One of the matters about which we could all stand to be a little more aware is that of the history of words, both the words of Buddhist culture in its Asian languages and the words of European languages into which Buddhist culture is now being translated. In the sections that follow I shall present just a few observations to serve as illustrations of the kinds of conceptual problems that scholars and teachers of Buddhism face as they interpret the Dharma in English. Perhaps the most basic problem of all is whether to call Buddhism a religion, a philosophy, a 'way of life', or a branch of the science of mind.

BUDDHISM: RELIGION, PHILOSOPHY, OR PSYCHOTHERAPY?

The United States Supreme Court has been called upon as part of one of its legal dispensations to make a decision on what exactly a religion is. The question is an important one in the United States, because one of the most cherished principles on which the nation was founded was that of the separation of Church and State. It is a fundamental principle of American political theory that neither the Church nor the State should encroach on the business of the other. The limits of this principle are constantly being tested by cases in which legislation is under review on issues about which religious institutions have moral stances. Two out of the many examples of such issues have been the legal status of performing or procuring abortion, and the rights of school boards to set the content of educational curricula that may include material offensive to some religious communities. A heated and highly emotional issue in recent years has been that of the legality of public prayer sessions in schools supported solely by State monies. In making decisions on such matters, the Supreme Court has been called upon to decide what prayer is. In particular it must be decided whether prayer is necessarily a religious activity or whether there can be non-religious forms of prayer. And that involves deciding what religion is.

The question of what religion is has been around for a very long time. St Thomas Aquinas (1225–74), the so-called 'Angelic Doctor' of the Roman Catholic Church, dedicated questions 81–100 of the second section of part two of his *Summa Theologiæ* to this question. There, as was always St Thomas's custom, he carefully recorded the views of his predecessors and weighed the matter methodically. Aquinas tells us that the great Roman statesman Marcus Tullius Cicero (106–43BCE) derived the word '*religio*' from the verb '*relegere*', meaning to read over and over again. For Cicero the essence of religion was careful pondering and reflection on what belongs to the divine. St Augustine, on the other hand, had derived the word '*religio*' from the verb '*religare*', meaning to fasten, bind, or connect. St Thomas did not wish to take sides in the dispute over the etymology of the word but did feel that whatever the literal meaning of the word, the essence of religion was in the relationship between man and God and that religion was not merely a moral or intellectual virtue like wisdom, justice, patience, and moderation. Anyone, even the pagan philosophers, could acquire these virtues. But religion was a special, indeed, a supernatural virtue. Such a view is still the official position of the Roman Catholic Church, as we can read in a modern catechism where religion is defined as 'the moral virtue by which we are disposed to render to God the worship he deserves.... Again, religion is often described as a composite of all the virtues that arise from our relationship to God as the author of our being, even as love is a cluster of all the virtues arising from our response to God as the destiny of our being.'[24]

Modern scholars of Latin, incidentally, tend to agree with St Augustine on the question of etymology of the word 'religion'. By studying how the word '*religio*' was used by a variety of Latin authors, lexicographers have determined that the word has the sense of exactness and careful attentiveness to detail as well as to conscience and moral scruple. The Protestant theologian John Calvin (1509–64), who also wrote in Latin, wrote that in his opinion the word 'religion' has the sense of self-restraint. 'I rather think,' wrote Calvin, 'the name is used in opposition to vagrant licence – the greater part of mankind taking up whatever first comes their way, whereas piety, that it may stand with a firm step, confines itself within due bounds.'[25] For Calvin, as for St Thomas, the essence of piety or religion, of course, was an attitude of deep respect for God. He writes, 'Such is pure and genuine religion, namely, confidence in God coupled with serious fear – fear, which both includes in it willing reverence, and brings along with it such legitimate worship as is prescribed by the law.'[26]

It is because of this association of the word 'religion' with the concept not only of God but also of divinely revealed Law that many people in Western society who have rejected traditional Judaism or Christianity have deliberately distanced themselves also from religion in general. This trend began well before Calvin's time, and he himself records the opinions of those men who believed that religion was the invention of crafty and cunning human beings who devised it as a means of keeping the unruly masses under control, a view that anticipates by several centuries the theory of religion that, in its bare outlines at least, both Freud and Marx endorsed. As Freud and Marx would do in the nineteenth and twentieth centuries, their forerunners in the sixteenth century expressed strong misgivings about basing morality on a belief in the supernatural. Their main fear was that when people began to question the truth of claims of the supernatural and discard them, they would also discard morality. Far better, they argued, to found morality on the basis of reason and common sense than on promises of future rewards and threats of future punishment.

It was also very much the view of the classical Buddhist thinkers of India that the concepts of God and divine revelation were the inventions of crafty priests whose main interest was in earning a handsome livelihood from the performances of rituals and ceremonies that God supposedly demanded of the faithful.[27] Of course, as Buddhist monks themselves began to profit from a lively trade in the performance of rituals and what amounted to the selling of merit, the once vigorous atheism became a little more subdued. In addition, tax advantages and the many other privileges that governments often confer on recognized religious institutions have a way of bringing out the piety in people who might be the least suspected of having such sentiments. Buddhism in Asia, like Christianity in Europe, was undoubtedly weakened from within by its very popularity among people who became ordained from less than noble motivations. But the fact remains that the way of life endorsed by Gotama Buddha was in some important ways religious and in other equally important ways rather anti-religious. If we take religion in the sense of moral scruple and self-restraint as opposed to self-indulgence and careless abandonment of good sense, early Buddhism was clearly a religion. But if we associate religion with obedience to divine commandment and restraint through fear of God, it is equally clear that Buddhism is not a religion in this sense and is even opposed to such ways of thinking.

The problem that Buddhists face in talking about the Buddhist way of life in Western society today is that the word 'religion' reverberates strongly with Catholic and Protestant overtones and with the notions of obedience to divine law and sacred institutions. To people who reject those institutions and the concepts upon which they are grounded, the word 'religion' therefore has rather negative connotations. It is too reminiscent of an era when every aspect of human life was dominated by a Church that claimed to have unique access to knowledge of the will of God. Many intellectuals who are deeply committed to self-restraint and adherence to such moral principles as altruism would strongly prefer to credit their restraint to common sense or philosophical wisdom than to anything religious. By the very fact of calling Buddhism a religion, we may turn away some of the people who would otherwise be most attracted to the teachings of Buddhism. A good many Buddhist teachers, sensing this aversion on the part of non-Christian Occidentals to the unpleasant connotations of religion, have presented Buddhism as a philosophy, a way of life, or even as a form of self-help psychotherapy – anything but a religion.

Other Buddhist teachers, on the other hand, noting that science and psychotherapy in Western culture have so often placed a premium on 'fact' rather than 'value' and recognizing that classical science is presented as amoral and value-free, have sensed a real danger in laying too much emphasis on Buddhism as a 'scientific' or 'therapeutic' path of self-help. They reason that if Western intellectuals are turned away from Buddhist wisdom out of a personal allergy to religion, they will find wisdom in some other form. The goal of Buddhism, after all, is to increase wisdom and happiness in the world, not to gain converts to the name of Buddhism. Whichever side one takes on this issue of what words to use in talking about Buddhism, it is important for Dharma teachers, scholars, and translators to have some sense of the emotional freight that the word 'religion' carries because of the turbulent history of Western society, in which millions have died over issues labelled 'religious'.

An interesting intellectual exercise that some scholars have indulged in is that of trying to find a Sanskrit word that comes close in meaning to the Latin-based 'religion'. Some have suggested 'yoga', because like 'religio' it has the root meaning of binding, and because such popular Hindu works as the *Bhagavad Gītā* speak of several types of belief and practice as so many kinds of yoga. The British Sanskrit scholar Monier-Williams, who compiled a comprehensive dictionary of the classical language of India, was motivated by an eagerness to translate the Christian scriptures into the sacred language of the Hindus. Given this motivation, he was naturally interested in finding good ways to translate such words as 'religion' and 'piety'. His English–Sanskrit dictionary offers several Sanskrit expressions for religion. At the head of the list is 'Dharma'. The remaining expressions in the list all had to do with devotion to God or divinities (*īśvara-bhakti, deva-bhakti*), service to God (*īśvara-seva*), and a few other expressions that he seems to have coined himself. To test out this correspondence between the words 'religion' and 'dharma', it might be fruitful to explore some of the connotations of the Sanskrit word which of course plays such a vital role in Buddhism.

The meaning of the word 'Dharma' depends a great deal on whether one is using it in a Hindu or in a Buddhist context. To get some idea of what the word means within the Hindu context, we can turn to one of the classical texts of orthodox Hinduism, Jaimini's *Mīmāṁsā Sūtras*, a lengthy work dedicated to the methods of interpretation of the Vedas, the supposedly revealed scriptures that, in theory at least, serve as the basis for all forms of Hinduism. Jaimini begins his work with the statement that it is written for those who wish to understand Dharma. He then defines Dharma as duty that is founded upon a command. Duty can never be discovered by man through experience or reason, he says, but can be known only through the statements of the Vedas, which are infallible. Jaimini did not believe that the Vedas were revealed to man by God, for he was an atheist, but he did believe that the Vedas were eternal. He believed they had never been written by anyone but were in some sense the blueprint that showed the very architecture of the universe. To live by the commandments of the Vedas was to live according to the cosmic order. Similar notions of Dharma are found in most Hindu works, with the exception that many Hindu sages argued that the Vedas were infallible because their source was God. It is the collection of supposedly infallible commandments in the Vedas that determines the duties of all men, women, and children of each caste in Hindu society. Living in accordance with these commandments that come to man from a source that is beyond experience and reason is what it means to be a practising Hindu.

The Buddhists of India had a very different conception of Dharma. The classical description of Dharma is found in this formula: 'Dharma is well taught by the Lord, it is self-realized, it is timeless, it is a come-and-see thing, leading onwards [to nirvāṇa], to be understood individually by the wise.'[28] Buddhists are encouraged to reflect on the Three Gems, Buddha, Dharma, and Sangha. The meditation exercise called recollection of the Dharma consists in reflecting on the meanings of the words of the above passage. In his explanation of this passage the great Theravādin master Buddhaghosa (early fifth century CE) says that the word 'Dharma' refers to two things. In common speech among Buddhists it means the collected sayings of the Buddha. But more precisely it means the wisdom that the Buddha tried

tried to convey in his sermons and poetry. This wisdom is 'well taught by the Lord' in that the Buddha's expression of his wisdom is articulate and pleasant to read, and it gives detailed instructions on how to live in order to attain the greatest possible happiness and fulfilment. Wisdom is 'self-realized' in the sense that it is simply there to be found in ordinary experience; it does not require revelation or scriptural authority. It is called 'timeless' because it is not necessary to wait any time to experience the results. In particular, it is not necessary to wait until an afterlife or next world. The Buddha said, 'If there is a next world, then one will be happy there because of having lived wisely in this life. But if there is no next life, one will still experience the benefits in this very life of living wisely.' The benefits of living a life of wisdom can be felt the very day that one begins to live wisely. The fullest joy of being wise, needless to say, can be experienced only by the fully wise, who have abandoned self-centred desires and attachments and habits of thinking and acting. But even reducing one's attachments leads to greater joy in this very life. This wisdom is a 'come-and-see-thing' in that each person can test it in their own life without having to rely on faith in another. The guidance of others may be useful when one is striving to gain wisdom for oneself, but the outcome of gaining it is to become self-guided and no longer to require guidance from anyone else.[29]

Given the above characterizations of the Buddha-dharma, we may be in a better position to think clearly about whether Buddhism is a religion or a philosophy or a means of psychotherapy. To my mind at least, no obvious answer to the question emerges. What does arise is a greater appreciation of the prices to be paid for being too quick to answer the question at all. As one who has taught university courses in comparative religions, I know at least one of the prices to be paid for saying that Buddhism is a religion. People tend to have rather fixed ideas about what religions have in them, and it is not only students who garble their accounts of religions on account of these fixed ideas, but the comparative religionists themselves who write the textbooks and set the professional standards. It is still not uncommon to find religious-studies accounts of Buddhism that use such terms as 'soteriology', 'salvation', 'sacred', 'sin', and 'heresy' with reference to Buddhism. Even Buddhists themselves, who perhaps do not know the full implications of such words, use them freely. English translations of Buddhist sūtras are full of these terms.

Every Buddhist knows that the goal of Buddhism is to get rid of the encumbrances of self-centred attachments and passions, and to be so disencumbered is called nirvāṇa; but what students of comparative religions often learn is that the search for nirvāṇa is an instance of soteriology. 'Soteriology' is a Christian word that means study of the nature of the salvation (*soteria*), and it has very strong associations with a theory of humanity whereby people are so weak that they require a superhuman saviour (*soter*) to deliver them from sin. To apply such a word to Buddhism makes very little sense and creates more than a little confusion.

First of all, there is nothing quite like 'sin' in Buddhism, for sin is a distinctly Jewish and Christian concept that means transgression against divine law; it is disobedience to God's will as expressed in commandments. There is, to be sure, a word in Sanskrit, *pāpa*, that is often translated as 'sin'. *Pāpa* means action that should be avoided. But the word itself is closely related in meaning to its Greek cousin *pema*, which means suffering or woe or hardship. *Pāpa* is any action that should be avoided, not because God or the Buddha or one's personal guru said not to do it, but because it is action that would be harmful or destructive and would cause misery. The goal of every living thing is to be happy. Causing misery stands in the way of that goal being achieved. But if we act so as to cause misery – if, in other words, we commit some *pāpa* – then there will be suffering. There is no undoing that particular bit of damage. It is not a matter of becoming defiled and requiring some purification, nor is it a matter of having to ask for forgiveness. There is no remission of *pāpa*, nor can *pāpa* be expiated or atoned for. It is, in short, nothing at all like sin in the Christian context.

I belabour these points because several times I have had the frustration of teaching Buddhism for an entire semester in an undergraduate course and at the end of that time realizing that even bright students, once they fix upon the idea that Buddhism is a religion, cannot seem to get the concepts of sin, salvation, and God out of their minds. Even after a semester of talking about such things very carefully, I find that students still have great difficulty breaking the habit of thinking of nirvāṇa as being like beatific vision, the Buddha as a giver of commandments like God or a prophet like Muhammad or a saviour like Jesus Christ, and karma as the divine retribution of sin. Do such misconceptions matter? To a professor, yes, because conceptual accuracy is part of what the professor is trying to impart. But to a practitioner perhaps it makes little difference how the outsider regards the practice. In any event, how one answers that question will largely determine whether one is willing to pay the price for calling Buddhism a religion.

Another thing to be considered, of course, is the price to be paid for not calling Buddhism a religion. There is certainly little to be said these days for calling Buddhism simply a philosophy or a therapeutic device. In the strictest sense of the word 'philosophy', as it was used in ancient Greece and in the Hellenistic age, Buddhism is a philosophy, a love of wisdom. But the word has become so vulgarized that it hardly means more now than either a set of opinions about something or a fondness for argument about matters that have almost no bearing on how we actually live our lives. On the one hand, the word is so trivialized that even managers of sports teams are said to have philosophies about how to have a winning season. On the other hand, professional academic philosophers often have a way of talking about problems in a manner so abstruse that only the highly specialized can follow them. Many of the real philosophers I know personally are in fact deeply concerned with genuine wisdom and with living in accordance with it, but most non-philosophers I know have a view of philosophers as people who have purely intellectual interests in purely abstract questions. Calling the Buddha a philosopher runs the very real risk of making his path seem to most people either trivial or irrelevant.

It has been a very long time since there existed philosophical guilds in Europe. At one time societies of people who separated themselves from ordinary society in order to live a life of pursuing wisdom were common. But such a level of commitment to a goal is no longer what we think of when we think of philosophers. Part of the reason for this is that, once institutionalized Christianity became politically strong enough to persecute rather than to have to be a victim of persecution, living in a philosophical guild other than a Christian monastery ceased being a healthy and attractive way of life. Consequently, when we think of a person having sufficient commitment to any positive goal to devote their whole life to it, we tend to call that person religious rather than wise. To lose sight of the importance in Buddhism of that all-or-nothing sense of dedication and commitment to wisdom is to lose sight of the essence of the Buddhist life. Perhaps no

English word carries that sense of commitment as much as the word 'religion'.

The verdict of the United States Supreme Court, incidentally, is that religion has a much broader definition than the traditional Christian criterion of religion as reverence for God. In the highest court in a nation that boldly inscribes 'In God We Trust' on its money, it was declared that the Buddha was not simply a philosopher or the founder of a funky little counter-cultural commune that lasted longer than most such movements, but that he was indeed the founder of one of the world's major religions. Even though in God he did not trust.

NAMES FOR OFFICES

During the first several hundred years of a religion's taking up residence in a new culture, the problem of finding the right terminology for all the offices and functions and rituals and concepts can be quite complex. In the early Christian church, for example, there was an office known as *presbuteros*, which is Greek for elder. This term was sometimes translated into Latin as '*sacerdos*', meaning one who offers a sacrifice, but this term conjured up associations of the old Roman paganism that Christianity was striving to replace. Eventually, Greek '*presbuteros*' was borrowed by the Latin language in the form of '*presbytes*', from which comes our English word 'priest' (by way of Old English '*preost*'). After the Protestant Reformation, the reformers tended to shy away from the word 'priest', since it was full of associations with the Roman Catholic Church and its rituals, most of which the Protestants disdained as base superstition. Rather than superstitious priests, the Protestants had pastors and ministers, who provided nurture but no magic.

Given this long and complex history of emotional associations in a predominantly Christian culture, what is a Buddhist to be called? Are ordained Buddhists priests, or are they pastors? Are they masters or doctors or teachers or friars? So far, many have settled for being called priests, and chief priests have opted to be called abbots, which is derived from an Aramaic word that means father and was used by early Christian ascetics in the desert monastic tradition. The Order of Buddhist Contemplatives, which has dropped the term 'Zen' from its terminology in favour of 'Buddhist contemplation' and other such locutions, is headquartered in Shasta Abbey. An abbey is where an abbot dwells, and an abbot, it will be recalled, was originally a father. The Vajradhatu organization too has elected to call its recently established complex in Nova Scotia an abbey rather than a monastery or seminary. According to one Vajradhatu representative, who was evidently blissfully ignorant of the etymology of the word 'abbey', the purpose of adopting 'abbey' was to avoid language with the patriarchal overtones that have become so offensive to the sensitive ear of the modern female! The people of Shasta Abbey also seem to choose to disregard etymology, for the abbot of Shasta Abbey is a woman.

Associated with Shasta Abbey are several priories. A priory is a monastery governed by a prior, which in traditional Christian circles is next in command to the abbot. The Buddhist Contemplatives of Shasta Abbey, incidentally, wear clerical collars like Catholic priests and chant the names of Bodhisattvas to melodies that sound remarkably like medieval Christian plainsong. The issues of cultural assimilation extend far beyond language into the realms of dress, artistic styles, music, and even table manners.

Calling a member of the Buddhist community of renunciants a monk is a bit odd, for the word 'monk' derives from the Greek '*monachos*', which means solitary or alone. But the Sanskrit term '*saṁgha*' means group, multitude, flock, or community, with the emphasis on togetherness and co-operation, so a member of the *bhikṣu-saṁgha* is hardly a monk. Rather, he is a *bhikṣu*, which means one who wishes to share; in ordinary language, the word simply meant a beggar. Nevertheless, it has become so customary to speak of renunciant Buddhists as monks that we had better abandon all attachments to etymological accuracy and simply learn to live with this adaptation of Christian terminology.

How about the Sangha itself? Under the influence of anti-Japanese sentiments around the time of the Second World War, members of Jōdo Shinshū in America chose to refer to themselves as the Buddhist Church of America. And they called their buildings churches. Presumably for similar considerations of conformity to North American expectations of what a religion should be, the Vajradhatu organization is now called the Vajradhatu Buddhist Church. Other Buddhist groups prefer to call their buildings either temples or centres. Between a church and a temple it is difficult to make a rational choice. The English word 'church' comes from Greek '*kurikon*', meaning house of the Lord; and the word 'temple' comes from Latin '*templum*', which was a section of sky or land set aside for the observation of omens. A place set aside for Buddhist meditation is neither a church nor a temple, strictly speaking. Perhaps for this reason many Buddhist organizations choose to call their places simply 'centres', a word that happily conjures up recollections of the concept of the Middle Path.

While one alternative would clearly be for all Buddhists to learn Pāli or Sanskrit and retain as many words as possible from the original languages of Buddhism, abandoning Indian names in favour of words from the local language was in the end what nearly all Asian cultures found most convenient. Following their example, it is likely that English-speaking Buddhists will continue to use familiar Christian names for religious items and people, gradually giving up such Asian words as 'zendō', 'choling', (from Tibetan *chos gling*, meaning dharma-land) and 'bodhi-manda'. What consequences that practice will have for the Buddhists' sense of distinct identity is a question that no one will be in a position to answer before several generations of North Americans have taken up Buddhism.

8

BUDDHISM IN THE NEW DARK AGES

Part of this essay appeared in 1986 under the title 'The Little Old Dharma Peddler' in Spring Wind: Buddhist Cultural Forum vol.6, nos.1–3. Although some of the individuals and organizations mentioned here have faded from memory, most of the trends they represented are still in evidence, and probably will be for some time.

ENLIGHTENMENT AND ENDARKENMENT

WHEN EIGHTEENTH-CENTURY authors such as Voltaire (1694–1778) and Denis Diderot (1713–84) popularized the ideas of their seventeenth-century predecessors such as René Descartes (1596–1650) and John Locke (1632–1704), much of the European populace acquired a new suspicion of anything that did not appear to be rational or empirically verifiable. The new intellectual climate came to be called the Enlightenment, and nearly two millennia of Western civilization was dismissed as the Dark Ages. Eighteenth-century confidence that the ages of darkness had become a thing of the past, however, proved unduly optimistic. A look at the world around us at the end of the twentieth century gives more cause to think that the Hindu and Buddhist views of history may have been more accurate. According to Hindu mythology we are now in the *kālī-yuga*, literally the age of blackness, in which people become increasingly incapable of discerning right from wrong and the beautiful from the grotesque. Buddhist mythology also designates the present age as the time of *mappō*, a Japanese expression meaning 'declining dharma'. Since the early days of Buddhism the prediction has been made that things would grow steadily worse until only a handful of people would even think it desirable to seek wisdom.[30] Whether or not one puts much stock in Hindu and Buddhist mythology, few would dispute the claim that the world in which we live is a sad, confused, and dangerous place. Nor is anyone likely to dispute the contention that at least some of those who claim to be part of the solution are in fact part of the problem. Where there is bound to be controversy, however, is on the matter of specific details. Just who, among all those who are offering us benighted souls a way out of the dark tangle of misguided human enterprise, is really showing us a means of arriving at a less confused state? And who among them are really only adding to our perplexity? These issues are at least as old as recorded human thought, and are in fact probably much older.

NEW AGE DARK AGE

Modern versions of the old question of whom to trust in the matter of how to conduct a sensible and productive life abound in the genre of literature that many, for want of a better name, call the alternative press. One small subsection of such alternative literature might be called the literature of alternative spirituality.

One of the wonderful things about spirituality is that no one knows for sure what it is. Apparently spirituality itself is an alternative – or, more accurately, a family of alternatives – to the unreflective pursuit of immediate gratification, which is according to most philosophers and religious leaders the pursuit in which the masses of human beings and the lower forms of animal life are almost constantly engaged. The problem with spirituality is that there is no standard form of it, and therefore nothing in opposition to which other forms of spirituality can rightly be regarded as alternatives. But in the 1980s that is not seen by many as a problem at all; 1980s human beings are among the most intellectually promiscuous in the history of our species, and in general they find little difficulty with the notion of pursuing a great plurality of claims to the truth, even when those claims are radically incompatible with one another. Random eclecticism and pluralism is the form of sad and dangerous confusion that appeals to the tastes of modern humanity. Just as we will eat anything, whether or not it is nutritious, we will believe anything, whether or not it makes sense.

In Washington DC there is a publication called *Pathways*, which bills itself as a 'journal & resource guide to personal and social transformation in the Washington area'. In the Spring 1986 issue one can find a number of items that were chosen, according to the editors, to provide the public with 'free access to local resources and specific tools for improving the quality of life physically, mentally, emotionally, and spiritually'. Examples of paths to spiritual betterment include workshops on an oriental massage technique that uses paths of energy that have somehow escaped the attention of systematic physiological research in the West, plus lectures and demonstrations and weekend retreats on numerology, magic wands, healing crystals, techniques for recalling past lives, tantric sex therapy, magic healing lamps, healing gems, acupuncture, holistic dentistry, ayurvedic medicine of ancient India, aura reading, astral travel, I Ching loving light massage, fourth dimensional chromatic healing, walking on a bed of hot coals to a destination of new spiritual realities and deeper capacities to love, vocational awakening group exploration, organic beef cookery, and native American shamanism. What a wonderful smorgasbord of junk food for the mind!

Pathways also carries personal advertisements, wittily entitled 'unclassifieds'. One such unclassified announces that a 'physically and mentally attractive' white female, aged 36 and single with a four-year-old daughter, seeks 'a unique single man'. This woman admits that she used to be a vegetarian but has now given up self-denial, although she still 'dabbles in "new age" thought', albeit not fanatically. She seeks a man who is a free spirit but who is also emotionally and financially stable. By all appearances, this lady is a definitive product of our age. One could hazard the guess that she may also be a little confused.

Also in the 'unclassifieds' of *Pathways*, placed right next to the ad from the white single female, is one that reads: 'Conference on Zen Buddhism, July 14 through 19, 1986. Examination of tradition and evaluation of current situation facing American Buddhist groups by leading scholars and Zen teachers.' This conference was sponsored by the Zen Lotus Society. Although it was not one of the issues discussed, one that certainly ought to have been discussed in the context of 'the current situation facing American Buddhist groups' is that they often advertise in journals that also feature advertisements for and articles on magic healing crystals and economically secure dabblers in spiritual alternatives. Why should this be so?

Before examining why Buddhist enterprises find themselves being advertised in the company of wish-fulfilling gems and seminars on how to achieve more meaningful orgasms, let us make it clear that Buddhism at the very outset deliberately tried to distance itself from other counter-cultural movements and spiritual fringe groups. In the *Brahmajāla Sutta*, at *Dīgha-Nikāya* i.11–28, Gotama Buddha stresses that he and his followers are unlike other groups who break away from the mainstream society and its concerns with wealth, status, comfort, and fame. Members of other breakaway groups acted as soothsayers, predicted the future, read and interpreted signs and omens, exorcized demons, cast spells, droned incantations, made charms, and sold love potions and aphrodisiacs. But Gotama and his monks were supposed to avoid all such low activity.[31] Why? Because all such activities are products of the very same delusion that is the root cause of all suffering. Rather than being part of the solution, these magical and occult practices are part of the problem. What these pseudo-remedies have in common with the disease that they are supposed to cure but cannot is that they are the product of sloppy thinking (*ayoniso manasikāra*). Those who practise these low arts bully their disciples and clients into accepting answers that are not backed up by sound reasoning; they claim to go into trances and learn things that ordinary people cannot know, which makes them immune from criticism; they tell people what people wish to hear rather than what is really so. An even more fundamental reason for the Buddha's rejection of magical and occult practices is that they really do not represent alternatives at all to the worldly goals of wealth, status, comfort, and fame. What they really amount to are alternative methods of arriving at the same old worldly goals.

The way in which Buddhism is a radical alternative is not in its methods but in its goal, namely, the goal of becoming free of self-indulgent passions and delusions that impede the ability to see things as they really are, which ability provides the only true form of lasting happiness available to ourselves and others. Buddhists, at least at the time of Gotama Buddha, had no use for the sixth century BCE counterparts of fourth-dimensional chromatic healing and astral travel.

Given the attitude of early Buddhism towards practices on the spiritual frontiers, we might expect that if modern Buddhists were faithful to the ways of their forefathers, a conference on Zen would be advertised in a journal such as *Skeptical Inquirer* rather than in *Pathways*. *The Skeptical Inquirer* is the quarterly journal of CSICOP, the Committee for the Scientific Investigation of Claims of the Paranormal. This non-profit organization comprises dozens of the brightest intellects in the world in the fields of physics, chemistry, psychology, mathematics, philosophy, and religion. The Committee 'does not reject claims on a priori grounds, antecedent to inquiry, but rather examines them objectively and carefully'. Among issues investigated in the past ten years have been countless UFO sightings, the biorhythm fad, the astrology industry, Creation Science and other aspects of Biblical fundamentalism, claimed recollections of past lives under hypnosis, alpha waves and biofeedback, firewalking, alternative medicine, and various types of psychokinesis. At the heart of CSICOP's scepticism towards these phenomena is the conviction that it is dangerous for people to be deceived, whether the deception is self-induced or inflicted upon them by crafty frauds who stand to gain from an uninformed public's willingness to believe anything that is too good to be true. CSICOP scepticism, being rooted in a healthy mistrust of wishful thinking, is very much in the spirit of Buddhism.

The Skeptical Inquirer does not carry advertisements, but it does carry news items. Even so, it is not likely that a conference on Buddhism would be considered a particularly newsworthy event to members of CSICOP, for a Zen conference would almost surely not be heralded as an important battle within the context of the continuing crusade against modern manifestations of mumbo-jumbo. CSICOP probably does not recognize Zen Buddhists as fellow travellers on the road to deliverance from muddle-headed thinking. One indication of this is the fact that the essayist on science and mathematics, Douglas R. Hofstadter, author of the best-selling *Gödel, Escher, Bach* and *The Mind's I*, is a great admirer of *The Skeptical Inquirer* but not of Zen. Hofstadter writes: 'To me, part of the challenge of Zen is very much akin to the challenge of the occult and of pseudo-science: the baffling inner consistency of a worldview totally antithetical to my own.'[32]

Why should a man who writes a brilliantly witty and thought-provoking book about questing for the essence of mind believe that the Zen world-view is totally antithetical to his own? This is a fascinating question. I suspect that the answer lies at least in part in the fact that Hofstadter does not have a very clear idea of what Zen is all about. And the reason for this must lie, at least in part, in the fact that Buddhism in modern North American society has been presented in the context of all those zany purveyors of clouded thinking that occupies the pages of journals of alternative spirituality. But why is Buddhism presented in that context?

The somewhat disingenuous answer that a Buddhist might give in defence of the common practice of peddling its goods to the spiritual fringe is that those are the people most in need of help. A good doctor takes his practice to where people are sick, and a good Bodhisattva is in Buddhist literature repeatedly likened to a good doctor. If Vimalakīrti visited prostitutes to preach the Dharma to them in terms that they could easily understand, why should modern Buddhists not post advertisements in the spiritually alternative press? People who dabble in the occult are obviously in need of a remedial dose of clear-headed receptivity to things as they really are, so it makes good sense to walk among such people and entice them to swallow the medicine they so desperately need. As good as this answer might sound, it is probably not the most honest one that could be given. The most honest answer to why Buddhists avail themselves of the alternative press is probably twofold. In the first place, the alternative press provides cheap and frequently even free advertising space, and that is all we can easily afford. In the second place, if the truth be told, quite a few North American Buddhists are actually fairly sympathetic to alternative spirituality. Two questions naturally arise at this point. Firstly, what price are we paying for making use of cheap advertising space? And secondly, why are North American Buddhists so receptive to practices and modes of thought that the Buddha himself claims to have disdained?

I cannot answer the second question at all. Perhaps others can. As for the first question, I suggest that one price we pay by advertising in the context of alternative spirituality is that we lose credibility among some of the more sensible people who might otherwise be our allies in the propagation of the type of thinking and behaving that the Buddha-dharma encourages. There is a very real problem to be faced in making Buddhism understood in a technological and fast-paced age. Buddhism is by nature the practice of cultivating a quiet, dignified, and sober mentality, whereas the mentality of twentieth-century mass culture is relatively hysterical, frenzied, and raucous. How can quiet and gentle people ever get the attention of all those noisy and busy beings whirling around on the wheel of life and death? Fundamentalist Christianity is perfectly suited to television, which is poorly suited to carry subtle messages. Thirty minutes of zazen, on the other hand, would make for comparatively dull TV, even for a zazen enthusiast. The only hope for Buddhism in our culture seems to be the intimacy of the printed word, a medium that our civilization appears to want to abandon altogether as soon as possible. The printed word is indeed the medium of choice for most of the Buddhist masters currently trying to make some impact on North America. And, for better or worse, the most commonly chosen form of printed word is the small advertisement in such publications as *Yoga Journal* and *Pathways*. We find, for example, in the May/June 1986 issue of *Yoga Journal* this advertisement:

> Zen training by correspondence. Authentic Japanese tradition. Free information. Zenji Abbey. PO Box 845, Greenville, RI 02828.

Another meditation master availing himself of the United States Post Office to transmit the Buddha mind is Seung Sahn Sunim, also known as Soen Sa Nim, founder of Kwan Um Zen School on Rhode Island. The July 1985 Newsletter of that organization carries a feature on Soen Sa Nim's 'Post Card Dharma', in which the Korean Zen master exchanges postcards with disciples in a sort of dharma combat by mail. One suspects that some of the spontaneity of dharma contact is lost somewhere in the bowels of Uncle Sam's mail service, but perhaps it will do some good there.

Another resourceful Dharma master who clearly became attuned to the gimmicky ways of North American life was the late Ven. Chögyam Trungpa, Rimpoche. In the January–February 1986 issue of *Yoga Journal* we encounter:

> Introducing Vajradhatu Home Study. Authentic Buddhist Meditation. The first home study course with taped lectures by Chögyam Trungpa, Rimpoche, Tibetan meditation master, author, and eminent teacher of Buddhism in the West. Also includes: meditation instruction, text, workbook, and individual attention.

In addition to postal order enlightenment Rimpoche also found a way to peddle Buddhist meditation without any references to Buddhism whatsoever in his Shambhala training programs. This slick presentation spoke only of basic human goodness, self-acceptance, genuine maturity, gentleness, and trust, breaking down habitual emotional patterns that could cover our natural dignity, developing self-confidence and alertness, learning to appreciate the opportunities for growth provided by even life's disappointments and irritations, and cultivating a broader perspective. Buddhism presented in such terminology, so palatable to the tastes of today's seekers for self-improvement, might seem even to Douglas R. Hofstadter a little less like a worldview totally antithetical to his own. Anyone who could manage to bridge the chasm between the conceptual universes of readers of alternative spiritual literature and readers of *Skeptical Inquirer* would have achieved a near miraculous accomplishment. If the product that is being sold by this clever marketing also succeeds in doing the task that the Dharma is designed to do, then it could be an example for other Buddhists to emulate. If not, then – like so many other feats of salesmanship in the world of alternative spirituality – it will be just another example of something that is part of the problem rather than part of the solution.

ZEN AND THE ART OF FREE ENTERPRISE

Although American civilization was founded on the principle of the separation of Church and State, the American Founding Fathers took great care in their wisdom not to advocate the separation of Church and Bank. The intimate, almost symbiotic, relationship between institutionalized religions and the economically prosperous has long been recognized by social observers and critics. Religious institutions nearly always have an insatiable craving for funds for the good works they perform, and the moneyed classes have an insatiable need to be reassured that their financial successes are not a spiritual impediment but are, on the contrary, a sign of divine approval. 'Yes, Virginia,' they long to hear someone say, 'camels can pass through the eyes of needles!' Since time immemorial the wealthy have been able to buy peace of mind by making generous donations to those who are by profession poor in spirit.

The system has worked wonderfully for millennia, and there is plenty of evidence available that it continues to work here in North America even in this New Age of spiritual rebirth that passes through our culture about once every six weeks. One particularly hot item on the markets these days is Zen. It is an elusive and mysterious commodity whose only known properties are the ability to banish failure and lack of fulfilment from one's life for ever.

There is probably nothing more heartbreaking in the modern technological age than the natural odours of one's own body. In past ages there was apparently very little one could do about one's natural scent, for we read in classical Buddhist meditation manuals that practitioners should strive to overcome sensuality by dwelling on the foul aromas of the human body. But nowadays such a bleak and dismal practice is no longer necessary, thanks to the modern miracle of capturing the spiritual essence of age-old traditions and putting them into Zen. Zen is a perfume made by Shiseido, which allegedly captures the 'lofty sensibility and spiritual purity' of the creative and spontaneous tradition of Zen practice. The result is said to be a 'unique perfume expressing quiet, purity, and traditional Japanese beauty'. There can be little doubt that it was to create just such a fragrance that Bodhidharma came from the West.

Some people may find the idea of achieving spiritual purity by putting a few drops of perfume behind the ears a little too simple. For these people the thrill is not so much in the goal as in the process of reaching it. Such people want the satisfaction of working for their spiritual purity. Fortunately, there is still the possibility for such hardy souls to take more rigorous forms of Zen training. The Toronto *Globe and Mail* carried an item not long ago about Club Med, an organization that is reportedly 'based on an uncomplicated philosophy of easygoing happiness and friendship, an attitude that encourages you to free yourself, [and] be yourself'. Among the many activities that Club Med offers in its excursions to the Bahamas, the Caribbean, and Mexico is instruction in Zen, if you can find time to squeeze it in between your classes in aerobics and skin diving. The *Globe and Mail* article featured a photograph of a slender young woman standing naked from the waist up (discreetly photographed from the back, of course, as befits a serious newspaper), holding a pair of skin-diving flippers. She had obviously learned to free herself and be herself, and it wouldn't be too surprising to learn that she both does Zen and wears it behind her ears.

Of course there are people who will find an entire week of classes in Zen in Caribbean pleasure spots a little difficult to work into their busy schedules. How many times do we say to ourselves 'I would love to be enlightened, but I just don't have the time!' So for those with tight temporal constraints a compassionate Bodhisattva has manifested himself in the form of Zen Master Rama. Zen Master Rama offers intensive one-night courses in 'Tantric Zen'. One can hardly beat the price, a mere $10 for an entire evening, according to promotional posters for his recent tour of major American cities. Or, for those sceptical souls who are dubious of the possibility of getting more than a little enlightened for a paltry sawbuck, Zen Master Rama also offers Rama Seminars for a little more. There is, for example, the One Evening Excursion (on Saturdays only) for $500, or the full weekend excursion for $1000. If cash flow is a problem, Zen Master Rama obligingly honours Visa, MasterCard, and American Express.

It would be rash to plunk down $1000 for a weekend of Zen without knowing what Zen is, so Zen Master Rama has thoughtfully prepared glossy photographs of himself with his magnificent head of trendily styled hair (who says Zen masters have to be bald?) and leather jacket so that potential disciples can see for themselves the obvious benefits of Zen training. Despite his Hindu name, Zen Master Rama claims that his form of Zen is neither a religion nor a philosophy. He also explains in the accompanying literature what exactly a Zen Seminar is:

> From my point of view it is an opportunity to challenge people. Most people are bored. They are bored with their jobs, their friends, their relationships, their sexual experiences, their academic and sports programs and themselves.... Your mind is never boring, particularly when you know how to use it.... No two seminars are the same. Otherwise I would be bored. The focus is on you: your career, your enlightenment, your ability to get the job done.... Zen. The thinking person's alternative to boredom.

Whether they are looking for the thinking person's alternative to boredom or the bored person's alternative to thinking, people reportedly flock to hear Zen Master Rama. His followers reportedly include 'a Sanskrit professor from Berkeley, an osteopathic surgeon from the

Midwest, a topless dancer from LA', and numerous other people of all ages and walks of life. Based in Hollywood, Zen Master Rama also does seminars in Aspen, Colorado and in major cities on the East Coast. In his public appearances he speaks, accompanied by electronic music, of how to keep track of one's energy flow and how to be sure the energy doesn't flow into 'holes' where it will be lost. According to the promotional literature, Zen Master Rama speaks in different voices using different accents, including one voice of an old Irish Zen master named Zen Master O'Flannagan. He informs people that in his opinion there is no such thing as death, and he performs Zen dances and tells jokes. His enthusiasts claim that when he meditates, the entire room fills with a light that reminds them of scenes from Steven Spielberg films. One person who has attended four of Zen Master Rama's seminars writes:

> He is a true Zen master in every sense of the word. I think he breaks all of the conventions of how we think a Zen master should dress, speak and live just to prove to us that our conceptions of a teacher are too limited. Zen Master Rama and his art of Tantric Zen Meditation stand outside of time and fashion. Meditating with him at one of his seminars is an experience not to be missed on your visit to the planet Earth.

The same enthusiast reports that Zen Master Rama, who paradoxically manages to be both timely and fashionable despite his standing outside of time and fashion, provides a refreshing change from the tone of the modern age that is 'filled with so much that is prepackaged, rude and crude'. Even for those of us who are not just visiting planet Earth but actually live here, it sounds as though Zen Master Rama provides a pretty dazzling show for a mere $500 per day, an experience that one can hardly afford to pass up.

Since the dawn of recorded history there has always been much money to be made in piety, and it is heart-warming to see that this age-old tradition of turning profits out of prophets has survived intact in the New World and in its New Age spirituality. But it would be unduly cynical to assume that this new spirituality is about nothing but making money. It should be borne in mind that it also has something to do with sex. Let's suppose you choose the Club Med Path and happen to meet one of those topless young ladies in your class on Zen. You'll be glad to know that after the retreat there is training available in Zen Sensualism. Zen Sensualism, unlike Rama's Zen, is a religious philosophy. It is not your average religious philosophy, though, for this one makes its contribution by 'uniting sexuality and spirituality'. Founded by Dale Watts of Oakland, California on the firm spiritual foundation of such pithy axioms as 'Love is the most direct path to enlightenment', 'Sexual repression leads to bigotry and hatred', and 'The feeling of oneness and unity resulting from sexuality is the most universally accessible spiritual experience', the Center for Zen Sensualism offers a range of seminars and workshops in meditation and sexuality.

The timid beginner in Zen Sensualism may wish to start off with group meditations in which the participants wear clothes, but the more adventurous will probably want to plunge into the more advanced group meditations in the nude. Even more advanced forms of sensual spirituality include Tantric masturbation while others watch, group masturbation while others participate and offer their aid, oral-genital sex, and intercourse with someone other than one's normal sex partner in intimate little gatherings of four or five people or in larger groups. Of course not everyone will want to limit their spiritual development to masturbation and group sex. Some will also wish to expand their intellects. The Center for Zen Sensualism therefore offers a reading list for those who would like to know more about Zen and spirituality. The list, while heavily weighted towards readings in science fiction, does include some books on psychology. The reading list also features Robert Pirsig's essay *Zen and the Art of Motorcycle Maintenance*, which was certainly one of the most interesting popular books on motorcycle maintenance to be published in the 1970s.

Zen Sensualist Dale Watts shares with Zen Master Rama a deep concern with the principal problem of our age: boredom. 'Monotony and boredom,' he writes 'are the great scourges of the human spirit. They require eternal resistance.' It is always encouraging to know that even in the spiritual desert of modern technological life, there are masters who have sought, found, and are willing for a modest fee to teach, remedies for these horrible scourges.

9

DOES A LOGICIAN HAVE BUDDHA NATURE?

This is a considerably expanded and revised version of an item entitled 'Zen Mind, Logician's Mind' that first appeared in Spring Wind: Buddhist Cultural Forum (1985) vol.5 nos.1–2.

WHEN CHINESE CHAN and Japanese Zen masters traced lineages of teachers who transmitted the Buddha Mind from Śākyamuni Buddha down to themselves, they nearly always included the names of such great Indian philosophers as Nāgārjuna and Vasubandhu. In the Patriarchal Line recitation adopted by the Zen Centers established by Rōshi Philip Kapleau, for example, Nāgārjuna is the fourteenth master after Śākyamuni Buddha, and Vasubandhu is the twenty-first, followed by Manorhita (*sic*).[33] A similar list appears in the patriarchal lineage recited by the Order of Buddhist Contemplatives, where Nāgārjuna and Vasubandhu appear under the Japanese forms of their names, Nagyaarajyuna and Bashyubanzu.[34] But the name of Ācārya Dignāga (c.480–540), father of the movement that has come to be known in the English-speaking world as Buddhist logic, does not appear in Zen lineages, nor do the names of later masters of logic such as Dharmakīrti (c.600–660), Dharmottara, Śāntarakṣita, and Kamalaśīla, all of whom figure prominently in the development of the scholastic tradition that was inherited and developed by the Tibetans.

To some people this absence of the names of the logicians among transmitters of the Buddha Mind seems perfectly natural. To the historically-minded, for example, it would seem obvious that Dignāga was excluded from lists of the transmission of Zen for the simple reason that Dignāga was probably not actually in the lineage of teachers between the Buddha and Bodhidharma, the first Zen patriarch to teach in China. But the historical issue is really irrelevant here, since very few historians of Zen regard these lists of teachers as historically accurate in any event. They are part of Zen mythology rather than Zen history, and as such they have much more to do with perceptions than with objective realities. So the interesting question is this: why did the Zen teachers of old perceive themselves as Dharma heirs of Vasubandhu, who is supposed to have been Dignāga's actual teacher, while they did not perceive themselves as Dharma heirs of Dignāga himself? Is it possible that Zen teachers of old were perpetrators of an anti-intellectual bias against the scholasticism and rationalism associated with the school of logicians?

There are representatives of the Zen tradition, and indeed of the wider Buddhist tradition, who express a degree of suspicion of logic and rational thinking. D.T. Suzuki identified logical thinking with dualistic thinking, the *bête noire* of Mahāyāna Buddhism, and warned his readers that dualistic thinking would prevent one from ever understanding the most profound messages of Buddhism. Logic, said Suzuki, operates in the realm of making distinctions between 'A' and 'not-A', between *asti* (being) and *nāsti* (non-being).

> This dualism goes on throughout our thinking. We can never get away from this so long as we stay within the conditions of thinking.... But, singularly, our heart or spirit never rests quietly so long as we do not transcend this apparently logically essential position ... we are dissatisfied with ourselves and with the whole world so long as we cling to the dualism of *asti* and *nāsti*, 'A' and 'not-A'.[35]

Perhaps one of the best-known opponents of logic in Western Buddhist circles was Edward Conze, one of the most influential scholars of Buddhism after the Second World War. Conze dismissed the logic of Dignāga as 'an utterly profane science' that only a small minority of Buddhists ever took seriously, because logic was after all 'at variance with the spirit of Buddhism'.[36] Logic, according to Conze, is a major obstacle to any kind of true spirituality, and indeed he seems to have had an almost neurotic dread of the basic axioms of traditional logic, namely, the axiom that two statements that contradict each other cannot both be true (law of contradiction) and the axiom that any given statement is either true or false (law of excluded middle). These axioms of logic, argued Conze, were foisted by Aristotle on to the Greek philosophical tradition, which before Aristotle had been spiritually alive but after the introduction of logic became spiritually dead, and Westerners have been slavishly following Aristotle's arbitrary rules ever since. But Conze's Buddhists were not bound by this false belief in the laws of logic. '*All* Buddhists' he suggested, 'depart from the Aristotelian logic in essential points.... The violation of logical laws is viewed as a small price to pay for spiritual freedom.'[37]

A disdain for and mistrust of logical thinking is nothing new to Western culture. The celebration of feeling, intuition, and imagination as more powerful forces than dry intellectual understanding; a contempt for all attempts by the faculty of reason to organize, analyse, and classify the rich and intrinsically intractable experiences of life; and a deep longing for the total freedom of the spontaneous spirit of the individual unrestricted by artificial social conventions: these were all hallmarks of several of the Romantic movements of the eighteenth and nineteenth centuries. These sentiments were in large measure reactions to the scientific rationalism of the Enlightenment, which sought to find the smallest number of principles to explain the greatest number of phenomena and in so doing tended to reduce the entire realm of experience to purely mechanistic principles. The idea of doing away with the spirit as a factor in the account of the human experience was repugnant not only to traditional Christians but also to many artistically-oriented intellectuals. Part of the reaction came to be embodied in the various Romantic movements.

Given a tendency, common among the Romantics, to love the exotic over the familiar, it is not surprising that it was they who were the first Western enthusiasts for Eastern thought in general and Buddhism in particular. Nor is it surprising that the view they had of Buddhism was not particularly accurate, but contained at least as much of their own rhapsodic enthusiasm for spiritual freedom as it contained any of the actual ideals and practices of the Buddha and his followers. Conze is a good example of a modern scholar who, though widely read in Buddhist texts, was still influenced at least as much by his Romantic predispositions as by the Buddhist texts that he studied and tried to explain. But Conze was by no means alone in this respect. It is probably safe to say that the majority of Westerners who have taken an interest in Buddhism in the post-Second World War decades have been heirs of European Romanticism. The most noteworthy heirs of the Romantics in post-war times have been the Beat Generation of the 1950s, the hippies or 'flower children' of the late 1960s and early 1970s, and some strains of the feminist movement of the 1980s; all of these groups have taken at least a passing fancy to Buddhism as a possible alternative to whatever they have identified as the root of all that is offensive in Western society.

It is probably only with the benefit of ignorance that one can maintain the view that Buddhism offers much solace to those of a Romantic nature. Well-informed feminists, for example, are likely to discover with Marilyn French that Buddhism typically encourages attitudes of self-restraint that are, in the eyes of at least some feminists who think like French, forms of 'extreme asceticism' that are opposed to all nature and therefore part of the dreaded patriarchy. The notion of patriarchy in feminist writing is often hopelessly murky, but as Marilyn French uses the term it is clearly enough defined, even if like the term 'unicorn' it is doubtful whether it actually applies to anything; the patriarchy is described by her as 'an ideology committed to the eradication of matricentric values and to the erection of a transcendent world. It was established in opposition to a specific morality, and all of its terms are designed to fabricate a reality that negates the reality of nature.'[38] Indeed, I have heard the view expressed recently by female academics that Buddhism is anti-family and anti-sex, and therefore anti-female and anti-nature, and the reason given was that it was a religion devised 'by males for males'. So feminists who find such rhetoric persuasive are sure to find Buddhism a poor ally in their struggles to slay the patriarchic dragons.

Feminists will not be the only disappointed neo-Romantics. Many are sure to find less spontaneous freedom of the spirit among most Buddhists than they first imagined they might find there; some may even discover that what the neo-Romantic sees as untrammelled spirit running joyously free, the average Buddhist regards with some alarm as self-indulgent ego running riot. As neo-Romantics become well enough informed to see what Buddhism is really like, and see that it is not what they had hoped it would be, they often move on to other things. Anyone who has been around a Dharma centre or Western Buddhist temple for any length of time has seen scores of them come and go. Often, unfortunately, when they go they go with ill feelings towards Buddhism. When they come to realize that Romanticism is often little more than a collection of firmly held opinions and prejudices that are best discarded in favour of more mature and considered thinking, we always welcome them back.

If one can still find enclaves of neo-Romantics among Buddhists in North America, it is most likely to be in Zen circles, where it is easier to remain ignorant for a fairly long time, since Zen practitioners are less strongly encouraged to become well informed about Buddhism than are those in most other Buddhist circles. So it is possible that one can still find people sitting on Zen cushions who firmly believe that Zen Mind is diametrically opposed to Logician's Mind. What I wish to do in the following paragraphs is to present some evidence that there is a great deal more similarity between Zen Mind and Logician's Mind than first meets the eye.

First of all, let us take a look at some of the mental qualities that Buddhist masters regarded as especially useful. The study of various systems of abhidharma, the advanced systematic study of the Buddha-dharma, shows that the early masters had made a number of observations about various types of mentality. Among the most basic of observations was that certain mental qualities always occur together. For example, a harmful mental quality such as anger was observed to occur with other harmful qualities such as conceit, pride, and self-centredness. A harmful quality (*akuśala-dharma*) is one that conduces to pain in oneself and pain in others. There was one set of harmful mental qualities that was observed to occur with every harmful mentality. That set of basic harmful states included mental rigidity, closed-mindedness, inflexibility, and unreceptiveness. Being emotionally and intellectually stiff, in other words, was observed to lead to a wide range of problems in the mental life of the unfortunate person who had not learned to loosen up and be more receptive and open. Most types of Buddhist meditational exercises can be seen as methods for breaking down the emotional and intellectual obstacles that stand in the way of our seeing things as they really are (*yathā-bhūta-darśana*). The logical methods devised by Dignāga and his followers can best be understood as a type of meditational exercise, one that is particularly well suited to breaking down harmful prejudices arising from long-standing habitual carelessness in one's ways of thinking, feeling, and speaking.

There is nothing that closes our minds to new information and new insights more than the feeling that we already understand. Understanding obstructs our experience of the immediate present. Our memory seduces us into seeing things as we have already seen them and as we expect them to be again, and we fail to note differences and changes. And when our old ideas and understanding are faulty, they may screen out the reality that surrounds us at each moment and tries to penetrate our awareness. Becoming open to what there really is, therefore, can begin with breaking down our false ideas. Zen practice, of course, incorporates a number of ways of breaking down our ideas. But the study of logic, which helps us break down our faulty ideas, is also a valuable means of becoming mentally open and flexible.

An examination of Dignāga's discussion of logic will show how that discipline can help to free the mind of unproductive ideas. Dignāga's own writings tend to be rather abstract and technical, but his key points can easily be discussed by using concrete examples of situations that we all encounter in daily life. Let us begin by considering the state of affairs that I imagine was behind Bodhidharma's leaving India and going to China. My guess is that Bodhidharma came out of the west after being turned down for a job as an instructor in logic at Nālandā University. The reason for his being turned down may have been that when the search committee looked at his application for the job, the following discussion took place.

CHAIRMAN: What do you think of this fellow Bodhidharma?
KUTARKA: He would probably make a rather poor logic teacher.

CHAIRMAN: Why do you say that?
KUTARKA: Well, it says here that he spends most of his time sitting in a cave and staring at the wall in meditation. People who do a lot of meditation make very poor logicians.

CHAIRMAN: I see your point. Toss his application in the fire.
KUTARKA: Where's the fire?

CHAIRMAN: Over there by that smoke. Wherever there's smoke there's fire.

The error in Kutarka's reasoning is fairly easy to spot. He reasoned that Bodhidharma would be a poor logician on the grounds that Bodhidharma did a good deal of meditation. Whoever meditates a lot, says Kutarka, does logic poorly. But what is Kutarka's justification for making such a statement? Most of us would recognize that in fact he has no real justification; his statement, we would say, was a careless generalization. But the Chairman in the above example also made a generalization when he said 'Wherever there's smoke there's fire.' Most of us would feel that the latter generalization is less likely to produce an erroneous conclusion than the former. So the question is: how do we distinguish careless generalizations from legitimate ones?

Kutarka's generalization can be seen as a statement that has a particular form. The form is: 'Whoever is A is B.' Another form this statement might have is 'Every A is B.' We use statements of this form quite often. 'All human beings are mortal.' 'Every passion is harmful.' 'Whoever smokes tobacco runs an increased risk of getting lung cancer.' 'Everything is impermanent.' Often we make statements that have this intention, even if we do not actually use the words 'all' or 'every' or 'whoever'. We occasionally hear people say, for example, 'People who do a lot of meditation make very poor logicians' or 'Christians are intolerant.' While it is possible that people who make statements of this sort intend to say nothing more than the rather unexciting but true observation 'Some people who do a lot of meditation make very poor logicians' or 'There are intolerant Christians,' it is most likely that someone hearing them will interpret them as saying 'All people who do a lot of meditation make very poor logicians' or 'All Christians are intolerant,' which is much more interesting, but false.

Even when we do not come right out and say such things as 'All Christians are intolerant,' and even when we would feel quite ashamed of ourselves if we ever were to make such a statement in a moment of careless anger, we often act as if we believe that statements of that form are true. Probably most of us have had an experience like the following. The telephone rings. You answer. Immediately on recognizing the other person's voice, your heart sinks. It is the boss's voice. Why does your heart sink? Because you are thinking something like 'The boss never telephones unless there is some extra work they want me to do.' Even if that little voice that is always talking inside your head is not saying these words, the sinking feeling in your heart is a quick intuitive reaction that betrays a well-entrenched habit of thinking that the boss never telephones unless they want to make some unpleasant request. It is an entrenched habit of thinking that has brought a moment of unhappiness into your life. In traditional Buddhist terminology, the habit of thinking was a karma, and the moment of unhappiness was the ripening of that karma. But however we choose to talk about it, please note well that it was not the boss that brought the unhappiness. It was your own entrenched habit of thinking, which in this instance took the form of a careless generalization.

But we still have not answered the question of how we distinguish the productive generalizations that help us conduct our daily lives sensibly from the counter-productive ones that block our paths to happiness. We are justified in believing that every A is B, says Dignāga, only if two conditions are satisfied. First, we must have seen A and B together before in our previous experience. And second, we must never have seen A without B. To give a concrete example, we are justified in believing 'wherever there is smoke there is fire' only if (1) we have seen smoke and fire together, and (2) we have never seen smoke without fire.

When we stop and think about it, not very many generalizations pass Dignāga's test. Very often we form generalizations and believe them when only the first of the two conditions is satisfied. We encounter, for example, a number of people who meditate regularly and we observe that they are inarticulate and seemingly poor in solving problems in formal logic. The seed of a generalization is sown, and the habit of repeating that generalization is strengthened each time we meet a meditator who is poor in logic. The habit may become so firmly established that we do not even notice it when we encounter people who do not conform to the generalization. When the habit of making the generalization is so well established that we fail to notice counter-examples, it is said to have evolved into a prejudice.

The logician's practice is to get into the habit of looking carefully for counter-examples to generalizations. If the idea pops into mind that meditators are poor at reasoning, the skilled logician will immediately begin to comb through past experiences in search of a memory that will prove that generalization false. 'Śākyamuni Buddha practised meditation quite regularly,' says the skilled logician, 'but he was consummately skilled in applying his powers of reasoning.' It is by deliberately recalling such counter-examples that one can make a generalization go away before it becomes a potentially harmful prejudice.

There is one more observation to make about Dignāga's test for worthwhile and useful generalizations. Note that the second part of the test can be stated like this: 'We are justified in believing that every A is B only if we have never observed A without B.' Here we must be very careful to realize just what that statement implies and what it does not imply. It does not imply this: 'if we have never seen A without B, then we are justified in believing that every A is B.' To see why, consider the following statements:

1. It rains only if there are clouds in the sky.
2. If there are clouds in the sky, then it rains.

The first statement is true, but the second is clearly false, since we frequently experience cloudy days without rain. So a statement of the form 'P only if Q' does not imply a statement of the form 'If Q then P.' What this means in practice is that even if we have never observed one thing without another thing, we are still not justified in concluding that the one thing always occurs with the other. Even if I have never seen a crow without black feathers, it does not follow that every crow has black feathers.

At this point we must make the important distinction between being *reasonable* and being *certain*. If I have seen many crows with black feathers and have never seen a crow without black feathers, then it is *reasonable* to believe that every crow has black feathers. But it is still not a matter about which I can be *certain*, for there is always the possibility, no matter how remote that possibility may seem, that some set of circumstances may arise to produce an event that does not conform to the patterns of my past experiences. So while it is reasonable to believe that every crow has black feathers, it is also reasonable to bear in mind that our own experiences of the world are quite limited and have undoubtedly led us into making a number of generalizations that may turn out on further observation to be false. Ignorance, according to the Buddhist logician, is the failure to be fully aware of how subject to error we all, including the Buddhas, really are.

There was probably no single doctrine that the Buddhist logicians took so much care to criticize as the doctrine of infallibility. In the days of Dignāga and Dharmakīrti the principal rivals of the Buddhists were the Brahmanical philosophers who believed in the infallible truth of the Vedas, which were believed to have been revealed to human beings by semi-divine channels known as the seven Rishis. The Vedas contained the elaborately detailed instructions on how to perform a wide range of rituals, specifying the occasions on which the rituals were to be performed, the purification exercises that were to be done in preparation for the actual rituals, the implements that were to be used, the words that were to be chanted, the gestures that were to be made by each of the several priests, and so on. The general belief was that performing these rituals was a duty (*dharma*) that had to be carried out; it was the duty of the priests to do the rituals, and it was the duty of the rest of society to cover the expenses of these rituals, which in some cases could be quite elaborate and very costly. Those who did their respective duties could expect a reward in the next life, but those who failed to do their duties could expect punishment in the next life.

Not all Brahmans used the same arguments to defend their confidence in the system of rituals commanded by the Vedas, but all agreed that these books were not of human origin but rather had been revealed to man. It was important for the Brahmans to demonstrate that the Vedas could not have been composed by human beings, because everyone recognized that human beings are capable of being mistaken and of fabricating deliberate falsehoods. Therefore, if the Vedas could be proved to have been written by ordinary human beings, there would be no guarantee that they had not been composed by people who were simply mistaken in their belief that performing the rituals would result in being reborn in heaven. Even more serious, if the Vedas could be proved to be of human authorship, the Brahmans would have no answer to those who claimed that the Vedas had been written for the sole purpose of serving the interests of a particular group of people, namely, the Brahman priests themselves.

In dealing with this system of beliefs in the Vedas, Dignāga, Dharmakīrti, and the other Buddhist logicians began by examining the belief that the Vedas were not composed by human beings. At the outset it must be admitted that it is impossible for anyone to be certain about this matter; there is simply no way that anyone can be certain that the Vedas were written either by one person or by a group of people or by God or by no one at all. Similarly it is impossible to be certain about whether people who do their duties go to heaven and those who fail to do their duties go to hell. Certainty about all such matters is beyond the reach of human beings. When certainty is impossible, we must settle for what appears most reasonable among competing beliefs. What is it reasonable to believe about the authorship of a body of religious scriptures? In answering this question, let us begin by making some basic observations.

First, we observe that scriptures are written in some language that has a vocabulary and grammar indistinguishable from the vocabulary and grammar of an ordinary language spoken every day by human beings. If one were to take any sentence from scripture and put it side by side with a sentence from ordinary language and compare the syntax and vocabulary, there would be no reliable means of deciding, without prior knowledge, which sentence was from scripture and which was not. Now we have observed repeatedly of sentences in general that they are spoken or composed by human beings, but we do not observe sentences composed by anything other than human beings. Therefore, given any sentence, it is more reasonable to suppose that it was written or composed by a human being than to suppose it was not.

The line of thinking just outlined may strike some as being somewhat superficial. Could it not be, some might argue, that the people who composed the sentences of the scriptures were indeed ordinary human beings but that in composing the sentences they received some special inspiration from a non-human source? Well, let us concede that such a thing might be possible. People do, after all, say things while under the influence of fevers, intoxicants, and hypnosis that they might never say while in ordinary states of consciousness. Speaking while influenced by a fever or an intoxicant is therefore an instance of being inspired by a non-human source. The question that arises, however, is whether being in one of these so-called altered states is in itself any guarantee that what one is saying in that state is any less subject to error than what one says under normal circumstances. Once again, we should appeal to experience. We frequently observe that people who are under the influence of fevers, intoxicants, and hypnosis are much more likely to make statements that are demonstrably false or even perfectly unintelligible than are people in ordinary waking circumstances. Rarely, if ever, do we observe that people's statements become more reliable and credible when they are delirious with fever or inebriated or in some state of trance.

But surely, someone is likely to point out, being inspired by a god is not the same thing at all as being under the influence of fever or strong drink or drugs. Perhaps that is so, but once again we must appeal to our experience, which tells us that seeing people who are undoubtedly in altered states due to fever, drink, or drugs is common, but we do not observe people who are beyond all doubt inspired by a god. So, in the final analysis, appealing to extra-human inspiration does more to cast the question of the authority of scriptures even further into doubt than it does to vindicate the view that scriptures are reliable.

There is a second observation we can make about scriptures, which is quite independent of the question of their composition. The second observation has to do with how people interpret the meanings of scriptural statements. When in doubt as to what a passage in scripture means, our methods of resolving the doubt are exactly the same as the methods we use to resolve any other kind of doubt. We reflect on our previous experiences in the light of reason. When, for example, two passages of scripture conflict when construed literally, we immediately conclude that one or both of them must be understood figuratively. This shows that even when appealing to scriptural authority we actually have as much confidence in reason to guide us into a sensible interpretation of scripture as in the scriptures themselves.

A further observation to be made about how we go about the business of interpretation is that we rely heavily on conventions of speech. But anyone who has lived for more than a couple of decades has observed that conventions of speech undergo changes through time, and that even at the same time different regions develop different conventions in the use of language. This means that each region and each generation derives a slightly different message from the scripture, which shows that there is no fixed and constant message in scripture. It is not, in other words, that the message of scripture is simply there waiting to be passively discovered, but rather that the human interpreter plays a most active role in making the scripture have some meaning. But if a human interpreter is capable of making errors in other matters, how can we be sure that the interpreter makes no error in giving a meaning to scripture?

The conclusion to be drawn from all these observations is, according to the Buddhist logicians, that no matter how hard we may try, we cannot escape our capacity to be mistaken. We can be completely certain about the truth value of positive generalizations only when we know them to be false. For example, given a statement such as 'meditators make poor reasoners', we can know whether or not it is true only when we know that it is false by observing a meditator who is a good reasoner. Otherwise, we have only to suspend judgement on the matter and keep an open mind.

Romantics and others who disparage logic often do so on the grounds that logic is very limited and that those who pay heed to it are therefore limited as persons. It goes without saying that logic has its limitations, and no one is more aware of these limitations than a logician, who has a very clear idea of what logic can and cannot do. Every logician knows that through reason and logic we cannot acquire new truths, nor can we even generate new ideas. But coming up with new ideas is not a problem that most of us face, for they invade the mind without invitation during every moment of the waking day. To be conscious at all is to be incessantly flooded with sensations, feelings, intuitions, impressions, imaginings, ideas, observations, inferences, and perceptions. No matter how rationalistic we become, this flood never dries up. And so the fear expressed by some Romantics, that rationalism will somehow impede the flow of intuition and creative imagination, is completely unfounded. The real problem we face as human beings is not a lack of imagination, for we all have that in abundance. Rather, it is a surplus of competing ideas and an overabundance of confidence in our own beliefs. Reason and logic help us not to acquire new beliefs and insights but to eliminate some of the errors in our thinking. Through the consistent application of the test provided by the Buddhist logicians to every idea that comes to mind, we may gain an insight into the Buddhist principle that ignorance is not the absence of knowing what is true. Rather it is the presence of carelessly formed ideas, such as prejudices and stereotypes, that make us overlook the obvious.

Breaking down prejudices, so that we can just a little more clearly see things as they really are, is the business of logic and reason. It is also the business of such Zen practices as working on *kōan*. It would be a sad mistake indeed to develop a prejudice over which of these two methods was more effective. To reject logic and rational thinking as inferior to Zen would be to adopt a most inferior type of Zen.

10

WHAT IS A FRIEND?

This essay was written in 1987 for my daughter, Jane Elizabeth Hayes, who at the age of eighteen asked me what, in my opinion, a friend should be. During the time this essay was written, I was feeling particularly strong determination to fulfil a lifelong fantasy of taking on the practice of celibacy, which I did for about a year. Some of the views on sexual relationships that are expressed in this essay have startled and even appalled some readers. While I might express more moderate views now – or at least might express the same views more diplomatically – I have decided to present this essay unedited as a sample of the kind of thinking that not only I but many male Buddhists have gone through. After the assault on sexual relationships in the first part, the rest of the essay on the more positive aspects of friendship is probably, of all that I have written, the one that comes closest to expressing my enduring thoughts on the most important issue about which I ever think.

OF WHAT USE to me is a friend who is not a constant source of irritation? For I am physically lazy, and given a choice in the matter I would prefer to sit passively under the shade of a large tree and simply watch the spectacle of a world that is on its way to nowhere in particular. I need to be goaded into physical action by necessities, little chores that must be done. All too often, even when I am aware of those necessities, it takes the prodding of an irritating friend to overcome my inertia and to put me into motion. Even greater than my physical laziness is my moral laziness. It often takes effort to do what is morally right, especially when doing what is right results in some immediate inconvenience or loss of comfort to oneself.

Doing what is right has many parallels to doing what one must do to remain physically healthy. Staying physically healthy requires at the very least paying attention to one's diet and making sure one gets enough good exercise. But eating just the right amount and then stopping is not nearly as much fun in the short term as is pleasing one's palate, especially when one is eating with companions. And eating what is nutritionally sound is often not as much fun as eating something rich and exciting to the taste buds. It is easy to overeat and get too little exercise, and somewhat harder to stay or become physically healthy. So, despite knowing what is necessary to be healthy, we often choose courses of action and inaction that result in being unhealthy. Similarly, despite knowing what is morally right, our pursuit of short-term pleasantness often leads us into choosing courses of action and inaction that result in being morally unfit. We need to be reminded and urged along. Being reminded is most irritating. Providing such irritation is exactly what good friends are for.

Not all people, judging from what I have been able to observe, really want friends. Many people, perhaps even most, would prefer tools, dumb and uncomplaining extensions of their bodies that will serve to enable them to achieve more swiftly whatever they believe they wish to achieve. But they do not want stupid tools. It is important that tools have enough intelligence of their own to require a minimum of instruction. After all, having to give instructions to a tool, as anyone who has tried to program a computer knows very well, is almost as tedious as doing unaided the task that the tool was designed to facilitate. Much better to have a smart tool, such as another human being, who does one's bidding by simply being told what to do in straightforward language.

Numerous are the tasks that people set out to perform with the aid of their smart tools. Through human companions people try to ward off the lonely and terrifying experience of solitude, for it is in solitude that one is most likely to call to mind such unwelcome realities as one's own shortcomings and mistakes, not to mention the inevitability of one's own death. People would usually prefer to do almost anything, no matter how otherwise pointless, so long as it serves as a diversion from facing up to one's own deficiencies in character and from the thought of the realities of decay and death. Entertainment, therefore, is one of the principal uses that people have for other people.

Of course, using an intelligent tool for one's own entertainment is not an entirely simple matter, for the fact is that the more intelligent one's tools, the more likely it is that they will have needs and desires of their own and will also have enough cleverness to use others to serve their ends. And so companionship among human beings is very rarely a simple matter of one person using another, but rather it is more usually a complex matter of each person using the other. Often when two or more people get together, all of whom have a need for diversion from thinking of their own mortality and their own moral shortcomings, they will spontaneously devise all sorts of activities to keep their little minds busy. One favourite pastime, enjoyed by people of all ethnic backgrounds at all times of history, is diverting attention away from one's own faults by talking of the faults of others. There is perhaps nothing more easy to find in this world than a fellow human being who is willing to complain about the shortcomings of a mutual acquaintance. Even total strangers can usually find someone whom they know in common, even if it is only a public official or a celebrity whom they know only through hearsay. This, in fact, is perhaps the most important function that actors, singers, novelists, sports heroes, politicians, and other celebrities perform in human society: they provide, from the simple conduct of their own perfectly normal imperfect lives, a constant supply of other people's faults for ordinary people to talk about. Nothing is more useless to the public than a politician who does nothing more than work hard, always remains sober, never speaks without thinking carefully beforehand, and always sleeps with the same partner. The public cannot live without scandal, and if politics and professional sports and the arts were by some act of magic or puritanical repression suddenly purged of all the seedy behaviour of the politicians, athletes, and artists, the public would at once lose all interest in those enterprises and would return to peeking into the windows and listening at the keyholes of their next-door neighbours to satisfy their craving for someone else's misconduct to speak about incessantly.

Perhaps even more of a diversion than talking of the sexual misconduct of other people is participating directly in sexual transgressions of one's own. Having sex together is not as frequent as indulging in gossip about other people, but it certainly ranks among the most common ways in which human beings use each other as tools. A great deal of effort has been made in recent generations to disguise the nature of sex by talking about it as a great opportunity for two people to express their love and concern for each other and to share their innermost noble feelings of magnanimity and nurturing compassion. No doubt it has been necessary to resort to such platitudes to counteract the tendency of previous generations, especially those within the fold of Christian Puritanism, to regard sex as something distasteful and offensive in the eyes of God. The Christians did, after all, have to take into consideration the somewhat neurotic attitudes towards sex that St Paul foisted on to them in the guise of divinely inspired revelation. Speaking of sex as something sinful and offensive in the sight of God is hardly to speak of sex as it is in its true nature, but neither is going to the other extreme of speaking of sex as the most fitting expression of all that is noble and good in the human soul. The real nature of sex is that it is, first of all, the means by which most life-forms reproduce, and second, a means by which individuals distract themselves from thinking about their own death and other unpleasant realities. It is above all a way that people use one another as tools, and it is only because two people so often use each other with mutual consent as tools that they can overlook the fact that sex is by nature a form of using other people to the end of escaping the unpleasantness of one's own existence. It is nothing to be condemned, equally nothing to be glorified, but it is something to be seen for what it really is, and if one chooses to engage in it then let one engage in it without sham and pretence.

Of all the types of relationship that human beings can enter into, none is more complicated than a sexual relationship, and perhaps therefore none is a more fertile field in which to plant the seeds of delusion. Let us, in trying to think clearly about this complex activity, first consider it from a purely biological perspective. The biological function of sex is quite clear: the continued existence of the species, through the production of new members to replace those who die, cannot take place in physiologically complex animals such as human beings without the fertilization of eggs, which only females carry, by sperm, which only males produce. One problem presented by human beings once so produced is that, owing perhaps to a flaw in their design, they remain relatively helpless for a good many years after birth and require almost constant attention and supervision by adults.

Moreover, it takes many years for them to be indoctrinated in all the silly prejudices of whatever social group they are born into.

The task of nurturing, protecting, and indoctrinating a small human being for at least a decade and a half is an enormous responsibility and not an enterprise that a reflective person would voluntarily undertake without very good reason. In order to overcome the hesitations that any thinking person would naturally feel on contemplating such an overwhelming commitment as that required to replace oneself with a younger member of the species, nature has developed a way to bypass reason altogether. This run-around reason is called the sex drive. The way it works is to make the act of sexual union seem so immediately attractive and pleasurable that the participants in the act momentarily lose all sight of the consequences of the act that might lie in store.

The consequences of sexual union are incalculably more grave for women than for men. A man can, and many men do, form an alliance with a woman for no longer than it takes to awaken her sexual desires and make her receptive to letting him use her to satisfy his own. Whereas the woman runs the risk not only of having to endure nine months of pregnancy but a further fifteen to twenty-five years of caring for and training a young human being (which is a very messy animal and difficult to train, and one that offers far less gratitude in return than a cat), the male runs almost no risk at all. For him sexual gratification has no consequences any more serious than that of becoming addicted to irresponsible forms of pleasure. Owing to this tremendous imbalance in the amount of risk taken by the male and the female in sexual congress, males and females tend to have rather different strategies and tactics in sexual encounters.

Because the woman is more prone to being rendered dependent during the time when she herself is nurturing a dependant, her overall strategy in a sexual encounter must be to secure the best possible hope of getting some help from the male who makes her pregnant. Therefore the woman's tactics tend to consist of ways of enticing the male with the long-term promise of readily available sex whenever he wishes to have it. Unfortunately, this promise is one that she is not likely to be able to fulfil, especially in the last stages of pregnancy and the early stages of infant care. Thus at the very times when she is most in need of holding on to her man, she is least capable of providing him with the sexual service that keeps him from straying.

Therefore women often have to provide a substitute for the sexual service by other forms of servitude to the male, such as preparing his meals, keeping his living quarters clean, and various other tasks that he could very well do for himself but allows the woman to do for him so that he can have more free time to devote to the pursuit of other women who seem more capable of fulfilling the promise of providing instant sexual gratification for him.

The feminine tactic of promising to be a source of physical pleasure to men has very powerful results, and a good many women become so adept at the art of promising pleasure that they can render males almost completely helpless. Enchanting and enticing men becomes a means by which some women can gain control over males for long enough periods of time to coax them into performing the most extraordinary deeds just to provide the woman with what she wants so that she will continue to provide him with what he wants. Not a little of the male behaviour that some radical feminists love to cite – whereby men are depicted as power-hungry brutes intent only on conquering and then controlling others – is in fact prompted by women who, lacking the physical strength of men, must somehow find a way to bring the strength of the male body under the control of the female will. It would of course be inaccurate to deny that men are often quite brutal and aggressive on their own, even without the aid of women, but it would be equally ridiculous to suggest that women are on the whole any less brutal and aggressive. Despite what some feminists have argued, aggression and assertion of power really is a human and not just a masculine trait.

The man's overall strategy in the game of gamogenesis, on the other hand, tends to be to entice the woman into taking the risk of becoming pregnant by trying to assure her that he intends to provide for her and to help care for any offspring that may result from his sexual congress with her. This assurance is only rarely backed up with the man's heartfelt sincerity, for when a man senses that a sexual opportunity is at hand he is liable to say almost anything to realize that opportunity. Since the woman's sexual drive is fulfilled through the expedient of making a promise that she probably cannot keep, and the man's is fulfilled by making a pledge that he rarely intends to honour, the sexual encounter is too often a game of deception from beginning to end. It involves systematic deception not only of others but also of oneself. The whole arrangement of human reproduction is so poorly thought out and badly designed that it alone serves as the most elegant refutation of the view that human beings were created by an intelligent maker. Reproduction through sex can only be seen as the outcome of a series of blind accidents.

Perhaps the most honest and therefore most healthy form of sexual encounter is that which is found in prostitution. Here the prostitute promises nothing more than one transitory taste of physical pleasure, and the paying customer promises nothing more than a finite financial reward for being given that taste. Each party in the transaction freely admits to acting on purely selfish motivations, and the whole relationship is openly based on the principle of mutual exploitation. For the purposes of this discussion I would include as forms of prostitution all the vicarious forms of sexual satisfaction, such as pornographic and erotic art and voyeurism. It is precisely because prostitution and pornography are so very sensible as ways of releasing sexual energy without pretence or ambiguity that society at large tends to discourage these activities. These means of satisfying the sexual urges of human beings stand to threaten the institutions built on deception and to expose them for what they really are. Prostitution is too honest a mirror held up to sexuality as a whole, for it reveals sexuality as such as an essentially exploitational form of behaviour. Thus people, and especially women, can be heard to decry pornography as demeaning to their entire gender. But there is no more reason to suppose that the willingness of a few women to pose nude for men brings shame to all women than to suppose that the willingness of some human beings to commit theft brings shame to all humanity. Surely theft dishonours only the thief, and sluttish behaviour shames only the slut.

Of course those who oppose free access to pornography do have at their disposal a far more cogent argument than the one I have just dismissed. The argument can be made that the widespread availability of pornography serves to teach males that treating women (or other men and even children) purely as instruments of sexual enjoyment is socially acceptable and reinforces all their exploitational instincts. This is a matter that requires very serious consideration indeed, and if it is demonstrable that pornography teaches its clients bad attitudes towards other human beings, it may also be demonstrable that a good many industries do even more damage by teaching these bad habits. For example a considerable amount of money is to be made by selling people clothing and cosmetics that are intended to render the user more sexually attractive by making the immature appear older, the middle-aged appear more youthful, the overweight appear more slender, the scrawny appear more fleshy, and in general to make everyone appear to be any way except how they really are so as to enhance their chances of entering successfully into an alliance of reciprocal exploitation. The products of the fashion and cosmetic industries are everywhere to be seen at all times in our society. Compared to the damage they do to honesty in human relations, the bad habits taught by pornography are trivial.

If prostitution is the most honest form of human sexuality, no doubt the least honest and therefore most unhealthy form of sexual encounter is that which is found in romantic marriage, founded on the mythology of mutual love and respect. It is one of the greatest tragedies of Western civilization that we collectively promote the myth that being in love with another person is anything other than a form of acute mental disease brought on by a temporary deflation of confidence in one's own ability to be emotionally self-sufficient and strong enough to face old age and death alone. It is only by a cruel accident of linguistic history that in the vulgar English language the same word, love, is used for one of humankind's most pitiable states, that of being in rut, and for one of the noblest of human sentiments, the dispassionate admiration that exists between two true friends whose interest in each other is founded solely on the recognition that both have as their highest aspiration the pursuit of truth and wisdom.

One of the most keen observers of the nature of human friendship was Aristotle, who argued that human associations can be based on three types of foundation: the pursuit of possessions, the pursuit of pleasure, or the pursuit of wisdom.[39] Those alliances founded on the pursuit of pleasure and wealth tend to be unstable, he observed, because pleasure and wealth are both fleeting things, and one who would use other people to help secure those things is not likely to have much loyalty to any particular means of acquiring them.

In his discussions of friendship Gotama Buddha outlined four types of companion who pose as friends but in fact bring us only to harm.[40] The first foe in the guise of a friend is the greedy person who makes many demands on one and offers very little in return; when such a person does seem friendly, the apparent friendliness is usually motivated by fear or by the hope that a show of friendliness will serve their own interests. The second sort of false friend is the hypocrite who makes great professions of concern and interest in being of service, but when actually called upon to help is always too busy or finds other excuses for not being able to help. The third kind of false friend is the person who offers much praise; those who flatter can usually be counted on to disparage behind one's back. And the fourth type of foe in the guise of a friend is the companion with whom one seeks all manner of fun and entertainment; such a person serves only to waste one's time and reinforce one's weaknesses.

The true friend, says the Buddha in this same dialogue, is the person who speaks the same to one's face as behind one's back, who offers the same help whether one is enjoying good fortune or suffering bad, who neither rejoices over one's misfortunes nor envies one's good fortunes, and who faithfully reminds one of the distinction between right and wrong and urges one to do what is morally right and counsels against what is harmful.

Acknowledging the influence of both Aristotle and Gotama Buddha on my thinking, let me reserve the word 'friendship' for just that kind of association with another human being that is based on a recognition in each person that the other is also a seeker of wisdom. Let me use 'companionship' to refer to all other forms of alliance, in which each party is using the other as a means to one's own achievement of pleasure or security or distraction from loneliness or other unwelcome realities. Regrettably, the state of being in rut, or 'in love' as they mistakenly say in vulgar English, is likely to occur whenever a sexually functioning male meets with a sexually functioning female, which makes it very difficult for men and women to develop dispassionate admiration for one another. Moreover, because women who are sexually involved with men almost by necessity regard all other sexually functional females as potential robbers of their security – since an attractive but as yet unconquered female can invariably turn the head of any sexually functioning man and distract him from his pledge of long-term support of whatever women he has already taken to bed – women have a difficult time truly admiring one another. Observing this state of affairs, Nietzsche wrote: 'Woman is not yet capable of friendship: women are still cats and birds. Or at best, cows. Woman is not yet capable of friendship. But tell me, you men, who among you is capable of friendship?'[41]

Having made these few preliminary remarks about friendship and other types of human alliance, let me get down to the central business of discussing in greater detail what a friend is. A friend, as has already been stated above, is being understood in this essay as a person who, like oneself, aspires above all else to wisdom and the truth. Now one who aspires to wisdom is not interested just in having wisdom as a personal achievement of some kind. It is not as if wisdom is a trophy that one can show off to others as a sign of one's prowess. Wisdom is not a static thing at all; on the contrary, it is a dynamic process. It is a way of engaging and interacting with the world as a whole. More specifically, wisdom consists in dealing with the world in a way that is beneficial not only to oneself but also to the world; in fact, it is dealing with the world in a way that recognizes there is no conflict between what is good for oneself and what is good for others. What is best for the world as a whole is exactly what is best for oneself. It is in the recognition of this that wisdom consists. But what is best for the world as a whole is never a mere abstraction. It does no good to realize something merely as a principle of the sort that is expressed in such slogans as 'What the world needs is love'. What does the world good is knowing quite precisely what to do about very concrete situations that arise in everyday life. What is needed is not some warm feeling in one's heart for all beings. What is needed is knowing where exactly we are and knowing where to go from here. What is needed at any given time is knowing what the next specific move must be in order to secure peace, justice, environmental health, and all the other things that we must have if we are to deliver planet earth to future generations. It is in just such knowledge that wisdom consists.

Therefore the essence of wisdom is action, and the essence of action is change. That is why wisdom can never be captured in creeds or formulas. That is, incidentally, why scriptures and the statements of teachers, if taken as definitive statements of the truth, serve more as hindrances than as supports in one's search for wisdom. But it is not sufficient to say that the essence of wisdom is action, for it must be emphasized that the essence of wisdom is beneficial, healthy action. The essence of wisdom is, in a word, morality. If the nature of a friend in the true sense of the word is to be one's colleague in the search for wisdom, it follows that the essential function that a friend serves is to help one to be a fully moral being.

There are few concepts in modern life that are more tragically misunderstood than that of morality, so I feel it may be necessary to clarify what is meant by this term as I am using it here. First of all let me note that we who live in the modern Western world are living in what has been described as a post-Christian society, that is, a society that is not only no longer founded upon traditional Christian doctrine but is founded to a large measure upon the deliberate rejection of many aspects of traditional Christianity. When it is remembered that a mainstay of traditional Christianity was morality, it is not surprising to learn that in the minds of many people one aspect of traditional Christianity that has been discarded is morality itself. It is common these days to hear people give expression to such views as the following. Each person, they say, has acquired certain habits from observing older family members and companions. We all acquire certain attitudes and habits of behaviour from the society in which we live. We all develop the habit of regarding some kinds of behaviour as socially acceptable and other kinds of behaviour as socially unacceptable. In the West, for example, children are taught to make a minimum amount of noise while eating, but in Japan it is considered perfectly proper to make a lot of slurping noises while eating. And so, the argument goes, since the attitude that one has towards eating soup silently or noisily all depends on the society in which one grew up, the notions of right and wrong are relative, dependent entirely on one's particular upbringing and training. 'What is right and good for me', people are fond of saying, 'may be wrong and bad for someone else. Therefore, I have no right to judge whether the actions of anyone are morally right or wrong.'

This line of thinking is often called moral relativism, and it has been very much in fashion for much of the twentieth century. A good many of the people in our society who become Buddhists think of themselves as moral relativists. Knowing that Buddhism is often described as an anti-dogmatic religion and thinking that non-dogmatism implies relativism, they think of Buddhism as a relativistic religion. One particular phrase that some Buddhists love to use in this connection is 'non-dualism'. Anyone who would make a distinction between morally correct and morally incorrect behaviour is apt to be reminded by a well-meaning Buddhist friend that one is being a victim of one's tendencies towards dualistic thinking. Since Buddhism is supposed to help one get beyond dualistic thinking, it is supposed to follow that

Buddhism helps one get beyond making these distinctions of moral right and wrong. This is a serious misunderstanding of the purpose of Buddhist teachings, and it is a misunderstanding to which modern Westerners seem especially prone.

In the following few paragraphs I shall try to show (1) that there is a fatal error in the position that we have called moral relativism that renders that position untenable by any rational person, (2) that the traditional Christian view of morality is also flawed, (3) that one can therefore reject the Christian view of morality without rejecting morality altogether, (4) that the Buddhist view of morality is different from the Christian view and that part of this difference consists in the Buddhist view being free of the weakness in the Christian view, and (5) that therefore the Buddhist teaching of non-dualism, understood properly, has nothing to do with transcending the distinction between right and wrong.

The position described above as moral relativism is a view that many people in our society believe they endorse. That is, they believe that they believe that what is right for one person may not be what is right for another person and that none of us, therefore, has any business deciding whether the actions of a person other than ourselves is right or wrong. Another form that this line of thinking sometimes takes is called situational ethics. Here the pattern of thinking is that what is right for a person in one situation may not be right for a person in a different set of circumstances. To cite a favourite example, suppose a family in a totalitarian state is hiding a political dissident in their attic. In the dark of night the secret police come round to ask whether the family knows anything about the whereabouts of the dissident. If they tell the police the truth, that they are in fact concealing the dissident in question, the dissident will surely be arrested and taken away to be tortured or even killed. In this circumstance, the argument goes, it would surely be acceptable for the family to lie to the police, even though such lying might put them at great personal risk. But for a person in a different set of circumstances, lying would not be acceptable. For example, a wealthy family might wish to avoid paying income taxes and might realize that by lying about the family income they could get away with paying lower taxes. Lying in these circumstances would not be as acceptable as lying to protect a political dissident from an oppressive government. Therefore, the argument goes, the rule that one ought not to lie is not absolute. Whether or not it is a rule to be followed depends very much on one's circumstances.

The principal reason that people are persuaded by the above line of reasoning is that they fail to make a distinction between general moral principles and particular rules. 'Avoid lying' is a particular rule, and like any rule it applies to many situations in which one has to make a decision about whether to speak what one knows to be true and what one knows not to be true. The fact that there may be some circumstances in which the rule does not apply simply means that the rule is not universally applicable. The moral relativist is often misled by this observation – that so many particular moral rules have exceptions – into thinking that no moral rules are without exception. What the relativist fails to take into consideration is that there may be higher principles, that is, more general moral rules, from which one can derive the more particular rules such as 'avoid lying', 'avoid having sex with partners who are married to someone other than oneself', and so forth.

The very fact that the moral relativist can distinguish the morally significant features of one circumstance from those of another circumstance shows that one is making an appeal to a higher moral principle to decide whether a particular rule applies to a particular situation. In the example of the situation in which a family is protecting a political dissident from the police forces of a totalitarian state, the decision that lying is acceptable is based on a higher principle. That higher principle might be stated in words such as 'protect the innocent from harm' or 'avoid acting towards other beings in a way that puts oneself at an advantage at their expense'. It might take a certain amount of careful thinking to arrive at the best wording for the most general principle, but the important thing to bear in mind is that if one does think about it, one can arrive at general moral principles that clearly have far fewer exceptions than more particular rules such as 'avoid lying' or 'avoid adultery'.

It was suggested above that the view of moral relativism contains a flaw that prevents a reasonable person from endorsing it. That flaw is simply that the position is not consistent with itself; it contains an internal contradiction. First the observation is made that moral rules have exceptions in some circumstances, and then it is usually concluded that therefore we have no right to pass judgement on the actions of other people. The internal flaw consists in the fact that the conclusion is itself a moral rule, which could be stated in the form 'avoid judging the actions of others' or 'judging the actions of others is wrong'. The reason one is supposed to follow this rule is that moral rules in general have exceptions. So we are entitled to ask now whether the rule 'judging the actions of others is wrong' is a rule to which there is an exception. If it does have exceptions, then there must be some circumstances in which it is in fact right to judge the actions of others. But if this rule has no exceptions, it should be made clear what characteristics this one moral rule has – unlike all other moral rules – that make exceptions to it impossible. This is a matter to which one should give a good deal of thought before arriving at any conclusion. Morality is too serious a business to be conducted on the basis of slogans that are blurted out without previous reflection. Rather than saying more about the issue of moral relativism myself at this point, let me simply invite the reader to make this a topic of regular reflection.

As was stated above, the position of moral relativism becomes much less attractive once one begins to realize that with thought it is possible to arrive at very general moral rules to which there are very few exceptions. One might even be able to arrive at a rule to which there are no exceptions, and it would certainly be foolish to assume that no such rule exists without first making every effort to discover it. Within those religions that had a great impact on the formation of the way that we think about morality in European society (and in those societies influenced by the Europeans through colonization and other types of interaction), there is no idea more central than the concept of sin. Implicit in this important religious concept is a moral rule of the sort that a moral thinker hopes to find: one that has no exceptions.

The Jewish and Christian systems of religious ethics are founded upon the concept of sin, which has been defined as 'the purposeful disobedience of a creature to the known will of God.'[42] According to ancient Hebrew mythology, the first man and woman, Adam and Eve, were expelled from the Garden of Eden because of their disobedience to the explicit order of God that they must never eat the fruit of the tree of the knowledge of good and evil. Despite God's order, Adam and Eve tasted of the fruit of this tree, in consequence of which God told Eve: 'I will multiply your pains in childbearing, you shall give birth to your children in pain. Your yearning shall be for your husband, yet he will lord it over you,' and he told Adam:

> Accursed be the soil because of you. With suffering shall you get your food from it every day of your life. It shall yield you brambles and thistles, and you shall eat wild plants. With sweat on your brow shall you eat your bread, until you return to the soil, as you were taken from it. For dust you are and to dust you shall return.[43]

So according to this ancient myth it was because of the first human beings' deliberate failure to obey the instructions of God that all human beings must not only struggle to live but also ultimately die; and because it was the woman who persuaded the man to disobey the rule, all women after her must hold a place subservient to their husbands. The price to be paid for disobedience to God was high indeed. The concern with heeding the will of God therefore became the central preoccupation of the ancient Hebrews, who believed themselves to be in possession of God's instructions to humanity in the form of the revelations contained in the Torah and the books of the Hebrew prophets, spokesmen who appeared occasionally among the Hebrews to remind them of the necessity of adhering to God's law as revealed in the Torah. The Hebrews, therefore, had a clear moral rule to which there were no exceptions: obey God's law.

Unfortunately, however, the moral rule implicit in the doctrine of sin also has its serious drawbacks. One of the most serious of these drawbacks has been apparent from the earliest records of Hebrew history. Stated in its simplest and most direct form, the problem is that we do not know what God's law is. In the Jewish community itself there were some who understood the law as the particular commandments and guidelines for the performance of sacrifice and the various dietary regulations contained in the first five books of the Hebrew Bible. But others understood God's law not as these particular rules but more as a general injunction to develop certain attitudes and habits of thought, such as the attitude of humility. One example of a Jew of this type was Jesus of Nazareth, who stressed that it was not the action of killing one's neighbour that was sinful, for that was only the effect of an underlying cause, namely, having hatred in one's heart. It is really this underlying cause, said Jesus, that is the violation of God's law.[44] Moreover, said Jesus, all of God's commandments could be derived from two basic principles: to love God with all one's heart and mind and to love one's neighbour as oneself. Jesus emphasized that adhering to these abstract principles did not release one from obeying the more particular expressions of God's will as contained in the many commandments of Jewish law. On the contrary, he said:

> The man who infringes even one of the least of these commandments and teaches others to do the same will be considered the least in the kingdom of heaven; but the man who keeps them and teaches them will be considered great in the kingdom of heaven.[45]

Jesus of Nazareth was still very much a Jew in his teachings and attitudes. In many ways the real founder of the Christian religion as it has come down to us was not Jesus but St Paul, who gave a distinctive interpretation to the life and especially the death of Jesus in his many letters to the Christian communities of the Hellenistic world. The Christians eventually accepted Paul's letters as having the status of divine revelation, so the Christians took Paul at his word when he claimed that his thinking in these matters was inspired by God. According to Paul, sin was introduced into the world through Adam, because of whose disobedience to God all humanity had to struggle and die. But the effects of Adam's sin were removed by the sacrifice of Jesus Christ. Paul summarized his views on the significance of the life and death of Jesus in these words:

> If it is certain that death reigned over everyone as the consequence of one man's fall, it is even more certain that one man, Jesus Christ, will cause everyone to reign in life who receives the free gift that he does not deserve, of being righteous. Again, as one man's fall brought condemnation on everyone, so the good act of one man brings everyone life and makes them justified. As by one man's disobedience many were made sinners, so by one man's obedience many will be made righteous.[46]

The Christians, said Paul, should see themselves as being like a widow who is free to remarry after her first husband has died. The former husband, now dead, was the specific laws and commandments of the Jews. The new husband is Christ. Therefore, those who accept Christ need not adhere to the old Jewish law.[47] But this does not mean that human beings need adhere to no law at all. Rather, all human beings, pagan and Jew alike, must adhere to the 'Law engraved on their hearts – they can call a witness, that is, their own conscience – they have accusation and defence, that is, their own inner mental dialogue.'[48]

The evolution of thinking within institutional Christianity during the past two millennia is well beyond the scope of this essay, particularly given that important differences emerged between the Roman Catholic and Protestant traditions. But what all forms of Christianity retained in their thinking about morality was that the principal form of sin was a person's turning away from God in the sense of wanting not to discover and live in accordance with the divine will. An action is sinful if the fundamental motive in performing it is to disobey the spirit of the divine law, which is understood as the law of universal love; love, in turn, is understood as the ability to put oneself in the place of others and to consider the effects of one's actions upon all creatures that might be affected by them.

There is no doubt that the sentiments of Christian moral thinking are as noble as one could possibly wish. The fundamental weakness in the basic moral principle of Judaism and Christianity is that the whole system is founded upon a belief in God. But whether or not a person is capable of believing in God depends very much on what exactly God is supposed to be. The concept of God is one that has had many variations through human history. There are some concepts of God that probably few people would reject, but there are many other concepts that only a few people would accept.

If the Christians had never made any claim about God other than that God is love and love is the capacity of putting oneself into the position of those who might be affected by one's actions, then few people would reject the Christian God. But there is much more to the Christian notion of God than the principle of universal love. Also associated with the Christian notion of God is that he is the creator of the universe, that man shares some essential characteristics with God in such a way that it can be said that man is created in God's image, that God is the source of inspiration of the words contained in both the Jewish and the Christian Bibles, and that reconciliation with God will result in eternal life. Clearly this concept of God is much richer than the bare concept of universal love. Any person of any faith can accept the principle of universal love as the highest of all principles, but one could easily accept this principle and still deny that, say, the letters of St Paul are divinely inspired. One could even admire these letters very much but still see in them nothing more than the thinking of a great human being. Similarly, one could very easily accept the principle of universal love and still deny that by striving to put that principle into practice anyone achieves eternal life. And perhaps easiest to deny of all the claims that some Christians have made is the claim that it is only through faithful acceptance of God's 'free gift' to humanity in the form of the crucifixion of Christ that one can please God and thereby gain eternal life and be fully moral.

The Christian moral theologians were well aware of the fact that their view of virtue and morality contained more than the corresponding view of the classical Greeks and Romans. The systematizers of Christian doctrine, beginning around the time of St Augustine, began to draw a distinction between the so-called cardinal or philosophical virtues and the theological virtues. The philosophical virtues were essentially those discussed by Socrates and the ancient Greeks. They were wisdom or prudence, or the knowledge of how to conduct one's life in such a way as to acquire what is beneficial and avoid what is harmful; justice, or the constant desire to have every being get what is due to it; patience or fortitude, or the ability to withstand great hardships and overcome obstacles that block one's progress to one's highest goal; and temperance, or the moderation of the desire for pleasurable bodily sensations and for the avoidance of discomfort. These philosophical virtues could be acquired, said the Christians, simply by human effort. But they were of little value in a human being's struggle to overcome sin and win eternal life. For the latter goal the theological virtues were required. There is nothing that a human being can do to acquire these virtues, but rather they come to people through the grace or gift of God. These virtues are faith, defined as acceptance of the revealed word of God in the form of the Christian scriptures; hope, defined as the aspiration to receive divine grace and to gain entry into heaven; and love, defined as the special form of friendship between man and God wherein God confers grace to man and man in return offers service to God. These theological virtues are sometimes called infused virtues, since they are poured into man by the grace of God. As a result of receiving this infusion of grace, Christians are also supposed to acquire far more prudence, justice, fortitude, and temperance than non-Christians.[49]

There is something very dangerous about confusing the issues of morality with the belief in revelation or the promise of eternal life or any other kind of reward. There is equally something dangerous in mixing the discussion of virtue with a discussion of the supernatural or transcendental as the Christians have done, for once morality and the supernatural come to be intimately associated in people's minds, it becomes difficult to reject one without rejecting the other. But the supernatural element is bound to be rejected by people, simply because it is so contrary to reason. It may be a serious mistake to assume that ordinary people without any training will naturally gravitate towards the reasonable, for there is simply too much evidence that people are prepared to believe almost any new idea that comes along. But it can be observed that people are not as a rule inclined to accept any particular absurdity for very long unless compelled to do so by brute force or dire threats. The view of God advanced by traditional Christianity is an absurdity of almost unparalleled proportions; the Christian theologians even celebrated how preposterous their notion of God was, for it was precisely this absurdity that made it necessary to have faith as a virtue that took precedence over ordinary human wisdom.

So long as the Christian churches were in a political position to make life hazardous for those who held views opposing the dogmas of orthodox Christian theology, few people dared to speak out loud of the dangers of founding morality on dogmas that do violence to all reason. But those days have passed when the Christian churches could exercise control over the thoughts of nearly all people. Although a little less than two-thirds of the population of North America still claim to be Christian,[50] one sees very little evidence that traditional Christian theological teachings permeate the North American ways of thinking about most things. People on the whole seem to have dismissed the supernatural, at least as the supernatural was traditionally portrayed by the Christian churches. Unfortunately, with the supernatural many people have also dismissed morality as if it were just another outmoded way of looking at the world. Or, adopting the commonly held view that the problems of metaphysics can never be solved, they assume that the issues of morality are equally beyond all solution. Familiar with the notorious difficulties attendent on proving the existence of God, and recognizing that theological doctrines ultimately rest upon the rather arbitrary authority of some scripture or other or on the interpretations of scripture by tradition, people assume that the defence of morality is equally full of thorny logical difficulties and rests in the final analysis only on the opinions of some people who are arbitrarily designated as authorities.

As we have already seen, moral thinking was already highly developed in the writings of the ancient Greeks such as Plato and Aristotle. A strong preoccupation with the question of how to live the good life, that is, a life of wisdom and justice and the other virtues, continued in the Hellenistic philosophical guilds such as the Stoics, Cynics, Sceptics, and various other schools that drew much of their inspiration from Socrates. The Christian thinkers grafted on to that Hellenistic moral philosophy an unnecessary accretion of essentially irrational views. It was not until the sixteenth and seventeenth centuries that large numbers of intellectuals in Europe began to rediscover the pre-Christian moral thinkers of the classical and Hellenistic periods. Members of the intelligentsia once again turned their thinking to the task of finding a system of morality based entirely on reason rather than on authority.

Buddhism has in common with some of the ancient Greek and Hellenistic moral philosophies that it bases the discussion of proper human conduct entirely within the domain of what we can observe in this world about the effects of our conduct on the beings around us. While acknowledging that human beings do perform actions in the hope of gaining some kind of future rewards beyond the present life, the Buddha emphasized that good actions performed in the hope of gaining a better birth in some future life were worth only a fraction of good works performed out of the motivation of simple *mettā* (friendship), that is, friendship or good will towards all other beings. The Buddha said: 'Monks, whatsoever grounds there be for good works undertaken with a view to rebirth, all of them are not worth one sixteenth part of that goodwill (*mettā*) which is the heart's release; goodwill alone, which is the heart's release, shines and burns and flashes forth in surpassing them.'[51]

Many discussions occur in the Buddha's discourses, as recorded in the Pāli literature, in which he is asked by monks and laypersons alike about proper conduct. People want to know, for example, why one should bother to be kind to others, why one should bother to take the welfare of others into consideration when planning or executing a course of action. In dealing with such questions the Buddha invariably avails himself of two lines of thinking. First, he points out that, if one thinks about it, one realizes that all beings are alike in that all wish to survive in safety for as long as possible. In that respect, all beings are just like oneself. And if one thinks about the matter just a little more, one will find that there is no basis whatsoever for treating ourselves in a privileged way. Being partial to oneself and one's own wishes is irrational; so is being partial to one's own family, one's own clan, one's own tribe, or one's own ethnic group, nation, race, or species. Partiality, also called attachment, is regarded, along with ill-will, folly, and fear, as one of the four motivations that lead to harmful results.[52] Harmful to whom? They are harmful both to oneself and to others. Acting in fear or panic, as we can all observe from the human and the non-human life forms around us, often leads the fearful being into an even greater danger than that posed by what caused the fear to arise in the first place. Stupidity and hatred also obviously lead to bad results. So does partiality or favouritism. Favouritism leads others to distrust the person who plays favourites; it leads to a breakdown in people's greatest potential strength, which is the ability to work together to achieve goals that no one person could ever achieve alone. A society in which there is little mutual trust and harmony, a society in which there is mutual suspicion, a society in which pettiness and selfishness are the norm, is a society in which life is very difficult to tolerate. But one wants to live in pleasant circumstances, and one recognizes that all beings want the same thing. These pleasant circumstances are impossible without mutual respect, and mutual respect is impossible when there is a climate of partiality and favouritism. Therefore, not only is it irrational to be selfish, but it makes positive good sense to promote social harmony. Being thoughtful of others turns out in the long run to be the best way to serve one's own interests. In the final analysis, there is no distinction between serving one's own interests and serving the interests of others, for what is truly good for oneself is precisely what is truly good for others and vice versa.

The theme that the world is a better place for everyone when all people adhere to the highest and most universal of moral principles is one that appears repeatedly in the discourses of the Buddha. In one of his dialogues, for example, the Buddha recites a myth explaining the division of society into different social classes.[53] According to this elaborate tale, the first human beings consisted only of minds without gross material bodies. Since they had only minds and no bodies, there was no distinction between males and females, for all differences between males and females are derived from the differences in their physical anatomy. But some of those early ethereal beings, the story goes, experimented with tasting the earth, to the pleasant taste of which they grew addicted. As they continued to eat pieces of earth, they grew more and more solid, and as they grew more solid they became more differentiated from one another. Some grew handsome, and others grew ugly. The handsome despised the ugly, and the ugly grew envious of the handsome, and as enmity grew between the handsome and the ugly, the earth lost its good taste. Life all round turned into more of a struggle. People had to work and their bodies grew ever more different. Eventually there arose a physical difference between males and females. The men and women began to lust after each other, and they discovered sexual intercourse. At first all decent people found sex disgusting, so those who practised it built shelters to hide their shameful activities from the decent folk. Eventually nearly all people began to practise sex, and even though only a few found the activity shameful, people continued the habit of building houses. But they put their houses to new uses. They began to hoard food in them. As more and more people began to hoard food, food became scarce. As food became scarce, the needy began to steal, and the wealthy demanded severe punishment of theft. Thieves learned to lie to avoid severe punishment. This state of affairs led the wealthy to choose strong men to protect their property. The institution of taxation was founded to pay these strong men to protect the welfare of the wealthy. The strong men evolved into the class of warriors, and gradually the remainder of society also developed into classes based on the occupations they performed. Each social class began to look after only its own needs, and members of each class adhered to the customs and duties (*dharma*) of their particular social group. As a result of this fragmentation of society into specialized groups, each with its own narrow interests, life in human society grew continually worse for everyone. The spirit of co-operation among human beings all but disappeared. And, says the Buddha at the end of this story, life will continue to grow steadily worse until people abandon their narrow interests and particular customs and dharmas and rediscover the universal dharma. The dharma that applies to all people of all times and all social groups consists in setting aside greed in favour of generosity, hatred in favour of love, and delusion in favour of wisdom. The Buddhist discussions of morality consistently appeal to common sense and observations of what kinds of conduct lead to general happiness and welfare. In this respect Buddhist moral theory has much more in common with the notions of the so-called philosophical virtues of prudence and so forth discussed by the Greeks than with the Christian notions of sin and redemption. Entirely absent from Buddhist discussions of morality is any appeal to God or to any other supernatural force. In fact, not only did the Buddha not base his own system of ethics upon a doctrine of divine authority, he also explicitly challenged the claims of those who pretended to know the divine will.

The Buddhist arguments concerning the existence of God were numerous and complex. In general the point is made that since the idea of God is capable of so many different variations, one might be better off doing away with the idea altogether and replacing it with concepts that are less subject to misunderstanding. Rather than speaking of God as love, for example, one would do better just to speak of love itself as the supreme good towards which all wise people strive. Nothing is gained and much is lost by personifying the good. Love and compassion are better left as abstract principles than as sentient beings who have their own desires and fears and aspirations and demands to make upon us.

From all that has been said up to here, I hope the distinctions between the Buddhist and the Christian views of morality have been made clear. I also hope I have made enough of a case for the advantages of basing morality on purely humanistic – rather than divine – principles for some people to give the matter further serious thought.

One promise that remains to be fulfilled is that of discussing the Buddhist view of non-dualism. This concept has caused a great deal of confusion to newcomers to Buddhism. As an aside, I think one of the greatest strengths of Buddhism is also its greatest weakness. The strength of early Buddhist teaching lies in its utter simplicity and its stark realism; the human situation is portrayed clearly and accurately, and it is made clear what one must do in order to improve the situation. Full responsibility is placed on the individual to achieve improvement in one's own way, but the advice on how to improve is given in a manner most plain and unadorned with false hope. This makes Buddhism enormously appealing to a relatively mature mind.

But to a somewhat less mature mind the message is perhaps too severe in its realism.

Plainness and simplicity is something we crave only after we have grown weary of the burdens of unnecessary complexity. It is, for example, only after we have grown weary of too many possessions that we really appreciate a simple life with the minimum of trappings. Similarly it is only after the mind has grown exhausted from pursuing one fascinating illusion after another that it comes to love the simplicity of ordinary truth. But most human beings in the world are poor and have not yet had a taste of luxuries that dull the senses, and it would be pointless and even cruel to suggest to the poor that their greatest treasure is their freedom from unnecessary possessions. Simplicity, like everything else of value, is something whose real worth we cannot fully appreciate until we lose it for a while. This is true whether we speak of material or of intellectual simplicity.

In the same way that the absence of possessions is a source of disgust to a person who wishes for possessions, the absence of supernatural elements is a source of disgust to a person who longs for the supernatural. The great simplicity of Buddhist moral teachings offers too little hope to those who would be immortal. But there is a further consideration. In the same way that a young man loves to pick up heavy objects just to feel the strain in his youthful muscles, while an older man is content to do only as much physical work as is necessary, the immature mind loves to be amazed with paradoxes and conundrums, while a more mature mind is content to deal with only the problems of everyday life. The simplicity of Buddhist moral teachings offers too little intellectual challenge to those who would test their mighty intellects against formidable riddles. So it is not surprising that Buddhist teachings eventually grew unnecessarily complex and arcane and filled with supernatural elements, for that is what most people craved.

The teaching of impartiality as explained above is simple. By playing favourites we create a society in which each group grows to mistrust the other, and society as a whole becomes a source of obstacles to people rather than a source of support. This teaching seems too obvious to be profound. Anyone could have thought of it. But the Buddha was supposed to have been a profound man. Therefore – the subsequent generations of Buddhists thought – there must be more to his teachings than these simple observations that a child can understand. Perhaps, they thought, if we work at it we can search through these teachings until we come up with something really unintelligible, something that nobody will ever be able to figure out. And so they went to work on the teaching of non-dualism and combed through it until they could find something that made no sense whatsoever. The teaching of non-dualism was transformed from an elegant and straightforward moral observation into a grotesque mystery. In the West we have inherited that mystery. Let us dissolve the mystery and rediscover the inner simplicity of this teaching.

What the teaching of non-dualism in its original simplicity stated was that people cause much misery by making false distinctions. We should not make false divisions of humanity into more specialized groups, because humanity is one. Between the level of human beings as a species of animal and the level of the individual there are no natural divisions. When we make artificial divisions in the whole species, we cause unnecessary suffering. What are the unnecessary divisions? Examples are: the family, clans, tribes, nations, ethnic groups, and groups based on profession, gender, native language, affiliation with organized religious institutions, and so forth. One could spend days just making a list of all the ways in which we human beings divide our species up into groups that become antagonistic to one another. The workers of a company divide off and make confrontation with the management; people who speak one language develop animosity towards those who speak another; the citizens of this nation despise the citizens of that nation; a group of women meet to discuss all the ways in which their lives have been worsened by men; the graduates of this university regard the graduates of that university as poorly educated. In just about every hour of every day one can hear someone making a statement or acting on a sentiment that is based on making an artificial distinction, a false division of humanity into subgroups. To make such distinctions is a form of madness. It is the product of a dysfunctional mind. It is a disease for which each person must find a suitable cure. That is really all there is to the Buddhist teaching of non-dualism. It is a plea to each one of us to work with all our efforts to purge our minds of all the stupid prejudices that we build up through careless thinking.

We should not understand the statement of the unity of humanity to say that somehow all individuals are but pieces or manifestations of one great cosmic person or mind. Some Buddhists in the past did actually construe the statement in that way. Each individual person, they argued, is but an aspect of the cosmic mind of the Buddha. The cosmic Buddha, being greater than anything in the universe, must contain all the universe. To contain the entire universe it must contain all that we consider good as well as all that we consider evil. It must contain all truth as well as all error. Therefore, to be as much in tune with this cosmic spirit as possible, we must overcome our tendencies to discriminate between good and evil, and between truth and error. Though it may be fun to say such things, such a view is really too silly and meaningless to be of any value to us except to relieve our boredom with reality for a few moments. But let us leave play behind us, for there is more serious work to be done.

The teaching of non-dualism is a doctrine based on the observation that the quality of life improves for all of us when we stop looking at the events around us in personal terms. Our outlook on life improves dramatically and we act better towards others when we learn to analyse personalities into their constituent parts and factors. Behaviour and personality are most complex, and we do violence to the people around us when we oversimplify. Examples of such oversimplification might be those situations in which our behaviour towards another person is governed exclusively by one dimension of the complex character. Suppose, for example, that I have a neighbour who lives alone and has few people to talk to. Whenever I meet this neighbour he tries to engage me in long conversations about things that are of very little interest to me. Because I am always in a hurry I do not welcome having my time consumed by a person who talks at great length. So I begin to think of the neighbour as a nuisance, and I avoid him whenever possible. The central mistake I have made in this case is to allow myself to develop the habit of reducing my thinking of an entire person and his whole life to one factor: the effect that person has on me when I am feeling pressed for time. Nearly all sympathy and concern for that neighbour evaporates in the heat of my irritation at having my time used in some way other than the way in which I wanted to use it. Thinking in this way is dualistic, for it makes a distinction between my wishes and another person's needs and then judges mine to be more worthy of being fulfilled. The more I think in this way, the more the neighbour bores, and the more dualistic I become in my thinking. If I am to escape this boredom, it becomes necessary for me somehow to break out of that cycle and to find a way of taking into account more of the factors of the neighbour's whole character. Without too much effort I might even find something interesting in the person's history, some common ground of interest and concern. Even if I cannot find anything of interest, I might recognize that loneliness is a horrible pain for some people. Rather than thinking of the person as a nuisance and someone to avoid, I begin to think of loneliness as a nuisance that ought to be avoided. Seeing that, I become willing to help the victim of loneliness avoid this nuisance by spending just a little time listening. Learning to see impersonal factors, such as loneliness and despair and hatred and selfishness, as irritations to be avoided not only by myself but by everyone, I learn to stop seeing people as the source of my feelings of annoyance. Just as a physician does not despise a person with cancer but does everything possible to help them become free of the disease, a wise person does not despise a person afflicted with hatred or worry or selfishness but does everything possible to help them get rid of those maladies. This is the spirit of non-dualism. It is simple and something that we harm if we try to make it too interesting or mysterious.

On the level of the individual, the teaching of non-dualism invites us to abandon making irrelevant distinctions based only on our selfish perspectives of the world. We naturally distinguish between pain and pleasure. But let us not be guided by nothing more than the consideration of what brings us individual pleasure and helps us avoid individual pain. Let us be willing to undergo hardship if doing so will help others be free of hardship. Let us be willing to forgo pleasure and convenience and comfort if our indulgence in them causes others to suffer under the yoke of poverty and deprives them of dignity. We in the technological age must above all else learn to conduct our lives in such a way that we do not render the very planet that sustains us infertile and incapable of supporting life. So far we have done a really pathetic job in this most important of our tasks. We have failed to understand the spirit of non-dualism as it is taught in not only Buddhist but most systems of morality. It is not a teaching that we can continue to misconstrue and fail to put into practice. We are too near death to frolic in the playground of delightful mysteries. We must come to our senses.

It is in the task of regaining consciousness from the collective slumbers of mystery religions and the individual slumbers of our own personal selfishness that a friend is most needed. The task of waking up is not particularly enjoyable, especially in its early stages. Like an adolescent awakened too early in the morning, we are inclined to grumble and to turn over for another few hours of sleep. A good friend will have the kindness to irritate us until we become fully awake.

We need two kinds of irritation. The first, as I said at the outset of this essay, is goading in the direction of doing what is morally right even when so doing results in personal discomfort or inconvenience. As a society we need gadflies, those people who go around pointing out the silliness of our social customs and the hypocrisies of the pillars of the community. No one should be immune from being stung by honest questions. The greater the social responsibility a person takes on, the larger should be the swarm of gadflies who come in for the sting. But let the gadflies be honest seekers of the truth and not the gossip mongers who fill our news services with the lurid and the spectacular for no reason other than that the tawdry pleases the infantile tastes of the masses. To keep the gadflies honest, society needs a flock of flycatchers on hand to pester the pests. Let there be no undeserved peace for anyone. Democracy – despite the fact that the very word brings a lump to the throat and a tear to the eyes of jingoistic Americans, who imagine somehow that their forefathers invented the democratic system of government and that it is still practised – has very little to recommend it as a form of efficient government. In republican democracies in which the uninformed and uninterested voters overpower the informed and the farsighted by staggering proportions, it is only by luck that any sensible person gets elected to public office. But there is one small virtue to democracy, which is really only accidental, and that is that democratic governments are often forced to pretend to tolerate dissidents. Gadflies have very short lives in most human societies. In democracies they have a fighting chance to survive just long enough to make one important sting before their wings are torn off.

But it is not only socially that we require the services of those people who vex and annoy the hypocritical public servants. Every one of us also requires the services of friends who make us a little uncomfortable with our own failures to live up to the lofty ideals that we claim to espouse. There is nothing more easy for most of us than to grow smug and complacent. We love to congratulate ourselves on how very noble and moral we are. But very, very few people manage to live up to the good reputations they acquire in their own minds. Few of us have the candour of a St Paul, who could say:

> I cannot understand my own behaviour. I fail to carry out the things I want to do, and I find myself doing the very things I hate. When I act against my own will, that means I have a self that acknowledges that the Law is good, and so the thing behaving in that way is not my self but sin living in me. The fact is, I know of nothing good living in me – living, that is, in my unspiritual self – for though the will to do good is in me, the performance is not, with the result that instead of doing the good things I want to do, I carry out the sinful things I do not want.[54]

Although few of us have the ability to see the discrepancy between our ideals and the realities of our own performance in such a clear light, what St Paul says of himself is what each of us could with truth say of ourselves. Seeing one's own mistakes clearly need not be an occasion for concluding, as St Paul did in the passage just quoted, that we each have a real spiritual self that recognizes evil and an unspiritual self that does the evil while the spiritual self looks on in dismay. One need not, in fact, conclude anything at all about why we all make mistakes and why we all take a very long time to develop the strength to live according to the highest moral principles. All one need do is to be aware of oneself and honest enough to admit individual mistakes as they arise; having done that, one can make an effort to avoid similar mistakes in the future. But even that is much easier said than done, because self-awareness is not easy to develop all by oneself. We need honest critics outside us to help us to see the differences between what we think of ourselves and how we really are. That is what a friend is for.

There is one further important function that a friend can serve, a function that is similar to that of acting as a moral gadfly. A friend can also help by pointing out the errors in one's reasoning. None of us, no matter how intelligent or well educated or skilled in logic, is immune from making serious errors in reasoning. We are all capable of being blind to our own fallacies, whether they be formal or informal. We are all prone to get into a mental rut and become incapable of seeing things in a fresh light. We are all liable to take shortcuts in our thinking that result in stereotypes and prejudices and unwarranted assumptions. Such shortcuts result from a variety of causes. Some are due to haste, but most are due to habitual attitudes of protecting ourselves from facing unwelcome realities. Whatever the cause may be, it takes friends to help us see all the errors we are capable of making. And if we are duly grateful for the services of friendship so rendered, we will perform a similar service in kind for our imperfect friends, for they too are prone to error.

At the beginning of this essay I said: 'Of what use to me is a friend who is not a constant source of irritation?' I did not say: 'Of what use to me is a friend who is not a source of constant irritation?' It is not constant irritation that one needs. Rather, what one needs is a friend who is always prepared to remind one what is right, who is fearless in the face of one's awful wrath when one is reminded of one's shortcomings. The worst one can do in the world is to have companions. Better by far is to be alone. Best of all is to be so fortunate as to have a friend.

11

FAREWELL TO THE RAFT

This essay was begun in the autumn of 1988 and completed the following spring. In the autumn of 1988 I had just moved to Montreal and shortly thereafter made the very painful decision to cut formal ties with the Zen Lotus Society and its founder Samu Sunim. Finding myself without a community with which to practise for the first time in several years was difficult, but it also gave me an opportunity to think in a new way about my relationship to Buddhism in general and to Zen practice in particular. Those circumstances may account for some of the apparently dissident tone of some of the passages in the essay. Not long before writing this essay I had followed a recommendation of Prof. William B. Powell to read Michel Foucault's fascinating book Discipline and Punish: The Birth of the Prison. Nominally about the history of the prison system in Europe, Foucault's book also has much to say about the institution of the monastery, which was the model upon which the modern prison was fashioned. Thinking about monastic discipline in particular and externally imposed discipline in general was a factor in my decision in 1988 to take a break from all Buddhist organizations for a while and to practise in a more solitary setting with my new partner (whom I eventually married). Part of this rethinking of what living according to Dharma meant to me involved also thinking about environmental concerns, which were continuing to dominate my thoughts at that time of my life. Like other essays in this volume, this one is preserved as it was first written, despite the fact that my current thoughts have evolved from the stage represented here.

ISLANDS AND A RAFT

> Be islands unto yourselves, be a refuge unto yourselves with no other refuge. Let the Dhamma be your island, let the Dhamma be your refuge, with no other refuge.[55]

This is a statement attributed to the Buddha with which nearly every Buddhist eventually becomes familiar. Judging by the frequency with which this passage is quoted, or at least alluded to, in Dharma talks and in Buddhist writings, it is considered one of the most important messages ever delivered by the Buddha to his followers.

Another equally celebrated and often quoted statement of the Buddha's wisdom is the analogy of the raft, told in a sutta called 'the Parable of the Water-snake'.[56] Here the Buddha tells the story of a man travelling along a highway who comes to a great stretch of water. The shore on which he stands is dangerous and insecure, but the man sees that the opposite shore is safe and secure. Wishing to cross the water to safety, the man gathers up some grass and twigs and branches and leaves, and builds a small raft. Lying on the raft for buoyancy, the man is able to swim across the river to reach the safety of the other shore. Getting to the other side, the man might think, 'This raft has been very useful to me. Depending on this raft, and striving with my hands and feet, I have crossed safely to the other shore. Now suppose I put this raft on my head or hoist it on my shoulders and carry it with me as I proceed on my journey.' But surely, points out the Buddha, it would be very foolish of the man to continue to carry the raft after it had served its purpose. The wiser thing to do would be to leave the raft behind on the beach or sink it in the river, so that he can proceed without encumbrances.

The raft in this analogy, as every Buddhist is aware, symbolizes all the verbalized teachings and formulas by which wisdom is transmitted. It also symbolizes all the various training methods and routines of formal practice. The raft stands for all the aspects of institutionalized religion that have become intermingled with a basic insight of the Buddha's, which is, ironically, that wisdom can never become an institution. Wisdom is incapable of being borne by a social structure or by an organization of human beings. Wisdom can be borne only by those individuals who have become islands and refuges unto themselves.

The realities of most of the Buddhism that is apparent in North America indicate that this message of self-reliance has been largely ignored, or at least placed far in the background, by many of our venerable Buddhist leaders. It is ironic that so many of the people who seek an alternative to the frantic competitiveness of North American secular life turn to Buddhist teachers only to find themselves overwhelmed by the even more frantic and demanding rat race of North American religious life. No one can seek shelter in a North American Dharma centre for very long without being reminded, sometimes none too gently, that there is no such thing as a free refuge.

Spiritual communities, like all other communities in the modern world, require financial support. And funding cannot easily be realized without effort. Consequently, modern North American Buddhists typically get drawn into donating as much money as they can afford, in addition to being expected to give countless hours to the Dharma centre. The hours are often spent addressing envelopes and licking stamps for direct mail solicitations of money, helping out with the organization's newsletter (which carries news of the centre's activities and reminders that such activities require financial support), or participation in innumerable rummage sales, homemade tofu sales, vegetarian cookbook sales, organically grown vegetable sales, whole-grain vegan baked goods sales, used book sales, art sales, handicraft sales, meditation robe sales, rosary bead sales, incense sales, special empowerment and initiation sales, and meditation course sales.

And what is done with all the money generated through all these sales and fund-raising campaigns? Usually it is used to build or buy or renovate physical facilities. If the Buddha-dharma is to flourish, the reasoning goes, those who live by the Dharma need larger, more comfortable, and more centrally located buildings filled with bigger and brighter Buddha statues and deeper donation bowls. Or sometimes the money is used to buy computers and photocopying machines to make the organization's newsletters more attractive and to make the mailing list for the next fund-raising campaign better organized and to make the letters themselves look more appealing.

The organized community of monks at the time of the Buddha is to the organized Buddhist community in North America as a one-person flotation raft is to an oversized diesel-powered ferry boat, belching pollutants into the air and befouling the water as it makes its crossing.

It is as if the only method that people in our society can devise for becoming free from the worldly struggle for material possessions and recognition is to go forth and strive for these same things for the sake of the Dharma. And so we find earnest Buddhists all over the continent who miss no opportunity to get some mention of Buddhism into the newspapers and on local television newscasts. It is important, so the justification goes, to inform the wider public of the Buddhist perspective on things, even though that Buddhist perspective has become indistinguishable from the perspective of mainstream society. The North American public must know that Buddhism has arrived on these shores, and Buddhists must therefore add their voices to the already deafening roar made by the tens of thousands of other religious institutions, political lobby groups, charitable organizations, and commercial enterprises that are incessantly shouting for our attention.

Surely the only way to stop madness is to become sane. If the madness of modern civilization consists in our individual and collective willingness to turn a planet into a wasteland in order to become just a little more comfortable and to have just a little more fun during our brief stay here, then the sanity that brings the madness to an end must take the form of rediscovering the simple and quiet life. Not only is the simple life more personally satisfying, but it is the only form of life that a person can live without contributing to the devastation of the planet, and without stealing the very possibility of life from future generations of birds, animals, fishes, and human beings. Modern civilization needs desperately to be *shown*, not just to be told, that this is still true. The life of simplicity, which it was the whole purpose of the Buddha's life to show in action, does not require large and centrally located temples, professional-looking newsletters, efficient fund-raising drives, and slick advertising efforts. On the contrary, the simple life is destroyed by all those things. The only thing the life of simplicity requires is to be lived in simplicity.

What is simplicity of life? It is living with a minimum of physical dependence on possessions, a minimum of emotional dependence on other living beings, and a minimum of intellectual dependence on unwarranted assumptions. It is being an island unto oneself with no other refuge. Living in such a way is wisdom itself. Wisdom takes no other forms than clarity of thought and simplicity of deed. Living in simplicity means being able to let go of all the material gadgetry and spiritual props with which too many people make their lives empty of all meaning. Wisdom consists in being able to leave the raft behind.

For Buddhists, the act of leaving the raft behind may involve developing a new way of looking at some of the most familiar teachings and practices of organized Buddhism. In the first part of this essay, therefore, I shall suggest a new way of looking at the basic ritual of Triple Refuge; in fact, this 'new' way is very old and traditional, although it is not often taught any more. And at the very end of this essay I shall make a few positive suggestions as to how one might replace the relatively pointless practices of organized religion with the much more rewarding practice of living simply and simply living.

THE THREE REFUGES RE-EXAMINED

Every formal meeting of Buddhists begins with the *tri-śaraṇa* (Pāli *tisaraṇa*) ritual, which has come to be called in English the ceremony of going for refuge. The ritual consists of reciting or chanting three short sentences: '*Buddhaṁ śaraṇaṁ gacchāmi. Dharmaṁ śaraṇaṁ gacchāmi. Saṁghaṁ śaraṇaṁ gacchāmi.*'[57] The Sanskrit word '*śaraṇa*' means a place where one can go for relief from danger or distress, so it is often translated as refuge, shelter, protection, or asylum. The word '*śaraṇa*' also means help and guidance. A Buddhist is one who recognizes that the so-called Three Jewels – the Buddha, the Dharma, and the Sangha – provide some kind of protection from pain and distress. But just what kind of protection from what kind of distress can the Three Jewels provide? Answering that question requires some understanding of how each of the Three Jewels is to be interpreted in the context of the Triple Refuge formula.

While the Buddha was alive, it was customary for those who became his personal disciples to pay their respects to him by affirming that they had come to the Buddha and his moral instruction for guidance. They did so by repeating the formula 'I go to the Buddha for guidance (*buddhaṁ śaraṇaṁ gacchāmi*); I go to his moral instruction for guidance (*dharmaṁ śaraṇaṁ gacchāmi*)' three times before witnesses.[58] After the Buddha died, of course, it became impossible for people to go to him for personal guidance or to receive personal moral instruction from him. All that remained of his career as a teacher were what people remembered of his sermons and conversations. These remembered teachings of Gotama Buddha, and of the disciples whose teachings the Buddha had approved, became the guidelines for all subsequent generations of Buddhists. Later Buddhist scholars, such as Vasubandhu and Buddhaghosa, acknowledged that after the death of the Buddha there was really only one refuge or source of guidance for Buddhists, namely, the Dharma. It was, they said, only because of the Dharma that the Buddha had been at all important; had he not discovered and taught the Dharma, then he would not have been any more worthy of being followed than any other teacher. Similarly, it was only because of the Dharma that the Sangha was important; for if the Buddhist community does not follow the Dharma, then it is not capable of offering guidance to anyone.

Dharma, then, is considered the essence of Buddhism in that without Dharma there would be no Buddha and no Sangha. It is, therefore, important to have a clear idea of what is meant by the word 'dharma'. According to Buddhaghosa, the principal meaning of the word is virtue (*guṇa*) or good character. Secondarily the word 'dharma' can mean any teaching that is intended to help someone develop good character. Since all the teachings of the Buddha were either directly or indirectly on the subject matter of moral integrity and how to achieve it, the recorded conversations of Gotama Buddha can be a tertiary meaning of the word 'dharma'. Other scholars, such as Vasubandhu, explain the meaning of the word 'dharma' in a way very much like Buddhaghosa's; some scholars add that since wisdom is the principal moral virtue, as without wisdom it is much more difficult to cultivate moral integrity, the principal meaning of the word 'dharma' in a Buddhist context is wisdom. And so, when Buddhists affirm that they go to the Buddha and the Dharma for guidance, what they are affirming is that they take moral integrity or wisdom to be the most important dimension of life, and they see in the life of Gotama Buddha an example of moral integrity that is worth trying to follow.

What it means to take guidance from the Buddha and the Dharma has been clarified, so all that remains at this point is to explain what it means to take guidance from the Sangha. This explanation must be somewhat more lengthy. In the Buddhist scholastic tradition there are descriptions of several stages that one normally passes through on the way to becoming completely liberated from the kinds of mentality that act as shackles and as causes of torment. This tradition offers a standard list of ten mental traits that serve to confine and restrict and imprison the mind with which they are associated. These mental characteristics are called the ten *saṁyojanas*, which means bindings or impediments. They are so called because they bind one to the experience of conflict and sorrow, and they impede one's search for contentment and fulfilment. These ten forms of mental bondage as described in the Pāli texts are:

Sakkāyadiṭṭhi. Traditionally, this expression is taken to refer to the belief in a real and enduring self or individuality. Literally, this expression means the opinion (*diṭṭhi*) that groups (*kāya*) are real (*sat*). Composite things are always bound to decompose. Any complex thing that is made up of simpler components lasts only as long as the components themselves. Therefore, it is a mistake to think that anything that is composed of more simple parts is durable. And since something that does not itself last cannot serve as a basis for lasting happiness, one can never rely on any composite thing as a source of enduring contentment or satisfaction. Because this belief that groups are real is such a serious obstacle to the search for contentment, we shall return to a discussion of it below, where I will offer a further interpretation to the one traditionally given.

Vicikicchā. This word literally means suspicion or intense doubt. It refers to the cynical mental habit of imagining, without having evidence or proof, that all people have ulterior motives and therefore no one can be trusted. It also includes the habit of believing in any kind of fatalism or determinism because of which one assumes that nothing can be done to improve one's situation. All of these underlying habits of mind tend to manifest themselves as an inability or unwillingness to make a commitment to spiritual practice.

Sīlabbataparāmāsa. This phrase means attachment (*parāmāsa*) to rules (*sīla*) and vows (*vata*). Buddhaghosa explains that this term refers to abiding by rules and vows for the sole purpose of gaining merit for oneself. One who does a good deed, or even one who is generally well behaved, in the hope of getting some reward for good conduct is still engaged in *sīlabbataparāmāsa*. More will be said below about why such an attachment is considered an obstacle to finding true happiness; I will also offer an interpretation that is different from the traditional one reported by Buddhaghosa.

Kāmacchanda. This term means desire (*chanda*) for sensual pleasure (*kāma*). Craving – not only the craving for pleasurable sights, sounds, odours, tastes, and bodily sensations, but also the craving for stimulating and fascinating ideas – drives one from place to place in an attempt to escape from boredom. Desire for new sources of stimulation is a form of alienation from things as they are. And since alienation is itself a form of discontent, it follows that desire is a serious obstacle to any kind of lasting contentment and satisfaction.

Vyāpāda. Malevolence (*vyāpāda*), which is the desire to see other beings unhappy or otherwise come to harm, is another form of alienation. The very act of wishing to see others suffer is a form of pain to oneself. As long, therefore, as one still harbours grudges or any form of wish that others might suffer, it will be impossible for one to be truly at peace.

Rūparāga. This phrase means the passion (*rāga*) for material (*rūpa*) things and material forms of existence. In this context material existence is understood to include any type of existence in the form of a physical body. The desire to continue existing in the future, whether in one's present physical state or in some other physical state, is a source of great distress, for the simple reason that it is a wish that may not come true. Having a wish that does not come true is a form of frustration, and frustration is a type of discontent which, as long as it lasts, prevents one from being content.

Arūparāga. This phrase means the passion for spiritual or non-material (*arūpa*) things and for non-material forms of existence. In Buddhist scholasticism certain kinds of very deep concentration, in which there is a complete lack of awareness of any stimuli from the external senses, are said to be non-material states of being. Some people may be under the impression that retreating into such states of deep trance may bring lasting peace and happiness. But these states, just like material states, inevitably come to an end. Therefore, the desire to continue to exist in such states is another wish that cannot come true and a wish, therefore, that serves only to impede the search for contentment.

Māna. This word means conceit, and it refers especially to the habit of constantly comparing and measuring (*māna*) oneself against others. The fully contented person, as the Buddha is reported to have said repeatedly, is one who has learned not to consider himself superior, inferior, or equal to others. Comparing oneself to others is a form of competitiveness, the desire to be better than others. Competitiveness is a form of dependence on others. If one's happiness depends on being better than others, then one is still dependent on them. Being in any way dependent on others for one's own happiness is far more risky than being completely self-sufficient.

Uddhaccaṁ. This term means agitation or excitement. It refers to all forms of emotional excitement, anxiety, and worry. The contented person is one who has learned to remain calm and composed and imperturbable in all circumstances.

Avijjā. This word means misconception or ignorance, and it refers to any kind of failure to see things as they really are. Typical misconceptions that serve as obstacles to happiness are thinking that impermanent things are lasting, or believing that happiness can be found by relying on things external to oneself.

In the classical Buddhist account of the stages that one normally goes through on the way to achieving complete happiness in this life, the first stage that one reaches is called Entering the Stream (*sota-āpatti*). Stream-entry is the name given in early Buddhism for the first step that one takes towards leaving behind the world of the childish masses of people (*bāla-puthujjana*), and freeing oneself from the obsessive search for recognition, power, possessions, and comfort. This first stage is said to have been reached when one has become free from the first three of the ten bindings outlined above, that is, from the opinion that groups are real, from suspicion, and from attachment to rules and rituals.

Entering the Stream is another expression for entering the Noble Path, which is noble in the sense that it is superhuman (*lokottara*), that is, superior (*uttara*) to the way of ordinary people (*loka*), otherwise called the childish masses. One who has entered the Noble Path (*ariya-magga*) is called a noble person (*ariya-puggala*). The collection (*saṁgha*) of noble persons is called the Noble Community (*ariya-saṁgha*). It is to this Sangha, which comprises all individuals who have themselves made progress in the journey to freedom, that Buddhists are supposed to go for guidance and for shelter from the troubles of life. It should be clear in the mind of every Buddhist that going to the Sangha for refuge is in no way to be construed as a sectarian action. Nor is it to be construed in any sense as an act of loyalty or respect or veneration for people who have undertaken some level of ordination to become monks or novices or priests in any formal Buddhist organization or society.

Going to the Sangha for refuge is not a sectarian action for the reason that the Noble Community is not a formally organized body of people. Rather, it is simply the set of all individuals who have succeeded in loosening at least the first three of the ten bonds that bind one to a life of pain. It should be obvious to everyone that there is no need to be an ordained monk to be a member of the set of noble people. It should also be obvious that there is not even a need to be in any way affiliated with any formal Buddhist organization or society to be a noble person in the sense described above. Since not all noble persons are Buddhists, and since one goes for refuge to noble persons rather than to Buddhists, it follows that going for refuge is not supposed to be a sectarian action.

If it is obvious that not all noble persons are members of a formal Buddhist organization, it is equally obvious that not all members of Buddhist organizations are noble persons in the sense of having made significant progress towards being free. The mere fact of undergoing an ordination ritual does not automatically make a person free of worldly obsessions, nor does it necessarily signify that one has a sincere desire to be free from worldly obsessions. People become members of religious societies for all kinds of reasons, sometimes for completely selfish and foolish reasons, and it can therefore never be taken for granted that a person has received ordination out of noble motivations. The fact that a person is wearing the style of dress required of ordained people does not necessarily indicate anything at all about the person's mentality. Going to the Sangha for refuge means seeking the guidance of people who have developed a certain mentality, rather than seeking the guidance of people who happen to wear a certain style of clothing. Fortunately, there are Buddhist monks, novices, priests, and laypeople who exhibit a noble mentality. Naturally, such people are to be respected, not because they are ordained but simply because of their noble mentalities.

THE MEANING OF SAKKĀYADIṬṬHI

The claim was made earlier that the belief in the reality of groups or composite things presents a serious obstacle to the search for contentment. There are two important ways in which the search for happiness by people living in modern society is hampered by a belief in the reality of composite things. The first way is rooted in the fallacy of group identity, which can be described as the false belief that a person's identity is determined by the social groups to which he or she belongs. The second way is rooted in the fallacy of individuality, which can be described as the false belief that an individual has any identity at all.

Let us begin by looking at some of the implications of the fallacious view that groups of individuals have some kind of existence as something more than convenient abstractions. For at least as long as any person currently living can recall, there has been a tendency throughout the world towards the centralization of political power. In some respects, this centralization has resulted in much greater efficiency and convenience for nearly everyone on earth. The establishment of the metric system as an international standard of weights and measures is an example of the benefit that can result from international co-operation. Because the metric system is very easy to learn, and because it is more simple to perform calculations in this system than in any other, the metric system is obviously far more practical than any previously existing system. Moreover, since the metric system has made it possible for people all over the world to exchange raw materials and manufactured goods with much greater ease, almost every nation on earth has gladly adopted it for both domestic and international use.

Not all aspects of centralization, however, have been welcomed by all people. Evidence of the resistance to centralization can be seen in the scores of nationalist and ethnic movements that have sprung up around the world. What most of these movements have in common is a central ideology which says that a person's interests are better represented and served by a smaller group than by a larger group. Most of these movements even go a step further and claim that a person's interests are actually being obstructed by human society at large. Members of a labour union, for example, are encouraged to cultivate feelings of 'solidarity' with their fellow workers and to regard the corporate management of their particular company as adversaries who are prepared to maximize corporate profits with no regard whatsoever to the cost that must be borne by workers and their families. This solidarity that workers are encouraged to feel with one another leads, almost inevitably, to periodic feelings of hostility towards not only the corporate management but also anyone in society who does not actively support the workers' cause. Members of corporate management, on the other hand, are encouraged to cultivate feelings of loyalty with their particular company and to regard as adversaries anyone who advocates public policies, such as environmental concerns, that would place an unwelcome restraint on the profits of their company or on corporate profits in general.

Modern society has come to witness thousands of special interest groups that promote an essentially antagonistic mentality like the one described above as the mentality of labour unions and corporate management. Thus, in their respective theatres of conflict, Armenians, Azerbaijanis, Basques, Georgians, Palestinians, Québecois, Serbians, Tamils, and Tibetans are aroused to believe that their interests can be served only by having states in which their cultural autonomy can be guaranteed. Of course the cultivation of feelings of solidarity between members of an essentially arbitrarily chosen subset of the human population is not restricted to ethnic and nationalistic movements or to religious organizations. In many countries, especially in the Western world, there are groups that form on the basis of the cultural bond that is supposed to be shared by all members who have similar sex hormones. There are, for example, feminist groups who try to persuade women that their interests and needs are so special that they are best served only by other women; in extreme cases, such a group may cultivate such a sense of alienation that both women and men who do not endorse the specific agenda of the group are characterized unflatteringly, and inaccurately, as misogynists. This type of group has become so popular in the West that various men's groups have formed based on the same supposition, that certain interests and needs of men are so special that only other men can fill them.

The result of the proliferation of such solidarity movements, whether based on occupation or gender or ethnic group or hobby, has been that human society has become divided into a number of tribe-like groups, each of which is potentially, and often actually, in conflict with other such groups. But when one looks carefully at the reality of human conduct, one begins to wonder whether there really is a basis on which to rest most of these feelings of solidarity. The reality of human conduct is that no matter where one goes and no matter with whom one associates, one finds that there are plenty of people whose intentions are far less than honourable, or who have good intentions but lack the competence to carry them out; and wherever one goes or with whomever one associates, one can usually eventually find individuals who have a combination of integrity and competence. As a general rule, those who are both well meaning and highly skilled are remarkable for the very fact that they are not very common. If one thinks carefully about it, one usually finds that this pattern holds good in any group of people that one cares to examine, regardless of the criterion for belonging to that group.

The basic flaw in the reasoning that leads to feelings of group solidarity can be exposed by considering oneself and all the possible groups to which one could belong. In principle, one could belong to as many different groups as there are names or labels that one could apply to oneself. Let us, for the sake of argument, consider a human being who is a thirty-seven-year-old left-handed male of fair complexion and hazel eyes, who was born in Boise, Idaho in early April of a mother of Swedish ancestry and a father descended of English ancestors who arrived in North America in the seventeenth century. Let us imagine that this man went to the University of Nebraska on an athletic scholarship and still maintains his physical fitness by running every day. Let us imagine also that he served in the US Navy and now works for a large corporation as a computer programming consultant.

Now already, in just giving this much of a description, we have described a human being who belongs to an astronomically high number of groups. Every single described characteristic gives him something in common with other human beings. His age alone makes him a member of several seemingly natural groups: people beyond the age of puberty, people of voting age, people over the age of legal alcohol consumption, people old enough to hold a seat in the US Congress, people old enough to run for election into the US Senate, people too young to be eligible for reduced fares on the public transit system, and so forth. Not only does every single characteristic define a group of comrades, but so does every possible combination of characteristics. He belongs, for example, to the group of left-handed former sailors under the age of forty, as well as to the group of hazel-eyed athletic corporate consultants. With any one of these groups our hypothetical specimen might feel a sense of emotional bonding. But none of them represents more than an insignificant fraction of his whole being. Why, then, would he be content to identify with any one group of people rather than with any other, by taking his month of birth as being a matter of more significance than his place of birth, for example, or taking his gender as a matter of more significance than his alma mater? Why would he identify with any group when doing so automatically distracts him from his own completeness and puts him in a state of potential conflict, both within himself and with the rest of society? And if our specimen were to make important decisions solely on the basis of his feelings of solidarity with the other members of these groups to which he belongs – his fellow Aries, for example, or his fellow alumni of Nebraska – he would almost surely be cheating himself out of his full potential as a living and thinking being.

Why would a toolmaker believe that his overall interests in life would better be served by another toolmaker than by anyone else? Or why would a woman feel that another woman would necessarily be better qualified to understand her personal needs than a man would be? Why would a Mohawk feel more secure being governed by other Mohawks than by anyone else? When one looks at the habits of thought and behaviour that predominate in human society, it is not surprising that so many people unthinkingly develop strong feelings of solidarity with some human beings and alienation from others. From the moment a child enters the world its feelings of loyalty to the family, the neighbourhood, the school district, the city, the province or state, and the country are constantly being manipulated, informally by childhood games and ditties and taunts and formally by the school system, organized sporting events, and various youth associations and clubs. By the time a person is a young adult, the habits of solidarity-alienation are so deeply entrenched that it may take a lifetime to break free of them.

Why would someone wish to break free of the habit of identifying with a group? Because becoming free of feelings of solidarity with a particular group is often the only reliable way of breaking the destructive habit of alienating oneself from the rest of humanity, from the rest of life, and indeed from the rest of existence. Because group solidarity, whether it takes the form of patriotism, racism, ethnocentrism, or sexism, is a form of incompetence that imposes a severe handicap on our development as morally responsible beings. Getting beyond the handicap of these forms of alienation is a necessary step in achieving any kind of lasting peace and contentment in the world. That is why the Buddha so repeatedly emphasized that one of the first steps towards a peaceful mind is the realization that families, clans, tribes, nations, occupational groups, gender affiliations, and religious organizations are all merely social conventions and not things that exist unless we insist on believing in them. Groups, the Buddha recognized, are fictions, and more often than not they are very destructive fictions. And so the beginning of the constructive life, of the noble life, is to learn to see groups as meaningless, senseless, tedious, and incompetent fictions made up by the mind as a result of carelessness in thinking. To realize that is to break the habit of *sakkāyadiṭṭhi*.

THE MEANING OF SĪLABBATAPARĀMĀSA

Very closely related to the realization that entry into the Noble Community begins with the removal of the obstacle in the form of the opinion that groups are real is the notion that such entry also begins with the removal of the bondage of attachment to rules and rituals. To see this relation, one need consider only one of the principal effects that following a specific set of rules and performing a particular set of ritual actions has on the individual. Following rules and performing rituals makes an individual the member of a community, that is, a group of individuals who are united into a whole by little more than the fact that they perform the same set of ritual actions. But if a collection of individuals is not a reality, it follows that whatever it is that apparently binds them together as a whole is an artificial bond.

The bond provided by ritual is artificial in two senses. Firstly, it is artificial in the sense that it is not a real bond at all. Secondly, it is artificial in the sense that it is contrived and invented by human beings rather than being part of the fundamental nature of the world as such. Individuals are born with an innate ability to breathe, see, smell, taste, and feel and do not need to be taught how to do these things. But people are not born with knowledge of how to perform ritual actions on specified occasions. Knowing how and when to perform rituals requires deliberate training and practice. Naturally, the more complex the ritual, the more extensive is the training required.

Ritual actions have something in common with language. As Buddhist philosophers never tired of pointing out, any language is a purely human convention. This means not only that there is no divine language but also that there is no human language that can be regarded as special or privileged. That language is a purely human convention also means that people invent names for things rather than discovering them. That is, it is not the case that all the various names we use for objects, actions, feelings, and relations are things that we discover about the universe as we explore it. When we examine a bird's feather, for example, we observe a good many things about it. But no matter how long and careful our examination of the feather may be, we will never discover that it is called a feather. The name is not part of the feather itself, but rather a sound that we assign to the feather. This much is obvious. What is less obvious is how we come to assign the sound 'feather' not only to one particular feather but to a wide variety of different physical objects. Without going into the rather complex arguments that various Buddhist thinkers used to arrive at their answer, let me here just state the answer itself that Buddhists gave to the question of how and why we use a single audible symbol to stand for a collection of objects. We do *not*, they claim, apply one name to many objects because all those objects are naturally bound together by a single property that is found in all the objects at once. There is in fact nothing that physically links, say, the tail feather of an eagle with the breast feather of a wren. These two objects may be quite isolated from each other in time and space. Furthermore, we can readily tell them apart by the way they look and feel, and probably if our noses and tongues are particularly sensitive, we would find that they also have very different smells and tastes. So what do they have in common that makes us apply the same name to both of them? The Buddhist reply to this question is that *they* have nothing in common. Rather it is we who use language who decide that they have something in common. We *make* them similar by the very act of giving them a common name.

Now how do we decide that two distinct physical objects have enough in common to warrant our giving them the same name? We do so, say the Buddhists, because all the objects to which we give the same name have a similar capacity to fulfil a human purpose of some sort. That purpose may be some sort of physical desire, such as hunger, or it may be a purely intellectual desire, such as curiosity or the urge to arrange and classify and bring order to our chaotic sense impressions. The desire to eat prompts us to seek a common word, such as 'food', to apply to all the objects of the universe that we can satisfactorily eat. Desire for particular tastes prompts us to divide the class of food into species by assigning them such names as 'artichoke' and 'rutabaga' and 'tofu'.

The desire to bring order to the chaos of sense impressions is very strong in human beings, for we tend to have a very low tolerance of disorder. This artificial sense of order that we impose on the random events of the world is called 'understanding', and the desire to understand prompts us to assign an enormous variety of names such as 'red' and 'square' to visible sensations, 'sweet' and 'bitter' to tastes, and so on. But whatever names we choose to assign, we apply them to a plurality of individual objects by ignoring all the differences that make those objects distinct. And the more we use language, the more we forget to observe – and the more we become even unable to observe – all the myriad subtle differences among all the individuals to which we apply the same name.

To illustrate how words make us blind to very real differences, one can try the following experiment. Place two apples and one plum on a plate and examine all three pieces of fruit with great care. Look at each individual piece of fruit very carefully, noting all its visible features. Explore each of the pieces of fruit with every other sense by which it is possible to detect particular features of the fruit under examination: touch each one, smell each one, etc. Examine the items alone through the physical senses. *Do not* give names to any of the features that are sensed. If names come to mind, dispel them at once and concentrate fully on the individual items. After examining each item carefully by itself, compare each item with each of the other two items. Take at least ten or fifteen minutes to do this experiment so that the examination is reasonably thorough.

On so examining the three items in this way, what people usually find is that they can see, taste, smell, and feel as many subtle differences between the two apples as they could sense between either of the apples and the plum. To be sure, the plum is usually of a different size and shape and colour from the first apple with which it is compared, but the first apple is also usually of a different size and shape and even colour from the second apple. The differences between the two apples might be less pronounced and more subtle than the differences between one of the apples and the plum, but the differences would, no matter how subtle, be quite apparent to the senses. Without much difficulty at all, one could tell the two apples apart.

Yet the fact that we apply the one word 'apple' to two of the three pieces of fruit serves to do two things. Firstly, it makes us begin to imagine that two of the pieces of fruit are somehow the same, or at least much more similar than our senses alone would lead us to believe. Secondly, the common name given to two objects leads us to exclude the third object from being of the same kind. Naming, in other words, leads us to believe in an opposition, a duality between the objects that we call by a particular name and the objects that we call by a different name. This habit of recognizing that opposition becomes so strong that we begin to think that opposition is somehow part of the objects themselves rather than something that we ourselves have created by naming them in the first place.

Now making an artificial opposition between apples and a plum may be relatively tame and harmless, and it is undeniably convenient for some purposes. But many of the oppositions that human beings create through language are not convenient and useful, and in some cases they are not at all harmless. Think for example of the damage that is done by the unmindful imagination of such linguistically generated distinctions as black man and white man, or Canadian and American, or male and female, or human being and animal. By holding that the distinction between human being and animal is a distinction in nature rather than a mere distinction of names, we learn to forget that every individual living being desires to be alive, healthy, unrestrained, nurtured, and allowed to reach its fullest potential as a being. Some human beings, forgetting the language-based artificiality of the distinction, begin to feel justified in confining animals, killing them for food and clothing and ornamentation, performing experiments on them to satisfy human curiosity, making them perform hard work, using them to test drugs and cosmetics to assess whether those products might harm human beings, and so forth. Of course, human beings also do such unpleasant things to other human beings, but usually only after putting them into a different, and presumably lower, class of human beings through the use of such words as 'enemy', 'foreigner', or 'alien', or some term of deliberate contempt such as 'infidel', 'traitor', or 'criminal'.

Names, rooted in the desire to fulfil some personal desire, lead us into willingness to use for our own purposes whatever beings we give a different name from ourselves. Names cause us to think of ourselves in opposition to others, then to be alienated from the supposed others, then to use those others for our own purposes and to our own advantage, often at great expense to themselves. It is for this reason that Buddhists so often associate true peace with silence. Peace, which may be described as the deliberate avoidance of avoidable damage and the providing of benefit to all beings without distinction, is a natural outcome of learning to be silent. Silence, in turn, is not simply being mute and desisting from speech. Rather, silence is the ability to experience the myriad sensible objects of the world without making artificial distinctions even in the mind.

With that brief account of the Buddhist view of language to serve as background, let us return to the discussion of ritual, which it was said has something in common with speech. Rituals, like names, serve not only to give a group of individuals an artificial sense of solidarity but also to reinforce the habit of alienating the individuals in a group from all beings who do not belong to their particular group. Everyone who lives in any modern nation is familiar with such rituals as singing the national anthem and perhaps reciting some formula of praise to the country. Everyone who has attended public schools in the United States has participated at one time or another in the ritual of pledging allegiance to the flag of the United States of America and solemnly proclaiming that theirs is 'one nation, under God, indivisible, with liberty and justice for all'. That ritual, carefully designed to promote a sense of patriotism and faith in the superiority of the nation's system of government, is extremely effective at inculcating in young people not only a feeling of solidarity with all other Americans of the past and present, but also a distinct conviction that the people of the United States are special among the people of the world. And the conviction of being a special people leads naturally to a belief that special people are more deserving of the world's natural resources than are other people. Such patriotic rituals lead also to the conviction that the collective interests of the people of one's own nation are naturally of greater importance than the interests of the people of any other nation on earth. The history of imperialism and global warfare that has characterized the past two centuries is a tragic testimony to the hideous consequences of the kind of patriotic thinking that is cultivated through the regular performance of nationalistic rituals.

The patriotic rituals of the modern national state are merely adaptations of the kinds of rituals that human beings have always used to promote systematic favouritism and prejudice. Such rituals have been part of human behaviour since at least the beginning of recorded history, and they have consistently been used to promote feelings of solidarity within the family, the clan, or the tribe. At least three of the world's major religions began with a realization that systematic forms of partiality such as tribalism impede both inner peace and peace among nations. Buddhism, Christianity, and Islam all began with the recognition that tribalism, and every other form of thinking that breeds mutual hostility among different groups of people, must be replaced by a new way of seeing humanity, a way of thinking that is based not on mutual alienation and hostility but on a sense of unity. In Buddhism the effort was made to promote a way of seeing not only all humanity, but all living beings, as one in every significant respect.

Ironically, the very attempt to overcome tribal parochialism and other forms of partiality often ends up giving rise to a new form of partiality, in which those who adopt the new way of seeing are regarded as distinct from and superior to those who still think in the old way. Thus early Christianity achieved a more universalist perspective at the unacceptably high price of denigrating the traditional Jews, those who did not accept Jesus as the Messiah. In order to cultivate a special awareness of the difference of this new religious community from the old, the Christians celebrated their distinctness from the other Jews by developing their own rituals. As a result of these attempts at self-definition through ritual, the Christian community failed to transcend tribalism and ethnic exclusivity; in effect, the Christian community became just another of the many tribes that cultivated feelings of solidarity by means of alienating themselves from the rest of the human race.

About seven centuries later history repeated itself in the Arabic world. To the citizens of Mecca, and later to the citizens of Medina, Muhammad delivered the Qur'ān, a series of recitations which he claimed was a revelation from God. In these new revelations the tribal customs of the pre-Islamic Arabs were roundly condemned. In the place of the old tribal mores and mythologies there was to be a new vision of the undivided family of human beings unified in their peaceful submission (*islām*) to a single God. But as had been the case with Christianity, the new sense of unity was achieved only by making what was in fact a new duality. The House of Peace (*Dar al-islām*) was distinguished from and elevated above the House of Struggle (*Dar al-ḥarb*). In effect, the Muslims became simply one more tribe that behaved approximately as most Arab tribes had always behaved. The brutal treatment of outsiders was justified on the simple ground that they were outsiders and therefore unworthy of being treated with the same civility that insiders were entitled to receive. The early Muslim community celebrated its unity with the Jews and Christians by bowing towards the holy city of Jerusalem in daily prayer. But when the Jews of Medina showed little interest in counting themselves among the Muslims, the Medina Muslims celebrated their difference from the Jews and the Christians by turning their backs to Jerusalem and bowing in prayer in the opposite direction, towards Mecca, the city of Muhammad's birth.

As anyone who has spent some time around a Buddhist centre has probably observed, Buddhism in practice has not done a much better job than either institutional Christianity or Islam in escaping the divisiveness created by rituals. Ritual became a part of Buddhism during the lifetime of the Buddha Gotama himself. It is reported that Gotama's followers once approached him and pointed out that all other people observed two days of fasting during the days on either side of the nights of the new moon and full moon. These other people, seeing that the Buddhists observed no such periodic fasting, concluded that the followers of Gotama must not be very serious about leading a noble life. In order to protect his followers from the ridicule they would receive as nonconformists, he reportedly allowed them to conduct a ritual ceremony at the same time as other people conducted their ritual ceremonies. While other people fasted and performed whatever other rituals they were used to performing, the Buddhist monks and nuns and lay supporters were encouraged to recite the set of training precepts by which they restrained their conduct. But since monks and nuns lived by slightly different training precepts, they were to meet separately and recite their respective sets of precepts, and lay supporters were to meet separately from the monks and nuns to review their training precepts. The Buddhist community thus became separated from the rest of society by the fact of performing a different ritual from mainstream society, and the Buddhist community also became divided within itself by the fact that different people within the community had different rituals to perform. Since the time of the Buddha, his community of followers has divided itself into uncountable compartments on the basis of very little other than differences in ritual. As a consequence of all these differences, there are some groups within Buddhism who do not regard other groups as being pure Buddhists, and there are even groups who do not regard some other groups as being true Buddhists at all.

It is said that the Buddha predicted that the words he used in his effort to express wisdom would remain among human beings for a long time, but that the wisdom behind the words would be lost within five hundred years. The present state of institutional Buddhism in the world leads one to suspect that the Buddha's prediction was accurate. The Dharma is scarcely anywhere to be seen in the world. Almost no matter where one goes in the world of organized Buddhism, the search for wisdom has been replaced by the chanting of formulas or the muttering of mantras. The quest for freedom from attachments has been replaced by a slavery to rituals. Direct compassionate action has been replaced by actions that are only symbolically compassionate. Thus, for example, one finds some Buddhists doing thousands or even hundreds of thousands of prostration exercises and other types of worship service that are said to generate religious merit which the devotee, in a pathetically shallow gesture of generosity, then dedicates to the welfare of all beings. Other Buddhists go off to meditation retreats and sit for hour after hour for days or even weeks at a time. This form of practice, like worship, can be very effective when conditions are right, but it is too often little more than a manifestation of attachment to the rites and rituals of a particular group of practitioners gathered around a particular teacher. Practices of this kind may do a great deal to keep an organization thriving, but they do not necessarily do much to promote wisdom, compassion, and the other virtues that characterize those rare individuals who have become members of the Noble Community.

A CRITICAL LOOK AT RITUALS

A ritual is nothing but an action, so one can think about a ritual in the same way that one can think about any other action. In the same way that one should reflect before undertaking any course of action, one should reflect before performing a ritual. And since we would say in general that a person who acts without thinking about the implications of the action is acting carelessly, we would say in particular that a person who performs a ritual without thinking about its implications is acting carelessly. Bearing these observations in mind, let us examine the sorts of questions that one could profitably ask before undertaking any course of action.

A careful person, before undertaking any course of action, is sure to ask what purpose it is meant to achieve. Once it has been determined what the intended purpose is, assuming one takes this purpose to be valuable, the thoroughly careful person is likely to ask whether that same purpose could be achieved as efficiently or even more efficiently by some alternative course of action. In choosing among various courses of action that could be followed, the careful person is bound to examine what some of the secondary consequences or side effects of each course of action might be. And finally, there may be much to be gained by reflecting on what hidden assumptions the actor would be making by acting in a given way. Once the actor determines what beliefs are being taken for granted in doing an action, it can be asked whether they are beliefs that the actor sincerely holds. Only after weighing all the above questions will a careful person finally choose a course of action that seems best suited to achieve the given purpose. Anyone who does not habitually reflect on such matters before acting is usually regarded by most people as an irresponsible person whom one is wise to deal with cautiously.

All the above questions can easily be asked of a course of ritual action. To illustrate how these questions might be applied, let me offer two concrete examples. The first example will show how Gotama Buddha applied questions very much like these to the Brahmans, who were the priests of his day in charge of conducting animal sacrifices. And the second example will show how modern Buddhists could ask exactly the same kinds of questions of their own teachers before performing any of the rituals that their teachers would have them perform.

According to the Pāli texts, the religion of mainstream society during the lifetime of Gotama Buddha was centred on the sacrifice of animals. Kings and wealthy merchants could sponsor a sacrifice by buying a number of animals and hiring a qualified Brahman priest to slaughter them in the ritually correct way. The carcasses of the slaughtered animals were usually burned on a special altar while the priests recited mantras and performed a series of prescribed gestures. The sacrificial ritual typically ended with the burned carcasses being cut up and eaten by the priests and the sponsor and his invited guests.

What is the purpose of the ritual? It is axiomatic in classical Indian thought that no action is ever performed by a sensible person unless the agent has a clear idea of some goal that is to be reached by performing the action. Since purposeless action is simply wasted effort, it is always legitimate to ask what purpose any action – including any ritual action – serves. Usually the answer to this question is not difficult to find, and in fact people who are about to act generally volunteer their motives. Typically when people sponsored an animal sacrifice they did so in order to increase their own lasting happiness or to gain a better social status. Occasionally a king might give as his reason for sponsoring a sacrifice that he wished to bring greater prosperity to society as a whole.

Can the purpose be achieved by some other course of action? Buddhist literature is filled with stories of Gotama Buddha examining a particular ritual and suggesting alternative courses of action that would achieve the stated goal more directly and efficiently. To give just one of many examples that could be given, in the *Kūṭadanta Sutta* the story is told of a very wealthy king named Mahāvijita who wished to use his wealth to sponsor a sacrifice in order to bring himself 'benefit and happiness for a long time'.[59] The king is advised that the purpose of the sacrifice could be realized much more efficiently if the king were to bring social and economic stability to the people of his kingdom. Bringing economic stability to the people could be achieved directly by making funds available to farmers to help them cover the expenses of planting and tending their crops. Further stability could be provided for the people if the king created jobs for labourers during the times of seasonal unemployment. By aiding farmers, labourers, and merchants in their efforts to earn honest livelihoods, the king would reduce poverty; and since poverty is the root cause of crime, reducing poverty would result in a reduction in theft and violent crime within the kingdom. As people became more prosperous and crime became less frequent, the people would naturally become more happy and secure, and they would praise the king. Being praised by the citizens would surely result in the king's lasting benefit and happiness. Therefore, as an alternative to the ritual sacrifice of animals as a means of securing his lasting benefit and happiness, the king is asked to consider providing a helping hand to his citizens.

What are the secondary consequences of the ritual? When someone performs an action for a given purpose, this aim may be called its primary consequence. But because events in the actual world are so intricately interconnected, actions invariably have many more consequences than just the one aimed at. Taking as many of these secondary consequences into consideration as possible when planning an action is what Buddhists call being mindful, and being mindful is the cardinal virtue of Buddhism. In the case of an animal sacrifice, the purpose of the ritual may be, as we saw above, to attain lasting benefit and welfare for the sponsor and perhaps even for all of human society. But the Buddha constantly reminded people of the secondary consequences of such sacrifices. The animals that are given to the priest for sacrifice must be captured and confined against their will, and the very act of rounding up the animals often results in physical injury to them; mothers are often separated from their offspring, which brings anxiety and sadness to both; the animals are terrified in the moments before they are slaughtered; and ultimately of course the animals die prematurely. The animals killed in this way are themselves innocent and harmless, and yet the sacrifice requires that they be treated by human beings in ways that no human being would wish to be treated themself.

What beliefs does the ritual take for granted? Any action that is done deliberately reveals something about the beliefs of the actor. If the king who sponsors an animal sacrifice does so for his own benefit or for the benefit of his citizens, then clearly he believes that the death of animals is somehow a cause of happiness to human beings. It may be that he believes that there are gods somewhere who are are delighted by the odour of the burning carcasses of the slaughtered animals and accept this odour as a gift for which they express their gratitude by doing some favour in return to human beings. When all the secondary consequences of an action are pointed out to the actor, a continued willingness to go ahead with the action reveals even more about the actor's beliefs. When told that animals suffer a great deal in the process of being offered up for sacrifice, the sponsor might go ahead and sponsor the sacrifice anyway. If so, this would show that the sponsor probably believed one or more of the following to be true: (a) the happiness of human beings is more important than the happiness of other kinds of animal, (b) animals do not really have feelings and therefore do not suffer the pain and anxiety they appear to suffer, (c) animals do admittedly suffer pain and their happiness is as important as the happiness of human beings, but animals that die in sacrifice go to heaven and enjoy eternal happiness much greater than any happiness they would experience on earth as animals, or (d) animals that die at the hands of human beings are liberated from whatever horrible karma resulted in their being born as animals in the first place. Please take note, while wiping away the tears of laughter prompted by what one might assume to be a manifestation of the author's demented sense of irony, that all of these beliefs have been held and defended in the course of human history. Given that a course of action, very similar to what in ancient India was called a religious sacrifice, is still performed in the West under the name of outdoor barbecue, it would appear that some of these apparently absurd beliefs are held by some people even now.

Can one sincerely hold the beliefs assumed by the ritual? Once a set of beliefs, whether explicit or assumed, has been identified, it is a relatively easy matter to test whether one is really prepared to hold them. In classical India, for example, the beliefs on which the ritual of animal sacrifice were based came under such heavy criticism that very few people found it possible to hold them with any sincerity. The beliefs were, it must be admitted, fairly preposterous. Consequently, the priests began to allow the sacrifice of an effigy in place of the actual animal. The belief that burning a flour paste figurine in the shape of a cow could bring human happiness may not seem much of an improvement over the belief that burning a real cow could bring human happiness, but at least the cows suffered less under the newer set of questionable assumptions. The Buddha himself, incidentally, found the whole set of beliefs underlying ritualistic sacrifice so absurd that he concluded that no sensible person could possibly believe them. This led him to conclude in turn that the institution of sacrifice must have been invented by brahmans for the sole purpose of extracting money from wealthy kings.

> The brahmins coveted the great enjoyments of men
> surrounded by herds of cows, groups of beautiful women,
> chariots with well-trained horses, well decorated with beautiful
> curtains and homes and dwelling places built to good
> proportion. Composing hymns, they then approached the king
> Okkāka and said 'You are possessed of manifold wealth; offer
> us your vast riches; offer us your immense wealth.' Then the
> king, the lord of chariots, persuaded by the brahmins,

> performed freely the horse sacrifice, the human sacrifice, the water rites and the sacrifice of liquor. Having performed these sacrifices he gave wealth to the brahmins.... And they having thus received wealth desired to hoard; and being overwhelmed by covetousness their greed increased. They composed hymns and again approached Okkāka. 'Like water, earth, gold and corn – even so are the cattle, for they are the necessary appendage of human beings. Therefore, offer us your immense wealth, give us your vast riches.' Then the king, the lord of chariots, persuaded by the brahmins caused to be killed many hundred thousand cattle in sacrifice.[60]

A CRITICAL LOOK AT THE RITUAL OF ZAZEN

There are many different kinds of rituals performed by Buddhists today that could be subjected to the same scrutiny to which the Buddha subjected the brahmanic ritual of animal sacrifice. Western Buddhists can be found who burn candles and incense, perform prostrations, chant, recite such formulas as mantras and dhāraṇīs, undergo tantric initiations or empowerments, or sit stoically like military generals for hours at a time in formal zazen. Without entering into the unprofitable and irrelevant discussion of whether the Buddha himself taught his disciples such things, let us simply examine one of them in the manner in which the Buddha is said to have examined the ritual of offering burned animals to the gods. Let us take the ritual of sitting in zazen as fairly representative of Buddhist rituals.

What is the purpose of the ritual? Before asking what the purpose of zazen is, it should be made clear that we are asking not about the purpose of meditation in general. Rather, we are asking specifically about the stylized form of sitting meditation practised by some Zen groups. Features of this stylized way of sitting vary from group to group, but typically they include such rituals as bowing to the master or to the master's sitting mat, bowing to one's own sitting mat before actually taking a seat, sitting in a particular posture with the hands held in a particular way, assuming a particular posture when a signal is given to begin meditation and remaining quite motionless until another signal is given to end the meditation, and so forth. A typical answer to the question of what purpose all these extra zazen rituals have is that such rituals help the disciple become less self-centred. By surrendering oneself fully to the rituals, it is usually said, one reduces the harmful influences of one's ego. In other words, doing rituals of this sort is supposed to make the disciple less proud and more humble.

Can the purpose be achieved by some other course of action? We can ask first of all whether it is possible to cultivate humility by some means other than surrendering oneself to the performance of the particular rituals of zazen. Presumably the answer is yes, for otherwise no one other than those who train in Zen would be able to become humble. But perhaps it could be argued that the particular rituals to which one surrenders are not what is important. What is important, it could be held, is just that one submit to a given routine and abide by that routine faithfully. But if that is the case, then one may ask whether there are any restraints at all on the kind of routine to which one submits. Could one just as efficiently cultivate humility, for example, by submitting oneself to the task of fulfilling all the requirements for a PhD in medieval Latin at Harvard? Or could one become equally humble in the same amount of time by training to run the marathon, or cross country skiing, or learning to make accurate sketches of beetles, or apprenticing in studio photography, or washing dishes?

A discussion of how one would go about finding an answer to this question might be as interesting as any actual answer that one might give it. How could one ever know whether the rituals of zazen are of any greater or lesser efficiency than any other method of becoming humble? Indeed, how could one know that the rituals of zazen are a method of becoming humble at all? The very most that one can know is that one has a subjective feeling that one has become more humble. But whether this feeling is accurate is difficult and probably even impossible to determine. Moreover, even if one could know with some certainty that one had indeed become more humble over a course of time, there would be no way of knowing whether the cause of the new humility was the regimen of rituals, the natural effects of becoming more mature, or some other set of circumstances.

What are the secondary consequences of the ritual? The rigid sitting routine and all the other rituals surrounding zazen are unnatural. It takes a certain amount of effort to adjust to them and learn how to do them properly. For most people the amount of effort required is considerable. As a rule, whenever people do something that requires much effort, they become attached to what they have done. In other words, people place a higher value on things they have accomplished with effort than they place on things that have come easily and with no effort. After all, reason most people, if a task was not worth a great deal, then no sensible person would invest a great deal of effort in doing it properly. Therefore, if one has invested time and energy and effort in a particular task, then either one is not at all sensible, or the task was worthwhile. Few people are willing to own up to lacking good sense, and so most people come to think that what they have done with effort has a high intrinsic value.

That being the case, it follows that most people who have learned with effort to adapt to the rigours of the stylized zazen way of sitting meditation will attach great importance to sitting in that way and to all that goes with it. For example, many people have difficulty overcoming the fear of facing the Zen master in interviews. The ritual of the interview, which is in almost every respect a perfectly meaningless experience, is often for the beginner a source of anxiety and terror. If one does not follow the good counsel of one's panic and quit practising formal Zen altogether, then when the fear subsides it is usually replaced by an exaggerated sense of gratitude towards the master. It is arguable that this new attachment that the disciple is likely to develop for the Zen master is not much of an improvement over all the attachments that the disciple had formerly. Given that the purpose of Buddhist meditation in general is to lessen the strength of one's attachments rather than just to change the object to which one is attached, it is questionable whether the formal zazen style of meditation achieves the purposes of Buddhist meditation in general.

One by-product or side effect that many practitioners of zazen have experienced is an exaggerated sense of obedience and loyalty to the Zen master. This should come as no surprise, since many of the rituals of Zen, and indeed of many other forms of organized Buddhism, were developed in feudal societies in which social stability was dependent upon the unfailing loyalty of vassals to their lords. Insubordination in such societies was simply intolerable, so virtually every social ritual that people performed served to reinforce the domination of nobles over peasants, royalty over citizenry, elders over youth, and men over women. These relations of social dominance were demonstrated and reinforced every hour of every day through such rituals as physically lowering oneself in the presence of a socially superior person. Thus disciples bowed deeply to teachers or even touched their heads to the teacher's feet to show their submissiveness to the teacher's authority.

These rituals of submissiveness, which were common throughout feudal society, were particularly important in military contexts, where insubordination was not only socially backward but also potentially dangerous. Disloyalty to one's military unit or disobedience to one's commanding officers is considered far more dangerous to group safety than even the commanding officer's potential errors; therefore, in a military setting it is preferable to obey a bad command than to run the risk of chaos brought on by wilful disobedience. Now it is worth recalling that in much of Asia, and especially in those parts of Asia in which Mahāyāna Buddhism took root, the Buddhist monastic community had a very close relationship with the government in general and with the military in particular. Therefore, in such countries as China, Japan, Korea, and Tibet it became common for Buddhist practice to evolve in ways that served the interests of the ruling military classes. Although the details vary from country to country and from era to era, it can be said that generally the power élite managed to adapt the practices of organized Buddhism to serve the needs of those in power. Kings were often regarded as manifestations of Maitreya, the Buddha of the future, and great generals were seen as incarnations of Bodhisattvas, who were themselves personifications of such virtues as wisdom, compassion, and courage. In such settings as these, obedience to the king and his generals could be regarded as a service as honourable in the present day as service to the Buddha and his personal disciples had been in days gone by. Such beliefs, and the practices associated with them, were quite valuable to governments that were authoritarian in theory and often totalitarian in practice.

Service and obedience, if they are to be as spontaneous as a physical reflex, must be trained into people. People must be made to go through the motions of submission repeatedly throughout the day so that they do so without even thinking about it. This is so important that it bears repeating. In a feudal or military setting, people must be trained to be obedient *without thinking about it.* Obedience must be a reflex that happens as quickly and as involuntarily as breathing. It was for the purpose of developing just this kind of reflexive obedience that many of the rituals of Asian Buddhism were devised. Examples of such rituals for reinforcing submissiveness are the rituals of prostrating before a teacher, avoiding eye contact with the teacher, and remaining silent in the teacher's presence unless invited to speak. Other rituals were designed to stir up feelings of group cohesion and *esprit de corps*. An example of this latter type of exercise is the common Zen ritual of reciting the names of the lineage of teachers from Śākyamuni Buddha down to one's own master. Another example is the common Tibetan ritual of praying for the speedy return of a recently departed lama and for the successful discovery of the lama's new incarnation.

Given that a number of Buddhist rituals of this kind were designed to ensure social stability by ensuring a passive and uncritical submission to authority, it is not surprising that they still have this effect on people who do them. If people do not wish to become uncritically submissive to authority, then they might consider whether they wish to engage in ritual practices that produce submission as a side effect. It is possible that, for both individuals and society as a whole, the good achieved by such rituals is outweighed by the bad.

What beliefs does the ritual take for granted? What does a person who is about to enter a room to practise formal zazen believe that the practice is going to accomplish? What has made the practitioner decide that sitting in formal zazen for an hour or an entire evening or a week is a more profitable use of their time than doing any number of other things? Presumably the belief is that others have followed the same path in the past, and by following just this path they have become wise, and in becoming wise they have become free of the burden of self-centred craving and all its consequent sorrows. But on what is that belief grounded? In many cases, those who stay with the rigorous training of formal zazen do so because they do believe the training is worth while, and they believe the training is worth while because they admire the Zen master under whom they are training. This leads us to ask: on what is the admiration of the Zen master based? Undoubtedly the admiration of the Zen master is founded on the disciple's belief that the master does indeed have many or all of the qualities that the disciple deems admirable. That is, the disciple believes that the master is kind, competent, wise, and trustworthy; the disciple may even believe that the master is enlightened. All these beliefs that the disciple has about the master are of course based in turn upon the disciple's confidence in his own ability to recognize true enlightenment when he sees it.

Can one sincerely hold the beliefs assumed by the ritual? Is the disciple's confidence in the Zen master justified? That is, is it founded upon beliefs that are likely to be true? I would invite any disciple of any master to perform the following exercise:

> Think for a moment about all the people you have dealt with during your lifetime. Think of all the taxi drivers, secretaries, social workers, soldiers, assembly line workers, veterinarians, teachers, shop supervisors, sales clerks, psychotherapists, repairmen, college professors, police officers, physicians, personnel managers, flight attendants, parking lot attendants, photographers, travel agents, lawyers, landlords, engineers, computer programmers, clerks, chefs, business managers, bus drivers, bank tellers, auto mechanics, and accountants you have had occasion to do business with. How many of the people that you have met in the world have impressed you as being competent and fully in command of their profession? How many of them struck you as having your own interests above their own? Do you find that as you look back over all these people in different professions it is difficult to find more than a few who have struck you as being really good at what they do? Probably so. Now, what makes you think that among all the Zen masters (or Tibetan lamas or other kinds of guru) there would be more people who are good at their job than there are people in any other profession who are good at their job?

It must always be borne in mind that part of the Zen master's job is to look like a good Zen master, just as it is part of a lawyer's job to look like a good lawyer. A professional's livelihood depends on looking good at what he or she does; indeed, in most professions it is more important to look good at what one does than it is actually to be good at what one does. Zen masters, lamas, monks, and priests all have in common with people who follow other callings that their livelihood depends on what they do, and the quality of their livelihood depends entirely on making the people who pay for their services believe that they are spending their money well. As is the case with any other professional, a Zen master's success in attracting customers depends very much upon being able to manage one's public image. And it is true of all professions, including any of the religious professions, that an ability to manage one's public image well does not always go hand in hand with one's ability to do one's actual job well. Deception is, unfortunately, always a very real possibility. To think otherwise would be tragically naïve.

It must be emphasized that every criticism that has been made above concerning formal zazen practice could also be made *mutatis mutandis* of virtually every other Buddhist practice that has made its way to the West through Japan, Korea, China, Tibet, or South-east Asia: tantric initiations, prostrations, chanting, reciting mantras or dhāraṇīs, or anything else that is supposed to help the disciple generate merit. The more one looks at all such practices with a critical mind, the more one is likely to conclude that most practices of this sort do very little other than make the disciple loyal to the teacher, which loyalty is of crucial importance for religious professionals to earn a livelihood. For the disciples these practices at best do little more than to mark time until the disciple is ready to join the Noble Community. And at the worst such practices may actually delay the disciple by retarding the development of the kind of critical thinking that is necessary to achieve the goal of becoming wise.

Gotama Buddha, it must be remembered, learned not to be deceived by the claims of the Brahmans of his day who performed religious ceremonies for a livelihood. A modern Buddhist would do well to follow his example in learning not to be deceived by all the Buddhist monks, priests, lamas, and masters whose livelihoods depend on selling meditation courses, giving empowerments, performing wedding services, blessing houses and finding auspicious names for children, praying for the dead, and generating merit to sell to those who are too busy to generate merit of their own through useful works.

BECOMING PART OF THE NOBLE COMMUNITY

There is no compelling reason to believe that human beings are on the whole any more sophisticated now than they were at the time of the Buddha. At the same time, there are no reasons to believe that human beings are any less capable of becoming members of the Noble Community now than they ever have been. The idea of progress is a myth without any basis in historical fact, but so is the idea of constant degeneration. Progress was the myth of wealthy European white Protestant Christians during the eighteenth and nineteenth centuries, and degeneration has been the principal myth of many cultures through history. But let us now put all such myths gently aside and look more squarely at what is currently before our eyes.

Human beings have collectively developed very efficient methods of satisfying their desires. But they have not collectively developed a very good method of deciding which desires are worth satisfying and which are better left unfulfilled. The vast majority of people, given a choice in the matter, have put as much energy as possible into seeking comfort and fun. This has probably always been true, no matter which society one considers at any given era of human history. Very wealthy and politically powerful societies usually manage to develop more efficient methods of providing comfort and fun to their own citizens than do economically poor and politically weak societies, and observation of this fact alone has encouraged many a person to believe that there is a great advantage to be had in being wealthy and powerful. If there is anything unique about the times in which we live it is only that the methods of acquiring immediate comfort and fun have become so efficient and so widely accessible that human beings have pampered and giggled themselves to the brink of extinction, exterminating tens of thousands of other species in the process. It is now time to pay the high price of the many excesses of ourselves and of the generations that have preceded us. We have begun paying already, through witnessing the early signs of what may very well be irreversible damage to the environment that supports life itself. But as a whole, human beings are hardly aware of the tremendous debts we and our children will be paying in future years. Most indications are that our planet is in much worse condition than most people had ever imagined even as few as five years ago. This is the situation that is squarely before our eyes.

What can be done? Well, if the damage that has been done to our planet is indeed beyond repair, as more and more scientists are beginning to believe, then nothing can be done to recapture the world of nature as it once was. But one need not take the view that the situation is absolutely hopeless. After all, as individuals we all know for certain that we are all going to die eventually and that there is nothing we can do (aside from dying young) to avoid the natural decay that comes with old age. But it does not follow from that knowledge that we give up and stop breathing right this moment. On a larger scale of time than that of our individual lives, we can be certain that with or without our help the earth will eventually stop supporting life altogether. But that is no call to hasten the death of this old chunk of spinning rock. Even as we die, we have the option of trying to live out whatever time we have left sensibly and with dignity.

What does it mean to live sensibly and with dignity? It means to live in such a way as individuals that if all other individuals were to follow our example, they would be able to live with as much happiness as we ourselves have. It hardly seems necessary to add that most Westerners do not live sensibly and with dignity. Our society transforms matter and consumes energy at rates that are proving fatal to the planet; ours is not an example that if followed would lead to happiness for other beings. Ours is an example that has been proven to lead to death.

It is time to stop living that way. It is time to stop blaming corporations and governments for failing to do something about pollution. It is time to stop buying their products, the vast majority of which are silly toys and distractions in the first place. In short, it is time to begin living lives of material simplicity. And it is time to stop consuming artificially generated forms of energy and to rediscover the experience of working with our physical bodies. To rediscover simplicity is to rediscover life. Not to rediscover simplicity is to kill and then to die. There are so many ways in which the life of an average Westerner could be productively simplified that one could fill several books with specific suggestions and tips. What all these suggestions and tips would have in common, however, is the message: consume less. It has been obvious to some people for a very long time that consuming less means taking less from the world, putting less waste material into the world, and in general doing less direct and indirect harm to human beings and other forms of life. There are plenty of efforts being constantly made to make us want to consume more. Most of us have lived our entire lives being bombarded by commercial messages encouraging us to think that buying more is an effective way to achieve happiness. It is now time to stop listening to such noise.

People all over the planet are waking up to the urgent need to reduce consumption. If Buddhists around the world wish to take part in this process of global awakening, they have a right to expect their own religious leaders to set the example for them by following the example of the Buddha himself. In virtually every dialogue attributed to the Buddha, he said: 'Learn to be content with little.' More specifically, he urged his followers to eat less and simpler food, wear more basic clothing and fewer ornaments and cosmetics and if possible eliminate them altogether, and to travel less.

The Buddha even taught that leading the moral life could be simplified. Being morally pure does not require hundreds of rules about what one may or may not do under given circumstances. Rules multiply beyond all control. But they can all be replaced by a single principle. Living a life of moral virtue, a life of Dharma, really involves following only one guideline for living: do not harm anyone anywhere. It takes no more than a few seconds to understand what that guideline means, but putting it into practice in every dimension of one's life at home and at work is the project of a lifetime. Our harm to others takes many forms, some obvious and some very subtle.

What Buddhists around the world, and especially in the West, desperately need is inspiration provided by members of the Noble Community who have mastered the art of living on very little and can show others not only that a simple life is possible but that it is far more attractive than the hideously entangled, cluttered, complicated, and deadly ways of living that most of us see around us every day. Unfortunately, however, there are not many good examples around for us to follow. Most of us must, therefore, learn to blaze our own trails back to simplicity.

Let me set out just one of many possible first steps that one might make towards the recovery of simplicity. Begin like this. Spend just one weekend, or even one day of the weekend, being very quiet. Turn off all the radios, televisions, stereos, computers, and other electrical tools and toys over which you have some measure of control. They are just unwanted distractions to a person who wishes to think clearly for a few hours. Unplug all the telephones and the answering machine. It is not really very important to hear from the outside world, and if anyone has anything really important to say, they will find other ways of getting through to you eventually. Turn off all the electric lights. The dark is not so terrifying, and there is nothing much to see anyway. After making all these preparations, spend a few hours just thinking about the way you live your life. Just think. Do not chant incantations. Do not sing hymns or songs. Do not pray. Do not burn candles or incense. Do not prostrate yourself. Do not do yoga. Do not read books. Do not putter in the garden or clean out the hall closet or vacuum-clean the living-room carpet. Do not do anything. Just think: why live like this? Is this really how any sensible person would choose to live?

After just thinking for a while it may be useful to walk around your living quarters and survey all the physical objects that have somehow managed to invade your dwelling as gifts, impulsive purchases, heirlooms, or by other mysterious methods. And it may be useful to review just a few pieces of information about the impact of the Western way of living on the environment. Libraries are filled with reference books on the subject. But if you do not have ready access to such information, you may begin with these few pieces of information:

A young fast-growing tree can recycle about forty-eight pounds of carbon dioxide per year. Carbon dioxide is the principal gas implicated in the so-called greenhouse effect, which is generally thought to be altering climatic conditions all around the planet.

Burning one gallon of gasoline produces twenty pounds of carbon dioxide.[61] Therefore, if one drives forty miles in a vehicle that consumes one gallon of gasoline per twenty miles, one is putting about as much carbon dioxide into the atmosphere as a young tree can recycle in a year.

A commercial airliner produces on the average half a pound of carbon dioxide per mile per passenger. Therefore, flying ninety-six miles as a passenger in a commercial aircraft produces about forty-eight pounds of carbon dioxide, the amount it takes a young tree to recycle in a year.

Even if one does not travel oneself but consumes goods that have been transported long distances by gasoline- or diesel-powered trucks or by kerosene-powered aircraft, one is indirectly responsible for contributing to the amount of carbon dioxide being produced in quantities greater than trees and other vegetation can convert back into oxygen.

Using one kilowatt-hour of electricity generated from the burning of coal produces two pounds of carbon dioxide. Therefore, using twenty-four kilowatt hours of coal-generated electricity will produce the amount of carbon dioxide it takes a tree to recycle in a year.[62]

The number of trees in the world is declining rapidly every year. People cut them down to make paper, to clear land for recreational purposes, to use as fuel, and to provide grazing land for cows that eventually end up being killed and eaten by human beings and other predatory animals. Owing to a decline in trees and a rising consumption of fossil fuels, the amount of carbon dioxide in the atmosphere is rising every year. It is suspected that this has the effect of trapping heat in the atmosphere, and therefore contributing to the warming of the planet. All the consequences of this so-called greenhouse effect are not fully known but are expected by virtually all scientists to be hazardous to most forms of life.

North Americans consume nearly ten times as much fossil fuel *per capita* as do the citizens of China, who in turn consume over twice as much *per capita* as the people of India.[63]

If you can manage to set aside just one weekend to look at your own dwelling and think about the implications of living as wastefully and as dangerously as most North Americans do, many of the ways of living more simply and less harmfully will become obvious. Becoming more simple in your life could begin with such things as buying fewer food products that have been transported from far away by ship, truck, train, or aeroplane; buying fewer unnecessary products of every sort, and buying those things that are necessary from nearby merchants in order to reduce or even eliminate transportation by artificially powered vehicles; reducing dependence on friends, relatives, and other forms of human company and thereby reducing the amount of travel that is done for purely social purposes; and depending less on technological stimulants, such as television, radio, cinema, recorded music, and video games, and rediscovering the joys of watching and caring for birds, squirrels, insects, worms, vegetation, rocks, and other forms of being. If you have already learned how to simplify your life by reducing your dependence on possessions and on other living beings, then perhaps you can spend some time trying to find ways to teach others to do the same.

Imitating the Buddha's example of utter simplicity in livelihood is by far the greatest service that any Buddhist can perform in these times. Compared to this, the activities of raising funds, building new temples, performing weddings, naming children, conducting funerals, chanting, lighting candles, burning incense, muttering mantras, droning dhāraṇīs, and gazing adoringly at gilt statues of Buddhas and Bodhisattvas are at the very best pointless, and at the worst quite counter-productive, for all these traditional activities are simply different forms of carrying around a burdensome raft that has performed its function but now serves only to impede our progress and obstruct our vision.

It is now time to say goodbye to the raft and to live as Buddhas.

12

PERILS OF A RAFT-DODGER

The essay entitled 'Farewell to the Raft' was written at a time when my interest in practising Buddhism as part of a community had reached a particularly low ebb. The following essay chronicles the resumption of my felt need for rafting with others.

AN EXPERIMENT

IN THE AUTUMN of 1988, I packed up my books and bought ten meditation cushions and moved from Toronto to Montreal. The books were for my new day job, teaching Buddhist studies at McGill University. The meditation cushions were for what I hoped would become a new kind of Buddhist centre in my new domicile. Having become disillusioned with the empire-building tendencies of the Zen group with which I had been affiliated in Toronto, I severed my formal ties with that group and gave thought to what kind of Buddhist practice I would take up in my new setting.

In a letter to a friend written in the summer of 1988 I outlined the central vision of what I hoped could be achieved and what could be avoided. On the positive side, the hope was to provide a place for quiet reflection in which participants would be encouraged to be particularly mindful of the environmental implications of their styles of living, their diets, and their modes of consumption. In addition to sitting meditation, there would be discussion groups in which people could exchange information about the environment and share their suggestions on how to live more simply, reduce waste, minimize the use of toxic products, and find alternatives to buying from large multinational corporations. On the negative side, the hope was to avoid any sense of group identity or any affiliation with a particular religious persuasion. While it was clear to me that my principal source of inspiration was the teachings of Buddhism, I hoped to create a setting in which people of all convictions, both religious and secular, would feel welcome. Because of this wish to avoid turning away anyone with a sincere desire to meditate and think about environmental issues, I planned the meditation room to be as sparsely furnished as possible. There would be no altars, no images, and no statues. During meditation we would burn no incense and ring no bells. There would be no chanting before or after meditation sessions. There would be no teacher or any other kind of leader. There would be no institution to maintain and therefore no officers to elect, no fees to collect, and no funds to raise. We would just meet regularly to sit quietly for two hours, each person doing whatever kind of meditative exercise seemed best suited for the needs of the moment.

When the plan was put into operation, the meditation room was almost as plain at I had originally planned. It contained no furnishings other than the ten meditation cushions. After much internal debate, I decided to put my small Buddha statue unobtrusively on the floor in a dark corner of the room, mostly because I could not think of any other room to keep it in. A simple poster was put up in the Faculty of Religious Studies at McGill University, announcing a weekly meditation group. Gradually people started attending the minimalist meditation sessions. During the first year, people came from all kinds of religious background. There was a former Theravādin monk, several Zen practitioners, an Anglican, a Muslim, a Jew, a former member of Subud, and several people with profound allergies to organized religion of any kind. A few came regularly; several came sporadically; most came once and never came back. In that respect, this group was not much different from denizens of the Zen temple from which I was a refugee.

For quite a while we conducted our sessions according to the original plan, but eventually one of the Zen people donated a small bell. Although I was initially resistant to even this tiny nod in the direction of Zen ritual, I eventually began using it, although I could not resist commenting that I really saw no point in signalling when meditation was to begin and end. After all, I explained, the whole idea is to make meditation a continuous process in one's life, rather than an event that begins and ends with a signal. My making an issue of the matter, predictably, led to disputes among the members of the group. The former Theravādin monk said he found the bell rather distracting and agreed with me that it was a bit silly to make an artificial distinction between meditation periods and the rest of daily life; the Zen people, on the other hand, liked the bell and said it helped them focus their concentration and reaffirm their resolve. Before long, the regular sitters were divided into factions over the issue of whether we should use the bell. Then, when people eventually tired of arguing about the bell, they began to argue about which forms of Buddhism were superior to which. I began to marvel at how harmonious we all were while sitting quietly together and how fractious we became as soon as the bell signalled the end of silent meditation and the beginning of the spontaneous informal free-for-all debate period that inevitably ensued. More than ever I became convinced that any ritual at all, even one as seemingly innocuous as ringing a bell, was inimical to the kinds of positive mental states that meditation is supposed to help cultivate.

REFLECTIONS ON THE EXPERIMENT

After three years, for a complex variety of reasons, I decided to stop holding these meditation sessions for a while and to reflect on the results of our little experiment in generic no-name-brand spirituality. Specifically, I began to rethink several of the issues that had been at the heart of my little manifesto entitled 'Farewell to the Raft'. As I thought about these matters, I realized that while wearing the sobriquet Mubul (No Buddha), I had managed to create a little island in which there was also no Dharma and no Sangha.

LAND OF NO DHARMA

Among the reasons I had decided against having Dharma talks or even readings from Buddhist texts as part of public meditation practice in my home, was that I did not wish to be perceived as a spiritual teacher or guide by anyone; I simply wished to be one of the meditators. A second was that I did not wish to alienate non-Buddhists by reading only Buddhist texts but did not wish to encourage too much spiritual eclecticism by reading texts from several different religious traditions. A third, and probably the strongest reason, was that I did not wish to read any text aloud to other people if it contained doctrines of which I was unconvinced, and my convictions about many key Buddhist doctrines were particularly weak in 1988 and 1989.

As a scholar and academic specializing in systematic Buddhist philosophy, I am in a particularly good position to observe how unsatisfactory the attempts have been to provide a sound rational foundation for the principal doctrines that have come to be canonical in most forms of Buddhism. If there is rational ground for the doctrines of karma and rebirth, I have not yet seen it. If there is any compelling reason not to be a materialist who believes that all mental processes require a highly organized central nervous system and that therefore a continuum of consciousness cannot continue after the death of the body that supports it, it has remained hidden from me. Despite their failure to provide convincing arguments, however, most Buddhists have traditionally seen materialism as an ideology that undermines the effects of Buddhist practice. Seen from a purely intellectual point of view, then, this raises the problem of whether it makes sense to follow a practice founded on a set of theories that one is not yet convinced are well founded. It would appear, then, that the theories of Buddhism must, to some degree at least, be accepted on faith rather than purely on reason. While reason may place some restraints on faith – for otherwise unrestrained faith becomes mere credulity or perhaps some kind of wishful thinking – it is also clear that if one were to rely on reason alone and refuse to entertain any doctrine for which no conclusive arguments could be provided, then one would have to be content to live within a rather cramped and pinched mentality.

My efforts to conduct a contemplative practice based mostly on the cultivation of *dhyāna*, with a bare minimum of doctrine and ritual, led to rather dry and unsatisfactory results; I did indeed begin to develop the cramped and pinched mentality predicted above. The change that was most obvious to me was a marked tendency to what I can only describe as intolerance and a hard-edged attitude towards others. For example, in order to reduce the amount of energy I was responsible for consuming, I stopped using heated water for personal use. This habit of taking cold showers during the early hours of Montreal's cold winter mornings had the psychological effect of making me much too conscious of my own virtue, with a corresponding disdain for the lack of virtue of others. In addition, I began to follow a strict diet made up mostly of raw grains and vegetables, the purpose being to avoid using animal products of any kind and to reduce the amount of energy used in cooking. This regimen almost completely eliminated pleasure from the act of refuelling my body, which increased my conviction that I was being terribly virtuous and a good planetary citizen. On the other hand, I also became aware of a subtle but persistent tendency to feel slightly contemptuous of people who ate more elaborate meals or who turned eating into an opportunity for social interaction with others instead of a mindful and solitary exercise in making nourishment available to one's own cells. Although not entirely lacking in affability, I became demanding of students and took a certain amount of pleasure in hearing that students had nicknamed me the Drill Sergeant. On one occasion a student came to me with a request that I consider giving her a higher mark, and I gave her such a scolding that she left my office in tears. Rather than feeling an impulse to comfort and encourage the worried student, I felt a mild scorn for her, as if her retreat into tears was a natural karmic result of her descent into moral laxity and psychological softness by pampering herself with too many warm showers and palatable meals.

Some people are capable of carrying firm discipline with much more grace than I was at that time, but the fact is that I was apparently not yet capable of such self-control without the side effect of an unpleasant tendency to feel disapproval for the behaviour of others. Fortunately, I knew enough about Buddhism to realize that this overly dry and rigid mentality was considered neither wholesome nor skilful and that in my zeal I had overshot the mark in aiming for the middle path. I was, after all, still the man who not long before had written in an essay on the religious politics of eating meat: 'Let us, in our eagerness to achieve justice through social reforms, be most cautious, lest the dictates of our own conscience result in condemning others to such a level of degradation that our attempts to establish justice end up making a mockery of justice.'[64] So, in hope of improving the condition of my mentality, I began to reintroduce various practices into my routine that I had earlier decided to reject. The most important of these was the cultivation of universal friendship (*mettā-bhāvanā*), which I soon discovered was much more powerful and transformative than I had previously recognized. In earlier days, I had tended to see *mettā-bhāvanā* mostly as an antidote to anger, which happened to be an internal enemy with which I had many a wrestling match. After anger had gradually subsided as a dominant trait in my mentality, however, I began to see that *mettā-bhāvanā* was much more than a mere antidote and was, in fact, the basis for cultivating a deeper understanding of the precepts and all the factors of the Eightfold Path. As *mettā* grows stronger, for example, the precepts cease to feel like rules or even guidelines and begin to emerge as a good description of how one behaves towards a friend; as one's feeling of friendship expands, the precepts are naturally a description of how one is inclined to act towards every being, whether human or non-human. Seen in this way, any given precept simply becomes a statement of fact about how friends are inclined to behave, rather than a rule for which rational justification must be provided.

This principle became especially clear to me one day when I had dinner with a friend who teaches ethics in a philosophy department. Noting that I ordered vegetarian food, he asked whether I was a vegetarian by choice or because of doctor's orders or because I happened not to like the taste of meat. When I answered that a vegetarian diet was something that I followed by conviction, my friend then demanded to know what my reasoning was for choosing not to eat animal products. I took the bait and provided a few reasons, all of which he found unconvincing. Finally I told him that I simply did not feel like eating the flesh of beings for whom I felt friendship and would therefore no sooner eat a cow or fish or bird than I would eat a human friend who taught ethics. He nodded and sat in silence for some time and then changed the subject. Regardless of whether my philosophical friend was convinced, I realized that for me ethical questions had ceased to be riddles to be solved through intellectual debate and had become matters that were spontaneously clarified through feeling positively towards sentient beings; the positive feelings themselves arose not from thinking things through but by imagining myself in the place of others and imagining how various actions might feel to them. Thinking about imagination in this way led me to think again about ritual and community.

LAND OF NO SANGHA

Although I had personally found it helpful to do such rituals as *pūjās*, prostrations, making offerings of incense and flowers, and chanting, when I first moved to Montreal I decided against including rituals as part of the public meditation sessions in my home. The reason I gave was that I feared that rituals might generate a mood of exclusiveness and particularity. By doing a given set of rituals in a certain way, I thought, our meditation group would come to see itself as different from people who did other rituals or who did similar rituals but in a different way. What I discovered by eliminating rituals altogether was that our meditation group had almost no sense of community. We were merely a collection of individuals who met once a week to meditate, each in our own way and for our own reasons. Although a few good friendships developed between some the members of the group, there was not enough sense of communal friendship or of shared commitment to enable us to cohere as a community. As time went on, I discovered that this lack of feeling that I was part of a community left me feeling rather empty and unfulfilled, as if some vital nutrient were missing from my diet.

In 'Farewell to the Raft' I discussed the artificial bond among people that can be produced by a ritual. I still believe it is often the case that ritual forms artificial bonds among people, by which I mean that it may create a rapport among people who have almost nothing in common except that they happen to perform the ritual. Speaking of artificial bonds, however, suggests that there may be such a thing as real bonds to which the artificial ones stand in contrast. An example of a real bond, I would suggest, is that of friendship based upon a shared commitment to the pursuit of a goal. Within Buddhism, for example, friendships are often formed around the nucleus of a shared commitment to the Buddha, the Dharma, and the Sangha. The Three Jewels, however, are for most people rather abstract ideals. While every Buddhist realizes, or at least knows intellectually, that the Three Jewels are associated with wisdom and compassion in some way, wisdom and compassion are themselves too abstract for most people to grasp very well. Usually what is needed is something more concrete and particular on which one can focus the mind.

A ritual, even if it is based on an abstract ideal, is necessarily concrete; it consists in a prescribed set of words that must be recited in a particular way, and a set of actions that are to be performed in a pre-established manner and order. Much of the point of a ritual is to be concrete and particular but to be so in a way that simultaneously disciplines the body, voice, and mind and provides an occasion for certain emotions to arise. Doing a prostration, for example, usually involves lowering the head or the entire body to the ground in a particular way while focusing the mind on a visible or imaginary object. Doing the action properly disciplines the body and mind; if the prostration ceremony also involves reciting a formula, it also disciplines the voice. There is, however, something more that usually occurs. The lowering of the head and body puts the physical side of oneself in a humble position. Since emotional states are in a complex state of interdependence with the physical body, a humbled body usually produces a more humbled mentality. A humble mentality, provided that it does not resent the fact of humility too much, generally becomes more open and receptive. The urge to speak and dominate gives way to a greater willingness to listen and be given guidance, and perhaps even to acknowledge that there may be someone higher, more accomplished, and more authoritative than what one can muster purely from within oneself.

My thoughts on this topic became a little more clear in 1992, when I was invited to a multidisciplinary academic conference at the East-West Center in Honolulu. The conference was on the theme of the self and self-deception, and I was invited to talk about Buddhist notions of self-deception. This was quite a new area for me, so I felt a need to read what others had said before trying to write anything on it myself. As I was reading what various people had written about weakness of will and self-deception, I noted that most people wrote of self-deception as something to be avoided. I began to wonder whether there might be areas in life in which some degree of self-deception might actually be positive, something that accelerates one's progress along a chosen path. As I thought about this, it seemed to me that some rituals can be seen as a kind of play-acting, a sort of make-believe in which one pretends to do such things as giving something to a Buddha, or offering one's merit to the benefit of others. Even pretending to do such things may very well help one develop the habits of thinking that make it possible eventually to do very real acts of charity and benefit. By doing a ritualized act of kindness again and again, one might unconsciously become more kind-hearted. I decided to write my paper for the conference on this topic and to flesh out some of the ways in which ritual could be seen as healthy-minded self-deception, a sort of voluntary participation in actions that one knows to be in some sense unreal or pretended.[65]

It often happens that as I am thinking about some issue, I discover that someone else has had the same ideas but has stated them much more clearly than I have been able to do. After I had attended the conference in Honolulu, help in thinking about the relationship between reason, ritual, and the imagination appeared one day as I was studying a Sanskrit text with a graduate student. He was writing a thesis on the place of yogic experience in the theory of knowledge of the seventh-century philosopher Dharmakīrti.[66] We came upon a passage in which Dharmakīrti states that any imagined thing becomes indistinguishable from a reality when the act of imagining is repeated again and again. The philosopher gives the example of a man who is separated from the woman he loves. He imagines his lover's face and body so often and so fervidly that he feels as if she is present with him. He speaks his thoughts to her as if she were there, he believes he hears her voice and smells her perfume, and he may even become sexually aroused. All these emotional and even physical responses occur despite the fact that the apparent cause is only an imagined being, and not someone who is actually present. Another example that Dharmakīrti gives is of a man who is apprehensive about being robbed by thieves. In the night he hears the creaking of trees and twigs falling upon his roof, and he imagines that these sounds are caused by a thief breaking into his house. Lying in his bed and imagining a thief, the home-owner becomes filled with panic; his heart races, and he breaks into a sweat. He interprets the play of light coming through a window as having the form of a man; he becomes convinced that he now sees the thief whom he had originally heard. He is sure that the thief is in the very room with him. He screams in terror. The 'thief', although just a figment of the imagination, begins to have the emotional effects of an actual thief. In an extreme case, the home-owner might even die of fright. At this point, the distinction between the real and the imagined is obliterated.

A yogin who takes up a subject of meditation, says Dharmakīrti, is acting in principle very much like the lover or the phobic home-owner; he repeatedly imagines a Buddha or a Bodhisattva, or even some abstraction such as friendship or impermanence or emptiness, with increasingly ardent conviction until he makes it real. Making something real is the literal meaning of the term *bhāvanā*. The yogin's experience in meditation is like the man's experience of his lover in that both experiences are generated by repetitious acts of imagining something that is, initially at least, not actual. The difference between the religious experience of the yogin and the erotic fantasies of the man in love is that the yogin's experiences gradually bring about a habitual flow of positive mental states and eventually result in an overall improvement of character. By using his fantasies to cultivate feelings of friendship, or the virtues associated with a Bodhisattva, for example, the meditator eventually begins to act spontaneously and unaffectedly as a friend or as a Bodhisattva. Without consciously thinking of the precepts and applying them to his decisions about how to act, the meditator simply begins to behave as if following the precepts were foremost in his mind. His friendship towards all sentient beings, which began as an exercise in the imagination, becomes a reality.

To someone with the mentality of a rational sceptic, Dharmakīrti's account of yogic experience is satisfactory in that it still allows one to regard many of the objects of religious devotion as unproved by the strict canons of epistemology. Many doctrines that shape spiritual practice may still be seen as ultimately insupportable dogmas for which no convincing arguments can be found. By regarding much of religion as a realm of make-believe, the sceptic can retain his sense of intellectual integrity. On the other hand, by realizing that make-believe does have the power to make one believe – and that some beliefs, even if dubious or outright false, do have the power to bring about positive transformations in one's character – the sceptic can, without fear of having compromised his rationality, enter into the realm of fantasy via the imagination and explore the consequences. Fantasies that have positive after-effects can be retained and explored more deeply; those that have negative after-effects can be set aside for the time being, perhaps to be left for others to explore with greater benefit.

Thinking about religious doctrine and practice as a kind of fantasy or make-believe had the effect of opening me up to a large body of Buddhist literature and practice that I had previously found uninteresting and unhelpful. It also had the effect of making me much more comfortable about speaking about things in ways very similar to how Buddhists have spoken about things for many centuries. Finally, it had the effect of making me feel more fully alive, as if I were making use of more of my potential than I had before. Part of feeling more alive was to feel more joy in sharing life with others who also felt alive. In short, a sense of community began to stir within me again.

As has been said earlier, the Sangha to which Buddhists go for refuge comprises only the so-called Noble Community, which consists of Stream Entrants up to Arhants; in Mahāyāna Buddhism, the third refuge also consists of those Bodhisattvas who, like Stream Entrants, have so consolidated their positive mentalities that they have no inclination ever to abandon the dharmic path. Those who practise Buddhism but have not yet attained to a state from which they cannot fall back into worldliness are normally called not a Sangha but a *pariṣad* (assembly or group). It could be said that one of the principal purposes of a *pariṣad* is to act as much like a Sangha as possible. It is, it could be said, a make-believe Sangha. This make-believe is done not only for the benefit of the individuals who belong to the *pariṣad*, but also for the general welfare of humanity. The individual members benefit by acting, as much as possible, as if they were Stream Entrants or higher, by consciously modelling their conduct on that of members of the Noble Community. By constantly repeating this make-believe, they eventually make the virtues associated with members of the Noble Community real within themselves. Society as a whole benefits by having a well-behaved *pariṣad* within itself as a source of inspiration and as a model for how all of society could conduct itself.

The make-believe in which the *pariṣad* engages takes many forms. Devotional services (*pūjā*), for example, consist in making offerings, often imaginary ones, to the Buddhas and Bodhisattvas, as if they were actually present to receive the gifts. In this way, the worshipper develops the habit of giving. Even though the giving is imaginary, it is practice for giving in the real world, in much the same way that an athletic scrimmage is a mock contest in which the participants hone the skills they will use in a real match. The make-believe involved in rituals may also be seen as similar to the rehearsal for a drama, in which the actors play their parts as if they were performing before a live audience, and in the process they learn to play their roles convincingly. The members of a *pariṣad* might also sit in group meditation, thus acting as if they are mentally collected and fully mindful; by so acting, they may eventually develop those characteristics in reality. By acting in this way collectively, the *pariṣad* may eventually come to make real the collective virtues of a genuine Sangha.

BACK TO REAL COMMUNITY

All of these reflections on ritual and community remained mostly at an abstract and theoretical level until the summer of 1994. By then I had spent six years without any formal connection to a Buddhist community. My wife and I had kept up a consistent meditation practice but had done so entirely on our own for more than a year. It had been a difficult year. My mother had died in 1993 after a two-year illness. My daughter and I had become alienated and were no longer communicating with each other. It felt as though I had too much work to do, and the stress of overwork and pressure that is so common in the modern workplace, including the workplace that some mistakenly call the ivory tower, was beginning to feel overwhelming. Fortunately, in the summer of 1994 I had a sabbatical leave coming up and was determined to spend at least some of that time trying to find a Buddhist community with which I might feel at home. There were several retreat centres I wanted to explore and several people I wanted to meet and old friends with whom I hoped to re-establish contact.

The first retreat facility I made contact with was Aryaloka Buddhist Retreat Center in New Hampshire. I had been there once before for a short visit in 1987 with my old friend, Alan Sponberg, to visit Manjuvajra, whom we had both met at a conference on Buddhism in North America at the Zen Buddhist Temple of Ann Arbor in July 1987. Aryaloka had made a good impression on me, and I had always hoped to find the opportunity to go there for a retreat. As it turned out, in the summer of 1994 there was a one-week study and meditation retreat on the theme of Sangharakshita's book *Wisdom Beyond Words*, and to make it all the more attractive, the study was being led by Alan Sponberg, who had recently been ordained into the Western Buddhist Order as Sāramati. While I expected the retreat to be interesting, I had not anticipated what an impact it would have on me, nor had I realized how ripe I was for positive changes in direction.

During the retreat, Sāramati gave a fascinating set of talks on Perfection of Wisdom and on Yogācāra philosophy. To keep the philosophical discussions grounded, there was a long *pūjā* every evening, and during the week our collective project was to use our imaginations to create a pure land in the shrine-room, specifically the land Abhirati associated with the Buddha Akṣobhya. Participants were also encouraged to make drawings, write poetry, compose music, or find some other creative outlet for their experiences of the material to be studied, and these creations were given as offerings during the *pūjās*. During my life I had done plenty of study and *pūjās* and meditation, but never had I seen these approaches combined with such skill and good taste to produce a strongly positive environment in which intellect, emotion, and imagination were all put into a dynamically healthy balance. I drank it all in like a thirsty desert traveller who had stumbled alone into an oasis and found not only refreshing water but also a caravan of good friends to continue journeying with. After six years of travelling alone, or at least without a strong sense of community, it was time to begin rediscovering the joys of being part of an extended network of *kalyāṇa-mitratā* (spiritual friendship).

OF TIGHTROPES, OF CARTS, AND AGAIN OF RAFTS

An image that often comes to mind in thinking about following the middle path is that of a person walking a tightrope. A tightrope walker maintains his overall balance by leaning now to the left and now to the right. He is constantly moving, for his balance is dynamic rather than static. At any moment one might take a snapshot of him walking across the tightrope. The chances are good that the shutter would click at a time when the tightrope walker seemed to be leaning too far in one direction or the other, and one might well think from looking at the snapshot that the person of whom it was taken was just about to fall. Similarly as one follows the Middle Path of Buddhism, one might sometimes need to move more to the left or more to the right in order to compensate for conditions that threaten to throw one more permanently off balance and perhaps off the path altogether. If one looks at just one small segment of a practitioner's life, it may seem that he is doing too much sitting meditation and not enough study, or too much study and not enough devotional practice. If, however, one looks at the practitioner's course for a longer period of time, one may see that over the longer course the person has somehow managed to steer a good middle way.

As I look back at much of what I wrote in the 1980s, I am inclined to see the constant appeal to reason in those essays as a needed compensation for the circumstances in which I was then practising, in which not enough encouragement was being given by people around me to careful thinking and systematic study. After leaving that context, I found myself in an atmosphere rich in study but relatively impoverished in such positive emotions as friendship and hope. It took time to discover that more was necessary than rigorous logic and severe self-discipline. By trying to pare Buddhist practice down to little more than *dhyāna* and rational scepticism, I managed to rediscover what has been obvious to most other Buddhists all along, namely, that something more than that is, if not absolutely necessary, then at least very beneficial and expedient.

It is possible to reduce the total weight of a cart by removing all the wheels, but this does not make the cart easier to pull. Similarly, one can reduce the bulk of the burden of the mind by removing all fantasies, unwarranted beliefs, and half-thought ideas, but this does not necessarily accelerate the process of becoming disencumbered of ignorance and confusion. On the contrary, by using fantasy creatively and imaginatively, I found, one may actually speed up the process. The process of liberating the mind from its own fetters is long and complex – far too complex for anyone to understand. Indeed, misunderstanding is far more probable than accurate understanding of the workings of the mind. Taking on the task of improving one's character so that one can become a gift fit to give to others is bound to lead to countless surprises along the way and innumerable muddles and missteps. One is navigating waters for which even the best charts are hopelessly crude. One must begin with a very sturdy raft, and with a willingness to make plenty of unpredicted repairs en route.

NOTES

1 *Sallekhasutta*, in Horner, p.54.
2 *Sutta Nipāta* 796–800. Author's translation.
3 *Dhammapada* xii.9. Cleary, p.56.
4 *Dhammapada* xv.1–3, Cleary, pp.69–70.
5 *Dhammapada* xviii.18–19, Cleary, p.83.
6 From an essay called 'Idea for a Universal History from a Cosmopolitan Point of View' in Kant, p.23.
7 Throughout these essays, I have used the pinyin system of transliterating Chinese names. Those who are not familiar with the pinyin conventions may be more familiar with the Daoist sages Lao-tzu and Chuang-tzu.
8 A good discussion of the Socratic notion of virtue and the development of that notion by Plato and Aristotle occurs in Copleston. My discussion here owes much to his observations on pp.125–134.
9 Hegel, p.125.
10 All the statistics cited here are to be found in *The Canadian World Almanac and Book of Facts: 1987*. Population statistics pp.199–200 and pp.242–3; energy consumption statistics pp.327–31.
11 See bibliography. On the title page of this work, the title 'Rimpoche' is spelled 'Rinbochay' in conformity with conventions followed at the University of Virginia.
12 Strictly speaking, a community of Buddhist practitioners is called a *pariṣad* (assembly), and the word 'sangha' is reserved for those who have attained to the state of Stream-entry or higher. In Western usage, however, it has become common to call almost any collection of Buddhist practitioners a sangha; such usage has the regrettable effect of devaluing the term.
13 See bibliography.
14 The translation is my own.

15 This passage is adapted from a selection from Chang, pp.391–2. I have made a few minor adjustments to this translation in accordance with what I think is a better interpretation of the technical terms.

16 See bibliography.

17 Walshe, p.93.

18 *Sutta-nipāta* i.7.22–4.

19 In saying that Buddhists reject revelation, what I am claiming is that Buddhists do not traditionally regard revelation as a source of knowledge that supersedes direct experience or reason. Whereas for conservative Christians and some Hindus revelation takes precedence over reason in case of a conflict between the two, Buddhists have generally insisted that experience and logical consistency take precedence over revelation. So if a supposedly revealed text were illogical or contradicted by experience, the text would have to be discarded or at least interpreted in such a way as to remove the contradiction.

20 I have taken liberties here with two quotations in different contexts. The first quotation is from the *Vinaya-piṭaka, Cullavagga* 10.1.6, where the Buddha tells Ānanda that the good doctrine (*saddhamma*) will last for only five hundred years, half as long as it would have lasted had women not received permission to enter into the homeless state. The second is from Vasubandhu's *Abhidharmakośa* 8.39, where it is said that the good doctrine (*saddharma*) is twofold, since it consists of (1) the transmitted tradition (*āgama*) of the teacher's words, and (2) the understanding (*adhigama*) of what those words mean. The words, say this text, are bound to last much longer than the understanding. It was Vasubandhu's claim that by his time, about a thousand years after the Buddha, only the words remained and that no one, including himself, could really be certain what wisdom the verbal teachings were meant to convey.

21 Some Buddhists use the word 'transcendental' to translate the Sanskrit *lokottara*, which traditionally refers to mental states in which the focus of attention is on the path of practice and its goal of nirvāṇa. These goals are seen as superior (*uttara*) to the goals of the general populace (*loka*). Needless to say, I am not suggesting that one should not focus on the *lokottara* path; on the contrary, focusing on that path is what makes one superhuman, superior (*uttara*) to the ordinarily human (*loka*). But the English word 'transcendental' also means 'beyond or contrary to common sense or experience'. If the Dharma were transcendental in this sense, it would not be described as something that everyone can come and see (*ehipassiko*) for oneself.

22 *Mahāparinibbāna Sutta, Dīgha-Nikāya*, ii.26. Maurice Walshe translates the passage in question as follows: 'Therefore, Ānanda, you should live as islands unto yourselves, being your own refuge, with no one else as your refuge, with the Dhamma as an island, with the Dhamma as your refuge, with no other refuge. And how does a monk live as an island unto himself,… with no other refuge? Here, Ānanda, a monk abides

contemplating the body as body, earnestly, clearly aware, mindful and having put away all hankering and fretting for the world, and likewise with regard to feelings, mind and mind-objects. That, Ānanda, is how a monk lives as an island unto himself,... with no other refuge.' Walshe, p.245.

23 Here I use the term 'transcendent' in the usual sense of that which lies outside the universe, as some Christians would say of God and as some Buddhists would say of Brahman. In views such as this, God existed before the universe and so must have been outside it. The words attributed to God as author of creation are, in these systems, believed to have a special authority over that of any human being, since they deal with matters that no human being could know were it not for divine revelation. It is revelation from a transcendent source in this sense that Buddhists have traditionally denied.

24 Hardon, pp.296–7.

25 Calvin, i.104.

26 *Ibid.*, i.42.

27 See Richard P. Hayes, 'The question of doctrinalism in the Buddhist epistemologists', *Journal of the American Academy of Religion* 52 (1984), 645–70; and 'Principled atheism in Indian Buddhism', *Journal of Indian Philosophy* 16 (1988), 5–28.

28 *Vatthūpamasutta*, in Horner, p.47.

29 The full commentary on all these points is found in Buddhaghosa, pp.246–52.

30 See, for example, the *Cakkavatti-Sīhanāda Sutta* and *Aggañña Sutta*, discourses 26 and 27 in Walshe, pp.395–415.

31 Walshe, pp.69–73.

32 Hofstadter, p.109.

33 Zen Center, *Daily Chants*, p.12.

34 Kennett, p.284.

35 Suzuki, p.270.

36 Conze, *Buddhist Thought in India*, p.265.

37 Conze, 'Contradictions in Buddhist Thought', p.45.

38 French, p.116.

39 See bibliography.

40 *Sigālakasutta*, in Walshe, p.464.

41 Nietzsche, p.57.

42 See bibliography, under Livingstone.

43 Genesis 3:16–19.

44 Matthew 5:21–22.

45 Matthew 5:19.

46 Romans 5:17–20.

47 Romans 7:1–6.

48 Romans 2:15.

49 A good discussion of the theological and the cardinal virtues as discussed by St Thomas Aquinas occurs in Glenn, pp.187–297. A shorter

but also good discussion occurs in Hardon, pp.193–4.

50 *The Canadian World Almanac and Book of Facts: 1987*, p.418. The population of North America, including Central America and the West Indies, is around 400 millions, of which 143.9 millions are Roman Catholic, 113.7 millions are Protestant, 5.3 millions are Eastern Orthodox. The number of Jews is 7.6 millions, and the Muslims number 1.8 millions. 350,000 people (less than one-tenth of one per cent) claim to be Buddhists.

51 Woodward, p.130.

52 *Sigālakasutta*, in Walshe, p.462.

53 *Aggañña Sutta*, in Walshe, pp.407–16.

54 Romans 7:15–19.

55 Walshe, p.93.

56 *Alagaddūpamasutta*, in Horner, p.173.

57 The formula in Pāli is better known. It is almost the same, except that '*saraṇa*' replaces '*śaraṇa*' and '*dhamma*' replaces '*dharma*'.

58 Eventually, after a number of people had gone for refuge to the Buddha and the Dharma, and after they had realized the goal set out in the Buddha's teaching, there was also a Sangha. This became the third refuge to which new Buddhists went.

59 Walshe, pp.133–41.

60 *Sutta Nipāta* 300–8, trans. Saddhatissa.

61 This figure may sound surprising, given that a gallon of gasoline weighs less than that in the first place. Gasoline is made up mostly of carbon and hydogen, both of which have atomic weights less than oxygen. When gasoline combusts, it is combined with oxygen, producing a quantity of carbon dioxide gas that weighs more than the original fuel.

62 Lighting two 100-watt electric bulbs for six hours and having a small television set on for two hours each day for a month would consume about 24 kilowatt-hours. Using electricity generated by nuclear power reactors or by hydroelectric dams does not produce carbon dioxide; but both of these ways of generating electricity damages the environment in other ways. Even using small batteries of the kind that power most cameras, pocket calculators, and quartz watches has been shown to contribute deadly toxins to the soil when they are discarded. There is no way of using electrical power that does not carry potentially serious environmental risks.

63 All these facts were featured in an article that I picked at random from a stack of magazines on my desk. The source of these particular morsels is James R. Udall, 'Climate Shock', *Sierra* (July–August 1989), pp.26–40. Food for similar thoughts is available in virtually every issue of *Sierra*, *Greenpeace*, and similar environmentalist magazines.

64 See above, Chapter 5.

65 See Richard P. Hayes, 'Ritual, Self-Deception and Make-Believe: A Classical Buddhist Perspective' in Ames and Dissanayake, pp.349–63.

66 Raynald Prévèreau, 'Dharmakīrti's account of yogic intuition as a source of knowledge', M.A. thesis, McGill University, 1994.

BIBLIOGRAPHY

The following translations and studies of the Buddhist Vinaya texts are useful for anyone wishing to learn more of this area of traditional Buddhist doctrine and practice.

Rhys Davids, T.W. and Oldenberg, Hermann, *Vinaya Texts* (Sacred Books of the East vols. 13, 17, 20), Oxford University Press, 1885, reprinted by Motilal Banarsidass, Delhi 1982. This is a goldmine of information on not only the Vinaya rules themselves, but also how and why they were formed. It contains an extensive history of the early Sangha from the time of the Buddha's first disciples through the early years after his death.

Holt, John Clifford, *Discipline: The Canonical Buddhism of the Vinayapitaka*, Motilal Banarsidass, Delhi 1981. This contains a study of the central role played by the Vinaya in the monastic life of Theravādin Buddhism.

Prebish, Charles S., *Buddhist Monastic Discipline*, Pennsylvania State University Press, University Park and London 1975. This contains a valuable comparative study of two of the major non-Theravādin Vinaya traditions that were in use in India. The Vinaya texts themselves are translated on facing pages for easy comparison, and there is an appendix that shows which rules occur and which do not in each of the four Indian Vinaya collections.

OTHER BOOKS CITED

Roger T. Ames and Wimal Dissanayake (eds.), *Self and Deception: A Cross-Cultural Philosophical Inquiry*, State University of New York Press, Albany 1996.

Aristotle, 'Nicomachean Ethics', book 8, in *The Basic Works of Aristotle*, ed. and introd. Richard McKeon, Random House, New York 1941.

Biblical quotations are taken from *The Jerusalem Bible*, Reader's edition, Doubleday, New York 1966.

Buddhaghosa, *The Path of Purity: Being a translation of the Visuddhimagga*, Pe Maung Tin (trans.), Pali Text Society, London 1975.

Calvin, John, *Institutes of the Christian Religion*, Henry Beveridge (trans.), Wm.B. Eerdmans, Grand Rapids, Michigan 1983.

The Canadian World Almanac and Book of Facts: 1987, Global, Toronto 1986.

Garma C.C. Chang (ed.), 'The Sūtra of Assembled Treasures' in *A Treasury of Mahāyāna Sūtras: Selections from the Mahāratnakūṭa Sūtra*, Buddhist Association of the United States (trans.), Pennsylvania State University Press, University Park and London 1983.

Cleary, Thomas (trans.), *Dhammapada: Sayings of Buddha*, Bantam, New York 1995.

Conze, Edward, *Buddhist Thought in India: three phases of Buddhist philosophy*, University of Michigan Press, Ann Arbor 1967.

Conze, Edward, 'Contradictions in Buddhist thought', in *Indianisme et bouddhisme: mélanges offerts à Mgr Etienne Lamotte*, Université Catholique de Louvain, Louvain-la-Neuve 1980.

Copleston, Frederick, SJ, *A History of Philosophy* vol.1: Greece and Rome, part 1, Image, New York 1962.

Foucault, Michel, *Discipline and Punish: The Birth of the Prison*, Vintage, New York 1979.

French, Marilyn, *Beyond Power: On Women, Men, and Morals*, Ballantine, New York 1985.

Glenn, Paul J., *A Tour of the Summa*, Tan Books, Rockford, Illinois 1978.

Hardon, John A., SJ, *The Catholic Catechism: A Contemporary Catechism of the Teachings of the Catholic Church*, Doubleday, New York 1975.

Hegel, G.W.F., *The Phenomenology of Mind*, J.B. Baillie (trans.), Harper Torchbooks, New York 1967.

Hofstadter, Douglas, *Metamagical Themas: Questing for the Essence of Mind and Pattern*, Basic, New York 1985.

Horner, I.B. (trans.), *The Collection of Middle Length Sayings (Majjhima-Nikāya)*, vol.i, Pali Text Society, London 1976.

Kant, Immanuel, *On History*, Lewis Beck White (trans., ed., introd.), Bobbs-Merrill, Indianapolis 1963.

Kennett, Rōshi Jiyu, *Zen is Eternal Life*, Dharma, Emeryville, CA 1976.

Lati Rimpoche, *Mind in Tibetan Buddhism*, Elizabeth Napper (trans., ed., introd.), Snow Lion, New York 1980.

Livingstone, Elizabeth A. (ed.), *The Concise Oxford Dictionary of the Christian Church*, Oxford University Press, Oxford 1977.

Nietzsche, Friedrich, *Thus Spoke Zarathustra: a Book for All and None*, Walter Kaufmann (trans. and pref.), Viking, New York 1954.

Saddhatissa, H. (trans.), *Sutta Nipāta*, Curzon, London 1985.

Sangharakshita, *Ambedkar and Buddhism*, Windhorse, Glasgow 1986.

Suzuki, Daisetz Teitaro, *Essays in Zen Buddhism: Third Series*, Rider, London 1985.

Walshe, Maurice (trans.), *Thus Have I Heard: The Long Discourses of the Buddha, (Dīgha-Nikāya)*, Wisdom, London 1987.
Woodward, F.L. (trans.), *Minor Anthologies of the Pali Canon*, Pali Text Society, London 1948, part 2.
Zen Center, *Daily Chants: including meal chants, repentance and precepts*, Zen Center, Rochester 1975.

INDEX

A

abbey 150
abbot 150
abhidharma 169
Abhidharmakośa 264
Abhirati 260
Adam and Eve 192
advertising 158
Aggañña Sutta 265, 266
agitation 217
Ajātasattu 112
Akṣobhya 260
akuśala-dharma 169
Alagaddūpamasutta 266
Alexander the Great 127
alternative press 158
Ambaṭṭha Sutta 115, 118
Ambedkar, Dr B.R. 97
Ānanda 107, 264
Aṅgaka 117
anger 20, 123, 253
animal sacrifice 102, 231
Aquinas, St Thomas 142
Aristotle 41, 86, 167, 186, 198, 263
ariya-saṁgha 217
arrogance 21
arūparāga 216
Aryaloka Retreat Center 1, 260
Aśoka 102, 128
atheism 134
attachment 199
Augustine, St 142, 196
authority, spiritual 85
avijjā 217
ayoniso manasikāra 156

B

Bacon, F. 35
Beat Generation 168
belief 234
Beloit College 14
Benedetta, Sister 125
Bhagavad Gītā 145
bhikṣu 151
birth 121
bodhicitta 95
Bodhidharma 161, 166, 170
Bodhisattva 94, 139
Brahmajāla Sutta 156
brahmans 113, 115, 116, 118, 121, 174, 234
  priests 102
brahma-vihāras
  see immeasurables, four
Buddha 34
Buddhaghosa 146, 214, 215

Buddhism 33, 37, 119, 145, 229
  advertising 158
  definition 147ff
  feminist views of 168
  values 50
Buddhist Church of America 151

C
Cakkavatti-Sīhanāda Sutta 265
Calvin, J. 85, 86, 143
carbon dioxide 245
Carver, G.W. 98
caste system 98, 99
Chaudhary, D. 97
Chögyam Trungpa 159
Christ 126, 193, 194, 228
Christianity 37, 43, 44, 125ff, 189, 194, 195, 197, 228
Chuang-tzu *see* Zhuangzi
church (the term) 151
Cicero 142
Club Med 161
companionship 181, 187
  see also friendship
competitiveness 216
conceit 216
consumerism 243
Conze, E. 166
cow 103
craving 215
creation 135, 265
criticism 206
CSICOP 157
Cullavagga 264
Cynics 17

D
death 31
democracy 206
Descartes, R. 153
desire 215
Devdas, Prof. N. 23
Dhammapada 124
dhāraṇīs 139
Dharma 34, 214
  definition, Buddhist 146
  definition, Hindu 146
devil *see* Satan
Dharma-centric 33ff
Dharmakīrti 165, 173, 257
Dharmottara 165
dhyāna ācārya 91
Diderot, D. 153
Dignāga 165, 169ff, 173
divine grace 196
doubt 215
drugs 19

E
education 43
effort 236
electricity 245, 266
energy 245, 266, *see also* fuel
environment 266
Erasmus 85
ethics 107, 116, 201,
  see also morality, virtue
etymology 150
excitement 217

F
faith 252
fantasy 258
feminism 168
fetters *see saṁyojanas*
Flower Ornament Scripture 139
Foucault, M. 209
Franklin, B. 98
French, M. 168
Freud, S. 143
friendship 179, 186, 206
fuel 53, *see also* energy

G
Gandhi, M.K. 98
gasoline 245, 266
gender differences 200
generalization 171

God 42, 129, 134ff, 142, 192, 195ff, 201, 265
of Israel 127
philosopher's 35
going for refuge 213, 217
groups 218ff
gullibility 51
guru 89, *see also* teacher

H
habit 171
Hebrew tradition 42
Hegel, G.W.F. 52
hierarchy, spiritual 86, 90
Hinduism 102
Hiroshima 26
Hobbes, T. 61
Hofstadter, D.R. 157, 160
Holy Spirit 130
hope 196
humility 236, 256

I
ideas 177
ignorance 217
imagination 80, 177, 257
immeasurables, four 95
impatience 70
inducements, four 95
injustice 47
inspiration 175
Islam 228

J
Jaimini 146
jāti 121
Jefferson, T. 32, 35
Jeffersonian democracy 43
Jews 126
Jīvaka 112
Judaism 195
justice 46, 98, 138, 196

K
kālī-yuga 153
kāmacchanda 215
Kamalaśīla 165
Kaṇha 115, 116
Kaṇhāyanas 115
Kant, I. 32
Kapleau, P. 165
karma 61ff, 76
Karuna Trust 101
Kāśyapa 94
Katsura, Dr S. 24
kindness 25, *see also* love
King, Martin Luther 98
Kṛṣṇa 115
Kūṭadanta Sutta 232
Kutarka 170
Kwan Um Zen School 159

L
lama 89
language 141ff, 223ff
Laozi 41
Lati Rimpoche 73
Laṅkāvatāra Sūtra 104ff, 109
Lincoln, A. 98
Lobsang Gyaltsen 74
Locke, J. 35, 153
logic 166
lokottara 264
Lord of the Rings 80
love 23, 186, 195, *see also* kindness, *mettā*
loyalty 237
Luther, M. 85

M
magic 156
Mahāparinibbāna Sutta 264
Mahāvagga 90
Mahāvijita 232
Maitreya 238
malevolence 216
māna 216
Manjuvajra 260

Manorhita 165
mappō 153
Māra 132
Marx, K. 143
Marxism 57
mass media 46
Mātaṅga 122
meat-eating 104ff, 110
meditation 23, 54, 66, 250, 257
see also mettā-bhāvanā, zazen
meditation, therapeutic 92
mental states 169
merit, transfer of 65ff
messiah 126
mettā 198, *see also* love
mettā-bhāvanā 23, 67, 253
Middle Path 131, 261
Mīmāṁsā Sūtras 146
Mind in Tibetan Buddhism 74
moderation 48, 196
monastery 88
Monier-Williams 145
monk 131, 151
morality 45, 143, 188ff, 197ff, 201, *see also* ethics, virtue
moral integrity 214
moral relativism 189
motivation 67
Mubul 7, 251
Muhammad 228
Muslims 228

N
Nāgārjuna 165
names 150
Nehru, J. 99
New Age thought 21
Newton 35
Nietzsche, F. 131, 133, 187
nirvāṇa 264
non-dualism 203

O
obedience 85, 238
occult 156
Okkāka 115, 234
open-mindedness 51
openness 170
Order of Buddhist Contemplatives 150, 165
Ottawa 19

P
pāpa 148
Parable of the Water Snake 210
pariṣad 84, 259, 263
partiality 199
Pascal, B. 79
Pathways 155, 159
patience 47, 196
Paul, St 127, 182, 194, 207
philosophy 149
Hellenistic 127
philosophical guilds 149, 198
Pirsig, R. 164
Plamintr 13
Plato 198, 263
Pokkharasādi 115
pope 85
population 266
pornography 185
Powell, W.B. 209
power 112ff
powers, five 95
pratibhāna 139
Pratyeka-yāna 5
precepts 107, 131, 254
five 84
prejudice 177
pride 108
priest 150
priory 151
prophet 136
prostitution 185
prostration 27, 255
Protestantism 43
pūjā 259

Q

Quakers 18
Qur'ān 228

R

raft 210
rākṣasas 105
rationalism, scientific 167
Ratnakūṭa 93
Reagan 52
reality 29
reason 58, 134, 167, 176, 177, 264
rebirth 61ff, 73ff, 113
Reformation Protestant 84
religion
  definition 142ff
  sacrificial 102
  see also Christianity, Islam
renunciation 131
resources 53 *see also* energy
restlessness *see* agitation
revelation 264
ritual 223, 227, 229, 230, 235ff, 255ff, 259
  Asian Buddhism 238
  Vedic 174
Roman Catholicism 44, *see also* Christianity
Romanticism 167
rūparāga 216

S

Sabhiya 93
sacrifice 102
sakkāyadiṭṭhi 215, 218ff
Sākyas 115
Sallekhasutta 263
Sāmaññaphala Sutta 112
Samu Sunim 7, 8, 209
saṁyojanas 215
sangha 88, 151, 217, 259, 263, 266
  monastic 87
Sangharakshita 1, 101, 260
Śāntarakṣita 165
Sāramati 260
śaraṇa 213
Satan 132
Sceptics 17
scriptures 175
self-deception 256
sense desire 215
Seung Sahn Sunim 159
sex 181ff, *see also* gender differences
sexual desire 108
sexual relationships 182ff
Shasta Abbey 151
Sigālakasutta 265, 266
sīlabbataparāmāsa 215, 223
silence 227
simplicity 202, 212, 243ff
sin 148, 192, 194
Skeptical Inquirer 157, 160
skilful means *see* tactical skill
social reform 110
Socrates 41, 45, 196, 198
Socratic virtues 45ff
Soen Sa Nim 159
solidarity 219ff
Soṇadaṇḍa 114, 116
Soṇadaṇḍa Sutta 114
sota-āpatti 217
soteriology 148
spiritual faculties *see* powers, five
spirituality, alternative 154ff
Sponberg, A. 260
Spring Wind 8
statistics 266
Stoics 15, 17
stream-entry 217
student–teacher relationship 90
suffering 26
Śūraṁgama Sūtra 107ff
Sutta Nipāta 21, 93
Suzuki, D.T. 166

T

tactical skill 68
teacher 83ff, *see also* guru
temperance 196
temple 151

temple religion 103
theft 108
Three Jewels 213
three refuges *see* going for refuge
Tolkien, J.R.R. 80
Torah 193
Toronto Globe and Mail 161
tradition 264
training rules *see* precepts
transcendental 264f
translation 141
tri-śaraṇa 213
truth 113, 129

U
uddhaccaṁ 217
universe 265
  origin 135
Uno, Prof. 25
Untouchability 99, 101ff
upāsakas (-sikas) 84
upāya-kauśalya 68

V
Vasubandhu 165, 214, 264
Vatthūpamasutta 265
Vedas 121, 146, 173
vegetarianism 103ff, 107ff, 254
vicikicchā 215
Vietnam 14
views, attachment to 22
vihāra 88
Vimalakīrti 158
Vinaya 88, 96, 267
virtue 117, 137
  philosophical 45, 196
  Socratic 263
  theological 196, 265
  see also ethics, morality
Voltaire 153
vyāpāda 216

W
Washington, B.T. 98
Washington, George 32
Watts, D. 164
wisdom 34, 35, 45, 46, 146, 188, 196, 214, 264
women 264
Woolman, J. 98

Y
yoga 145
Yoga Journal 159

Z
zazen 235ff
Zen 157, 161, 235ff
Zen Lotus Society 155
Zen master 89, 237, 239
Zen Master Rama 162
Zen Mind 169
Zen Sensualism 164
Zenji Abbey 159
Zhuangzi 41

The Windhorse symbolizes the energy of the enlightened mind carrying the Three Jewels – the Buddha, the Dharma, and the Sangha – to all sentient beings.

Buddhism is one of the fastest-growing spiritual traditions in the Western world. Throughout its 2,500-year history, it has always succeeded in adapting its mode of expression to suit whatever culture it has encountered.

Windhorse Publications aims to continue this tradition as Buddhism comes to the West. Today's Westerners are heirs to the entire Buddhist tradition, free to draw instruction and inspiration from all the many schools and branches. Windhorse publishes works by authors who not only understand the Buddhist tradition but are also familiar with Western culture and the Western mind.

For orders and catalogues contact

WINDHORSE PUBLICATIONS
11 PARK ROAD
BIRMINGHAM
B13 8AB
UK

WINDHORSE PUBLICATIONS INC
540 SOUTH 2ND WEST
MISSOULA
MT 59801
USA

WINDHORSE PUBLICATIONS
P O BOX 574
NEWTON
NSW 2042
AUSTRALIA

Windhorse Publications is an arm of the Friends of the Western Buddhist Order, which has more than sixty centres on five continents. Through these centres, members of the Western Buddhist Order offer regular programmes of events for the general public and for more experienced students. These include meditation classes, public talks, study on Buddhist themes and texts, and 'bodywork' classes such as t'ai chi, yoga, and massage. The FWBO also runs several retreat centres and the Karuna Trust, a fund-raising charity that supports social welfare projects in the slums and villages of India.

Many FWBO centres have residential spiritual communities and ethical businesses associated with them. Arts activities are encouraged too, as is the development of strong bonds of friendship between people who share the same ideals. In this way the FWBO is developing a unique approach to Buddhism, not simply as a set of techniques, less still as an exotic cultural interest, but as a creatively directed way of life for people living in the modern world.

If you would like more information about the FWBO please write to

LONDON BUDDHIST CENTRE
51 ROMAN ROAD
LONDON
E2 0HU
UK

ARYALOKA
HEARTWOOD CIRCLE
NEWMARKET
NH 03857
USA

ALSO FROM WINDHORSE

P.D. RYAN

BUDDHISM AND THE NATURAL WORLD:
TOWARDS A MEANINGFUL MYTH

P.D. Ryan takes a fresh look at our relationship with the living world and offers a radical analysis of our consumerist attitudes. Applying the Buddha's fundamental message of non-violence to these crucial issues, he draws out a middle way between destructiveness and sentimentality: a way which recognizes the truth of the interdependence of all life and places universal compassion at the very centre of our relationship with the world.

In *Buddhism and the Natural World* Ryan emphasizes the importance of living in accord with this truth – and reminds us of the Buddha's insistence that to do so calls for nothing less than a revolution in consciousness.

144 pages
ISBN 1 899579 00 1
£6.99/$13.95

KALYANAVACA (editor)

THE MOON AND FLOWERS:
A WOMAN'S PATH TO ENLIGHTENMENT

This book brings together essays by nineteen women who have been ordained within the Buddhist tradition. They come from different countries and have very different lifestyles. Their firm commitment to Buddhism is perhaps the only thing they all have in common.

Here they demonstrate how they are trying to bring the various aspects and concerns of their daily lives into harmony with their Buddhist ideals and practice. They talk about feminism, motherhood, work, sexuality, friendship, and many other issues. The wide variety of personal experience woven together with key principles and practices makes for a vivid and richly textured portrait of what it means to follow the Buddhist path as a woman in the modern world.

304 pages, with photographs
ISBN 0 904766 89 6
£11.99/$23.95

PARAMANANDA

CHANGE YOUR MIND:
A PRACTICAL GUIDE TO BUDDHIST MEDITATION

Buddhism is based on the truth that, with effort, we can change the way we are. But how? Among the many methods Buddhism has to offer, meditation is the most direct. It is the art of getting to know one's own mind and learning to encourage what is best in us.

This is an accessible and thorough guide to meditation, based on traditional material but written in a light and modern style. Colourfully illustrated with anecdotes and tips from the author's experience as a meditator and teacher, it also offers refreshing inspiration to seasoned meditators.

208 pages, with photographs
ISBN 0 904766 81 0
£8.50/$16.95

SANGHARAKSHITA

A STREAM OF STARS: REFLECTIONS AND APHORISMS

A Stream of Stars is a collection of aphorisms, poems, and writings by the eminent Western Buddhist teacher, Sangharakshita. Encompassing culture and society, relationships and the human condition, these incisive teachings illuminate many aspects of life.

With clarity, insight, and flashes of humour, Sangharakshita provokes us to thought and then to aspiration: an aspiration to true happiness and freedom.

136 pages, with photographs
ISBN 1 899579 08 7
£6.99/$13.95

SANGHARAKSHITA

WHAT IS THE DHARMA?

THE ESSENTIAL TEACHINGS OF THE BUDDHA

Guided by a lifetime's experience of Buddhist practice, Sangharakshita tackles the question 'What is the Dharma?' from many different angles. The result is a basic starter kit of teachings and practices, which emphasizes the fundamentally practical nature of Buddhism.

In turn refreshing, unsettling, and inspiring, this book lays before us the essential Dharma, timeless and universal: the Truth that addresses the deepest questions of our hearts and minds and the Path that shows us how we can renew our lives.

272 pages, illustrated
ISBN 0 899579 01 X
£9.99/$19.95

SANGHARAKSHITA

AMBEDKAR AND BUDDHISM

The remarkable and stirring story of Dr Bhimrao Ramji Ambedkar, lawyer, politician, and educationalist, who, in 1956, started the most important social revolution occurring in India today: the conversion from Hinduism to Buddhism of millions of Indians wishing to escape the degradation of the caste system.

Sangharakshita knew Ambedkar personally, and has himself played an important part in the 'Mass Conversion Movement' that Ambedkar set in motion. In this book he explores the historical, religious, and social background to that movement, and assesses the considerable contribution made by Ambedkar to the spiritual tradition in which he placed his trust.

192 pages
ISBN 0 904766 28 4
£5.95/$11.95

SUBHUTI

SANGHARAKSHITA: A NEW VOICE IN THE BUDDHIST TRADITION

Sangharakshita was one of the first Westerners to make the journey to the East and to don the monk's yellow robe. In India he gained unique experience in the main traditions of Buddhist teaching and practice. His involvement with the 'mass conversion' of ex-Untouchable Hindus to Buddhism exposed him to a revolutionary new experiment in social transformation. More recently he founded one of the most successful Buddhist movements in the modern world – pioneering a 'living Buddhism' that seems ideally suited to our times.

Highly respected as an outspoken writer and commentator, he has never been afraid to communicate his insights and views, even if they challenge venerated elements of Buddhist tradition.

But what are those insights and views? How have they arisen and developed? Here one of Sangharakshita's leading disciples offers an account of his evolution as a thinker and teacher.

336 pages
ISBN 0 904766 68 3
£9.99/$19.95

ROBIN COOPER

THE EVOLVING MIND:
BUDDHISM, BIOLOGY, AND CONSCIOUSNESS

As both scientist and Buddhist, Robin Cooper has a unique perspective on evolution, and his detailed account of this meeting between two apparently different worlds makes an entirely new contribution to the field of evolutionary science.

This is a fascinating study of the evolution of consciousness from the simplest organism through the self-aware human being to Enlightenment. Viewing the latest theories from a Buddhist standpoint, it sees evolution as a process of perpetual self-transcendence. This book will appeal to those interested in the natural world, the mind, and self-development.

288 pages, with diagrams and illustrations
ISBN 0 904766 74 8
£10.99/$21.95